Short Historical Sketches of Page County, Virginia and Its People

Volume 1

A Collection of Articles from the
"Heritage and Heraldry" Column of the
Page News & Courier
August 1997–September 2001

Written and Compiled by
Robert H. Moore, II

HERITAGE BOOKS
2007

HERITAGE BOOKS
AN IMPRINT OF HERITAGE BOOKS, INC.

Books, CDs, and more—Worldwide

For our listing of thousands of titles see our website
at
www.HeritageBooks.com

*Cover illustration from a postcard c.1920
"The Road to Stony Mountain, Luray, Virginia"
by D. L. Kauffman*

Published 2007 by
HERITAGE BOOKS, INC.
Publishing Division
65 East Main Street
Westminster, Maryland 21157-5026

Copyright © 2005 Robert H. Moore, II

All rights reserved. No part of this book may be reproduced or transmitted in any form or by any means, electronic or mechanical, including photocopying, recording or by any information storage and retrieval system without written permission from the author, except for the inclusion of brief quotations in a review.

International Standard Book Number: 978-1-58549-954-4

Dedication

To My Grandparents –

Polly & Bill Bricker

A Note to the Reader

As indicated in the title, this book is a compilation of all of the articles that I wrote for the *Page News & Courier* from August 1999 through September 2001. As you will note, these articles have been reorganized from their chronological sequence of appearance in the *Page News & Courier* to a historical chronology to allow for easier reading.

Some of the articles that I have written for the paper during this time have roots in Harry M. Strickler's *Short History of Page County* in that, while he may have lightly touched on a topic, I made an effort to expand upon it. In some sense, Strickler gave me just enough information to strike a sense of inquisitiveness in me that led me to find more on my own.

Just as Strickler points out in his Author's Forward of his *Short History of Page* County, the county's history is far more complex than many may realize; much like the magnificent river that runs through it, with each turn and bend there is an even more fascinating aspect to discover and enjoy. Strickler made it clear that the task of writing a county history was a large one and that, in his book, he "boiled down the mass to an economical size and at the same time" kept "it readable and worth while." In turn, I am making a series of "installments" on the county history through my articles in the newspaper and then, through these volumes that will contain the articles for all to have the opportunity to have on hand, enjoy and reference for generations to come.

I hope that you enjoy what I have discovered. The history of our county and its people belongs to all of us and is worthy of remembering. My many thanks to the *Page News & Courier* for allowing me to bring it to you for over seven years!

R.H.M., II
November 2004

TABLE OF CONTENTS

Pre-Colonial, Early Colonial & the Revolution (10 Articles)

Living Back in the Mighty Shenandoah, 10

The Plight and Flight of Page County's German Immigrants, 12

A People or a Liquor? - the Scots/Scotch-Irish Debate, 14

Was John Lederer the First European to Lay Eyes on Page?, 16

Development of the "Massanutten Tract" – a German-Swiss Colony, 18

The 'Fort Homes' and Historical Interpretation, 20

The Connection Between Rev. John Casper Stoever and Elder John Koontz, 22

Setting the Record Straight: Native American Raids in Pre-Page, 24

Slavery in the 'German Element' May Have Rooted from an Influential Minister, 26

Muhlenberg's Revolutionary Inspiration to Valley Germans, 28

Early 19th Century Page County (8 Articles)

The Legacies that Accompany Page County's Name, 30

Early Geographic History and Roadways of Page County, 32

In the Wake of Nat Turner: Controversy over Slavery in Page, 34

The Controversial 19th Century Murder of John Wesley Bell, 36

How the Slave Woman "Old Sill" Ran the Charles C. Dovel Household, 38

A Forgotten People – Page County's Antebellum Population of Free African-Americans, 40

Clarifying a Few Details in the Narrative of Bethany Veney, 42

A Review of the Family Profiles of the Antebellum African-American Population in Page County, 44

American Civil War: Events & Personalities (30 Articles)

A Former Page Citizen, Abraham Lincoln and the Winds of War, 46

A Yankee Represented Page in the 1861 Secession Convention, 48

Thomas Jordan – Page County's Earliest Accomplished Military Leader & Noted Journalist, 51

Gallant Leaders of the "Page Volunteers" – Company K, 10th Virginia Infantry, 53

Marching with Stonewall – Leaders and Men of the 'Page Grays', Co. H, 33rd Virginia Infantry, 55

Page County's Sole Artillery Battery – The Dixie Artillery, 57

Page County's Confederate Reserve & Militia Organizations, 59

Page's Soldier-Farmers and the Militia Dilemma in the Civil War, 61

An Early History of Page County's White House Bridge, 63

Bloodshed on the River – A Little Known Civil War Action in Page, 65

One Yankee's Recollections of Marching through Page, 67

Price's Mill – Witness to the Last Days of the 1862 Valley Campaign, 69

Page County and the Insult of Two General Orders, 71

An Unwelcome Summer Expedition to Luray, 73

White's 'Comanches' included Leaders, Men of Grabill's Company E, 35th Battalion Virginia Cavalry, 75

The Grand 'Parade' and the Last Passage of Stonewall from the Valley, 77

The Stern Discipline of Stonewall Jackson and the Hard-Luck Page Grays, 79

A Sad Tale of Two Civil War Soldiers, Part 1, 81

A Sad Tale of Two Civil War Soldiers, Part 2, 83

Some on the Retreat from Gettysburg Found Passage through Page, 85

Federal Cavalry and the December 1863 Raid on Luray, 87

Though Page's VMI Cadets Didn't Fight at New Market, They did Distinguish Themselves in Service, 89

Action at Overall May have Prolonged the Civil War, 94

An English Yankee and the Only Medal of Honor Earned on Page County Soil, 96

One Page County Confederate's Tale of the War, the "Burning" and Comrades, 98

Page Execution: Marylanders Fall for Defying Barn-Burners, part 1, 100

Page Execution: Marylanders Fall for Defying Barn-Burners, part 2, 102

Page Execution: Marylanders Fall for Defying Barn-Burners: The Conclusion, 104

Page County Graycoats Dispatched at Rude's Hill (Summers-Koontz Execution), 106

Misc. Stories relating to Page Co. in the Civil War (16 Articles)

Who was the Man Behind the Summers-Koontz Execution?, 112

County had Not-So-Pleasant Prisoner-of-War Experience, 114

Did Page County African-Americans serve for the Confederacy?, 116

Why did Page take a Stand? Seeking an Answer to the Confederate Question, 118

The Return of Union Soldiers to Page . . . after the War: Part 1, 120

The Return of Union soldiers to Page . . . after the War: Part 2, 122

A 'Clasping of Hands' – the 1881 Luray Reunion, 124

The Original Summers-Koontz Memorial of 1893, 126

Page County's Civil War Claims Amounted to Only One Percent, 128

Former Page Confederate Served as Speaker of U.S. House, 130

James Huffman's 'Ups and Downs of a Confederate Soldier', 132

"But I Know my Great-Great-Granddaddy Served in the Civil War", 134

Sources Abound for Information on Local Civil War Ancestors, 136

Daughters of the Confederacy in Page County, 138

Early Confederate Veteran & Descendant Organizations in Page, 140

The Winnie Davis Cottage (Luray Orphanage), 142

Surnames & Genealogical Research Tools (22 Articles)

The Origins of the Aleshire/Aleshite/Elscheit Family, 144

Origins of the Broyles Family in Page County, 146

Patriarch of the Cave Family in Page County, 148

The Other Residents of the Ruffner House – the Chapman Family, 150

Page's Fighting Chapman Brothers – Postwar Life, 152

The Irish Dorraugh-Dorrough-Derrough Family of Page, 154

The Dovel Family & an Introduction to the Terror Experienced by the French Huguenots, 156

The Early Hillyard/Hilliard/Hilliards Family Lines, 158

Five Brides, a Witch and a Deadly Curse (re: Charles Robert Hilliard), 160

Current Genealogical Work Regarding Michael and Mary Kiser, 162

Discovering the Roots of the Page County Nauman Families, 164

The Trek of the Nicholson Family – Whitehaven, England to Virginia to the Valley, 166

Thomas Purdom and his Role in the American Revolution, 168

The Roudabush Family of Page County, Part I, 170

The Roudabush Family of Page County, Part II, 172

The Hessian and a Case of Good Fortune – the Strole-Keyser Connection, 174

"Surfing" Your Way to Page County Genealogical Research, 176

Researching Your Family History May be Just a Web Site Away, 178

America's Wars Have Left a Long Paper Trail for Genealogists, 180

Interpretation of History Often Strays from Documented Fact, 182

Pass Down those Nostalgic Tales to Future Generations, 184

Genealogical Research May Also Include World Wide Web, 186

About Me (1 Article)

So Just Who is this Upstart Columnist?, 188

Miscellaneous (17 Articles)

Striving to Keep Tradition and History Alive, 190

Researching a Civil War Ancestor, and Where to Begin, 192

Virginians Get to Your Posts for Gettysburg's 135th Anniversary Reenactment, 195

Anniversary Date Targeted for Summers-Koontz Roadside Marker, 197

History, a Researcher, and One of Many Spooky Ironies, 198

The Need of Keeping Page County's Documented History in Page County – Part 1, 200

The Need of Keeping Page County's Documented History in Page County – Part 2, 202

Page's Part in the Early History of the Baptist Church in Virginia, 204

That which is Important to Preserve and Why, 206

Page County Civil War Commission Update, 208

Milam's Gap and the Legendary Milam Apple, 210

Page was Once Known for Orchards and New Apple Varieties, 212

Honoring Our Veterans with a Headstone is an Easy Process, 214

What's in a Name: Luray and Shenandoah, 216

Virginia Civil War Trails and Marking Page County History, 218

Belsnickling – When Dressing in Costumes Wasn't Just for Halloween, 220

Fall Celebrations of Heritage and the Spirit of America, 222

Index, 224

About the Author, 242

Pre-Colonial, Early Colonial & the Revolution

Living Back in the Mighty Shenandoah
(1155 – 1688)
Article of 10/7/1999

As an early fall air begins to make its sweep across the blue hills of the land of the Shenandoah, so too do I sweep in and take up residence once more in the place that I have always called home. After 10 years of service in the Navy, I have joined the staff of the Frontier Culture Museum in Staunton. So then, as an added inspiration in writing these articles, I now have as the most perfect surroundings in my work environment. Just within sight of my office window weaves a magnificent chestnut split rail fence, which, in fact, is just in front of the American homestead that portrays the synthesis of the three cultures that helped to make-up the Valley – the Germans, Scotch-Irish and English.

But before I ramble on, I thought it appropriate to give a brief description of the area from whence a large part of Page County's Germanic ancestry immigrated, The Palatinate.

Known best as German PFALZ, The Palatinate area included the lands that lay on both sides of the Middle Rhine River between its Main and Neckar tributaries. Once the land of the County Palatine (a title held by a leading secular prince of the Holy Roman Empire), the land was actually divided between two small territorial clusters: the Rhenish, or Lower Palatinate, and the Upper Palatinate.

Overseen by Hermann I, as the first Count Palatine in 945, The Palatinate was continuously ruled by his descendants until after 1155. The title "Count Palatine" was not a hereditary one, so following the line of Hermann I, the Bavarian Wittelsbachs took over as ruling Count Palatine. In 1356, the Count Palatine was made an Elector of the Holy Roman Empire with the Golden or papal bull (an official document from the Pope and sealed with the official Papal seal called a Bulla). But during the Reformation, the Palatinate accepted Protestantism and became the foremost Calvinist region in Germany.

Following the publication of Martin Luther's 95 Theses on the door of the castle church at Wittenberg on October 31, 1517, many Lutherans immediately fell under severe religious persecution for their beliefs and concentrated as a people of one belief in The Palatinate. In addition to those people relocated from within Germany, the population of The Palatinate also swelled with new groups of Lutherans from Holland and Switzerland.

In 1619, the Protestant Elector Palatine Frederick V (1596-1632), also known as the "Winter King," became King of Bohemia and the clash between Catholics and Protestants in Germany escalated with the Thirty Years War. While not the exact cause of the war, Frederick's ascension to the throne was the "straw that broke the camel's back" in the long-running political and religious hatreds established over the years. Frederick was driven from Bohemia in 1623 and deposed as Elector Palatine, but the war continued through 1648 and devastated the Palatine country and other parts of Germany. As the warring armies rolled across The Palatinate, the residents suffered immeasurably, not only from constant pillaging and plundering by the French army, but also at the hands of desperate and unpaid "friendly" armies.

Though the Thirty-Years War drew to a close, the citizens of The Palatinate were yet to see a real peace as the War of the League of Augsburg (1688) and the War of the Grand Alliance (1689) loomed on the horizon, both lasting until 1697.

The Plight and Flight of Page County's German Immigrants
(1688-1709+)
Article of 10/21/1999

In a previous article, you may recollect that we left our friends of the Palatinate (many of whom ultimately found their way to the area that became Page County at a much later time) in the midst of a most horrific Thirty Years War. As you will also recall, this was not the end of their hardships in Germany. While there was indeed a brief intermission between wars, by 1688, The Palatinate was once again in the midst of yet another war - the War of the Grand Alliance. Once again, troops of the French monarch Louis XIV ravaged the Rhenish Palatinate, causing the first great effort by Germans in that region to take leave of their homeland. Many of these people ultimately made their way to America, creating the first of the group of people later better known as Pennsylvania Dutch.

But this one was just one of two that the residents of the Palatinate would endure until 1697. The War of the Palatinate or War of The League of Augsburg, began in 1688 when Louis XIV laid claim to The Palatinate. Ultimately, havoc ruled and the Palatines were devastated until the wars drew to a close in 1697. Though the Palatines had sustained unspeakable hardships, there was more yet to come – specifically the War of the Spanish Succession that began in 1702 and lasted until 1713. To make matters even worse, the winter of 1708-1709 was extremely severe, destroying many of the lush vineyards of the region.

Therefore, the time was ripe for an exodus from Germany. Beginning with an invitation from Queen Anne in the spring of 1709, approximately 7,000 Palatines sailed down the Rhine to Rotterdam – a trip that took from 4 to 6 weeks with tolls and fees demanded by authorities of the territories along the way. Rotterdam, in turn, would be the main "distribution point" for all emigrants bound for America by a special situation worked out by William Penn. Soon overflowing with approximately 1,000 Palatines per week, Rotterdam was overcome. While some took a direct route to America, others were making the transit via England. However, overcome there too, the British government issued a Royal proclamation in German that all arriving after October 1709 would be sent back to Germany. Despite the action, London had swelled with 32,000 former Palatines by November 1709. Most were forced to winter over in England until arrangements could be made for transportation to America.

While the majority made flight toward the "New World" full of hope and promise, a sizeable amount ended up in Ireland as permanent residents in order to strengthen the protestant interest on that unstable island. Many of these people, however, opted later to make their way to Pennsylvania and Canada.

Therefore, an abundant number of these hard-shipped Palatines, at least those fortunate enough to have survived wars and winter, desired to take their chances in a new and alien world. Some left for individual reasons, many left for a combination of reasons (did I forget to mention taxation as an added incentive to leave?) Nevertheless, the English colonies offered another chance at survival, in what would hopefully be less hostile. But did they really realize the hardships that lay ahead since they would form a nice buffer between the English and French in an untamed environment with hostile Native Americans?

A People or a Liquor? - the Scots/Scotch-Irish Debate
(Early 17th Century)
Article of 11/18/1999

There is a story of a tour guide in Scotland who enjoyed poking fun at Americans. On one of his motor coach treks, he made a point of commenting that "scotch is a beverage, Scots are persons." While I cannot personally attest to the validity of the story, there definitely seems to be a bit of confusion when it comes to calling a certain group of people by a certain name. Some people get down right offended over the matter of being called "Scotch-Irish" vice "Scots-Irish." However, lets get right down to the records and see what history tells us.

The Ulster Scots, more commonly identified in America as the "Scotch-Irish," were a group of people that made their way from Scotland to North America by way of Ireland. Following a nine-year war, Ulster's Gaelic lords had given up their control of lands in the early 17th century. Leaving the land open for colonization, King James I established the "Plantation of Ulster" which redistributed the lands from Roman Catholic lords to Protestant English and Scottish lords. In turn, these English and Scottish lords recruited Protestant settlers from among tenant farmers, laborers, and craftsmen in England and Scotland to settle among the displaced Irish tenants in Ulster. As a result, Scots Presbyterians, French Protestants (Huguenots), and English Protestants created a stir by establishing their religious practices in a land that was use to Catholicism. It was only the beginning of a long and vicious clash between the two religious groups in that region. But that will be another article - back to the central theme of this story . . .

Early immigrants to the British colonies from the north of Ireland came from the province of Ulster, which at the time of the 18th century consisted of nine counties. According to many 18th century documents, upon arriving in the colonies they generally – despite their origins – referred to themselves simply as "Irish." In rare instances did they refer to themselves as "Scotch-Irish," but even more rare was use of the term "Scots-Irish."

By the mid-to-late 19th century, the usage of the term "Scotch-Irish" was quite heavy. The reason for the sudden "boom" was that those of that descent wanted a clear distinction from the masses of Roman Catholic immigrants who had begun to pour into America in the wake of the 1840 potato famine. By adding "Scotch-" to "Irish" the self-entitled peoples made it clear that they were not of Irish stock, nor were they Roman Catholic, but typically Protestant and Calvinist – Presbyterian. Additionally, "The Scotch-Irish Society of America" was formed in the late 1800's – a self-entitled organization of the distinctive descendants of those immigrants. Certainly, the people that founded the society meant no offense to their ancestry and were in fact honoring their ancestors.

In Ireland today, there is an organization entitled "The Scotch-Irish Trust of Ulster," showing no deviation from the trend. This organization consists of trustees who have been knighted by Queen Elizabeth II, their vice president being the Duke of Abercorn. Being a prominent group of citizens who still reside in the United Kingdom, these people apparently do not take offense to the "Scotch-Irish" title anymore than their distant cousins in America.

So while you should make certain that you call the people of Scotland – "Scots", it would appear that history is in your corner if you call those that made the trek from Scotland to Ireland – "Scotch-Irish."

Was John Lederer the First European to Lay Eyes on Page?
(1699)
Article of 12/2/1999

While not receiving wide acclaim for his explorations during his lifetime, physician John Lederer has only in this century been given praise and credit for having been the first white man to lay glimpse upon the area that became known as the Shenandoah Valley. A native of Hamburg, Germany and former student of the Hamburg Academic Gymnasium, Lederer was originally commissioned by Governor William Berkeley to make explorations into the frontier beyond Virginia's Tidewater settlements. His first expedition to the Blue Ridge leaves a question as to exactly what portion of the Shenandoah Valley he actually had an opportunity to behold.

In his book *A History of Rockingham County* (1912), John W. Wayland explained that Lederer March 1669 journey brought him to the area at or near Waynesboro. However, forty years later, with the publication of *A Short History of Page County*, Virginia, Harry M. Strickler made a different claim, stating that Lederer's first march landed him in the neighborhood of Big Meadows. Being a native of Page, had Strickler been writing on wishful thinking and did his inspiration rest upon the marker that honors Lederer in the vicinity of Big Meadows?

Five years later, Wayland's *Twenty-Five Chapters on the Shenandoah Valley*, included more detailed information on Lederer's expedition.

Whether the two Valley authors had come together in discussion over the matter is not readily known, however, Wayland had shifted Lederer's 1669 arrival some distance to the north along the Blue Ridge. Specifically, Wayland wrote:

"From Lederer's narrative . . . as well as from his map it seems that he reached the top of the Blue Ridge on his first tour at or near Swift Run Gap. He had come up the Pamunkey River and followed its main branch, the North Anna, to its first spring. There or near there he first described that Apalataean mountains. The next day he passed over the south branch of the Rappahannock River (the Rapidan), evidently near its head. There he must have been near the site of Stanardsville. Within the next three days he climbed to the top of the mountain, where he wandered around for several days, seeing higher mountains to the north and west."

Of his discoveries on March 18, 1669, Lederer wrote:

". . . to the north and west my sight was suddenly bounded by mountains higher than that I stood upon. Here did I wander in the snow, for the most part, till the four and twentieth day of March, hoping to find some passage through the mountains; but with the coldness of the air and the earth together, seizing my hands and feet with numbness . . . I returned back the way I went."

Whether Lederer had wandered north or south along the Blue Ridge was never made clear in his journal, leaving historians with the question as to what areas of the Valley he had the opportunity to view from the crest of the mountains.

Lederer's three expeditions were covered in a journal that was translated from Latin to English and published by Sir William Talbot in London in 1672. Not until 1902 did the work resurface in a reprinted edition limited to 300 copies. While not specifically commenting on his expeditions, Lederer's comments on another similar situation mirrored his efforts and lack of recognition in the explorations he made beyond the Blue Ridge: "I have lost nothing by what I never sought to gain--popular applause."

Development of the "Massanutten Tract"
- a German-Swiss Colony
(1669 – 1726)
Article of 10/23/1997

There were numerous Germanic influences that made the German and Swiss immigration to the Valley inevitable.

As early as 1669, German-born John Lederer entered the Shenandoah and dared fur trade in an unknown and "untamed" region. Following his efforts and explorations, Lederer made his accounts well known through publication that was received by the German and Swiss people.

The second most significant explorer was also of German-birth. Franz Louis Michel explored and mapped the middle and northern Shenandoah Valley in 1709, leaving suspect of a silver mine somewhere in the area that became known as Massanutten. Interestingly, Michel did not mingle with the British, but rather first purchased land in the French Huguenot settlement of Manakin Town.

Michel's work, in turn, was exploited by Baron Christopher von Graffenried upon his release from the Tuscarora by Governor Alexander Spotswood. Whether a concocted hoax or not, Graffenried appears to have seen an opportunity for yet another Swiss colony, like his colony of New Bern in North Carolina, and exploited the tale of the silver mines in the Blue Ridge. Though Graffenreid's attempt to coerce Spotswood did not totally succeed, Spotswood had been interested in iron mining for sometime prior and favored the idea of using the knowledge and skill of the well-known ironworker of Germany. Upon this initiate, Graffenreid cooperated with Spotswood in exporting Germans from the Nassau-Siegen district, who would later comprise a large part of the population of the Germanna colony.

It is important to note that Spotswood, from Germanna, initiated his own exploration into the Shenandoah Valley with the "Knights of the Golden Horseshoe." Though nothing concrete remains of Spotswood's reasoning, it is important to note that he entered the

Valley opposite Massanutten, possibly in the hopes of exploring the prospects for the earlier proposed venture by Graffenreid.

With Jacob Stover (Stoeber), the long sought after hope of opportunity arose. Though his appeal for a colony named "Georgia" west of the Blue Ridge as far as the present day site of St. Louis was not agreed to by England, he did receive over ten-thousand acres of land in 1732 to distribute to German immigrants that had already begun to arrive or had resided in the Shenandoah Valley since at least 1726.

The Massanutten settlement, once initially settled, continued to fill with German immigrants well into the years prior to the American Revolution. Some of these German and Swiss immigrants arrived late due to their self-imposed indentures to people in England to pay for their passage to the colonies.

Despite the interaction of some with the English, the colony of the Massanutten tracts remained isolated for years, preserving the ethnic identity of the Germanic people that resided therein. Nevertheless, the German and Swiss settlers did need to communicate in order to vote and voice their opinions through representatives in political positions. Furthermore, the same was to hold true in the courts and trade. Interaction with British speaking people was inevitable.

The 'Fort Homes' and Historical Interpretation
(1728 – 1827)
Article of 2/24/2000

After making a recent tour, there appears to be some controversy over the true definition of a "fort" house. Undoubtedly, the structures made of huge logs and/or limestone were much more defensible than the common homes throughout the Shenandoah Valley during the 18th century. The arched cellars would have made an excellent refuge for citizens who did not have as substantial a homestead as that of a "fort". However, can all of these homes with arched cellars really be considered "forts"?

Of these "fort" structures or arched cellars, historical architecture specialist Edward Chappell states:

"The most dramatic accommodation . . .is a variable cellar form drawn from Rhineland and Pennsylvania precedents. As an integral part of their houses, the Massanutten builders constructed single-and two-room cellars employing techniques that protected large quantities of perishable food from changes in temperature. The cellars housed functions that were relegated to detached springhouses in the nineteenth century, and two Massanutten cellars, as well as a number of Pennsylvania examples contain springs. The primary insulation method involved construction of a rubble stone barrel vault rising from low walls. These vaulted rooms, or die Gewolbkeller, were provided with small vaulted and trabeated [wedge-shaped] window openings that were tapered toward the exterior [believed in most local lore as "rifle slots"]. Iron and wooden hooks embedded in the vaults carried wooden poles for suspension of foods such as meat and cheese."

As to the extra structures found in the cellars of a few of the homes, Chappell comments that "a fireplace in the outer room at the Abraham Spitler House and an underground access to a well from the lower of two vertically stacked cellars at Fort Philip Long suggest that those rooms were also the scenes of productive activities. Full-size windows in the cellars at Philip Long and in the outer rooms at the Spitler House and Fort Stover further evidence them as work rooms."

As to the positioning of the homes – Chappell: "This method of hillside siting, with relatively direct entrance into two floors, is a distinguishing feature of the Rhenish house in America. Multilevel dwellings and farm buildings that take advantage of sloping ground exist in Britain, but the form is seldom found in English-settled areas of Tidewater and Piedmont Virginia. The occasional appearance of the siting choice in nineteenth-century Shenandoah Valley houses can be attributed to the persistence of a Germanic minority trait."

A comparison can be made between the "forts" surveyed and the home of Adam Miller – "Green Meadows." Miller's home is still standing and is believed to have been one of the earliest homes in the area (ca. 1728). This structure has never been given the title of "fort" and does not represent the more typical "sturdy" homes that bear the name. Another structure, Fort Harrison, near Dayton in Rockingham County, is neither Swiss-German immigrant-built or typical of the "forts" built by Swiss-German settlers in the Massanutten settlement.

Perhaps Chappell sums it up best when he states:

"In both Pennsylvania and the Shenandoah Valley, early houses have sometimes acquired the term fort, and present use of the prefix may have been encouraged by conjecture about the defensive functions of the vaulted cellars. Despite the improbability of this function, it is of interest that White House was referred to as a "Fort house" as early as 1827 (Shenandoah County Land Tax Book 1827)."

The Connection Between Rev. John Casper Stoever and Elder John Koontz
(1733 – 1831)
Article of 10/1/1998

The first spiritual inspiration among the early congregations of Lutherans in Page Valley probably came from the Rev. John Casper Stoever, Sr. Born Jan. 13, 1684 or 1685 in Frankenburg, Hesse, Germany, Stoever was the son of Deitrich and Magdalena Eberwein Stoever.

The grandson of the Rev. Andrew Reveberwien, it seemed inevitable that John Casper would play a role in the Lutheran Church. By the time Stoever was nearly 35-years-old in 1720, he moved to Annweiler in the Hardt Mountains in Bavaria.

Accepting a call to be minister at the Germanna Colony of Virginia, Stoever arrived in Philadelphia on Sept. 11, 1728, on the ship *James Goodwill*. Soon after arriving in Pennsylvania, the Rev. Christian Schultz ordained both John Casper and his son, John Casper Stoever, Jr., on April 8, 1733. The elder Stoever became the first pastor of the Hebron Lutheran Church, founded by the first Germanna colonists in 1717 and the first permanent Lutheran Church in the United States. His son became one of the most prominent Lutheran ministers in Pennsylvania during the 18th century.

The elder Stoever's stay in Virginia was relatively short. In 1739, after returning to Germany to raise funds for his Virginia congregation, Stoever died during his passage back to Virginia and was probably buried at sea in the Atlantic Ocean.

The roots of Elder John Koontz were also deeply entwined in the history of the Germanna Colony and early German-American religion. The first generation born in Virginia, on March 26, 1739, Elder Koontz's father, John Cuntz, had arrived in Philadelphia on Nov. 30, 1730, aboard the *Joyce*. His mother, Elizabeth Catherine Stoever Cuntz, was the daughter of the Rev. John Casper Stoever, Sr.

Not unlike his grandfather, Elder Koontz also had a greater calling for religion in Virginia. While originally Lutheran, Koontz was highly influenced by the Baptist revival that spread like wildfire throughout Virginia in the latter half of the 18th century. While living near Front Royal and attending one of these revivals, Koontz was so moved that he traveled to Fauquier County for baptism in December of 1768.

Returning to the Shenandoah Valley, Koontz began teaching the gospel according to the Baptist faith in the area of Mill Creek. Preaching in both German and English, Koontz's sermons were moving and eloquent enough to convert many, including Martin Kauffman and many of his Mennonite flock. Reportedly, his efforts to convert so many subjected Koontz on more than one occasion to beatings by "ruffians" of the Massanutten neighborhood.

Koontz reportedly preached to his Massanutten flock at Mill Creek Church from 1772 until 1824. Elder Koontz died less than a decade later between December 1831 and April 25, 1832. The controversy over the death date stems from the date of probate on his last will and testament. Buried in the Shuler-Koontz cemetery within site of his home near Alma, Koontz's stone was removed in later years to the Seekford cemetery. The old home place of Elder Koontz, better known as the Shuler-Koontz homestead, deteriorated significantly in this century and collapsed in the 1960s.

Setting the Record Straight: Native American Raids in Pre-Page (1758 – 1765)
Article of 3/23/2000

Yes Page County, at one time these lands were considered a part of the "wild, wild west!" But lets not get carried away – no James West, Artemus Gordon or Dr. Loveless here. Rather, there was a time of territorial disputes between Europeans and unsettling affairs with the not so local Native American population. Of the former, there are at least two prominent "Indian Raids" that stand at the forefront of Page County history. However, not all of the attacks made by Native Americans in "pre-Page" were made in the French & Indian War. Additionally, these Native Americans weren't necessarily a band of local tribes (in fact there is some debate over when the last tribe to actually make the valley a long-time residence resided here).

The French & Indian Wars were actually territorial campaigns that spread from European conflicts and effected activities in the English colonies. While somewhat unimportant to Europe at that time, the wars that took place in America from 1689–1763 did put Canada, the American West, and the West Indies up as stakes. However, the fighting that took place in this arena would not carry the same weight as the fighting that took place in Europe.

As a stark contrast to what Europe believed however, this time of history was horrifying to settlers on the frontier of the English colonies. Not only would these people sustain raids from the French but many would also fall victims of tribal border warfare. One source states: "The conflict may be looked on, from the American viewpoint, as a single war with interruptions. The ultimate aim—domination of the eastern part of the continent—was the same; and the methods—capture of the seaboard strongholds and the little Western forts and attacks on frontier settlements—were the same."

Page County CAN claim the Stone/Holtiman/Brubaker Raid of 1758 as a raid that occurred during the French & Indian War. However, the attack made upon the Rhodes family in the latter part of August 1764 should not be considered as an event of the French & Indian War. With the war having ended in 1763, the attack was most likely a spin-off raid made at the tail end of the Pontiac

Conspiracy – influenced by the Ottawa chief named Pontiac.

From 1763 into 1765, small bands of Native American's that sided with Pontiac's beliefs attacked forts and outlying English settlements. After an unusual but unsuccessful 6-month siege of Fort Detroit, many Indians that sided with Pontiac became discouraged and returned home to prepare for the coming winter. Pontiac then tried unsuccessfully to obtain aid from Commandant Neyon de Villiers at Fort de Chartes. According to local tradition, Pontiac then reluctantly met with George Croghan, Sir William Johnson's representative in July 1765 to make preliminary arrangements for peace. Following the meeting, the two men traveled to Fort Quiatenon (LaFayette, Indiana) and on to Fort Detroit to smoke a peace pipe and sign a treaty ending the uprising.

Ultimately, in the English colonies, the French & Indian conflict & the smaller affairs such as the Pontiac Conspiracy led to a feeling of less military dependence upon England. Additionally, a spirit evolved from the fighting that left the settlers feeling more American than British – yet another spark for a fight for American Independence.

Slavery in the 'German Element' May Have Rooted from an Influential Minister
(1739 – 1764)
Article of 7/27/2000

While not the sole reason for its establishment within Virginia's Germanic community of settlers near and within the Blue Ridge, the church may have played a role in the introduction of the institution of slavery, and the ultimate seed for this introduction came from Rev. George Samuel Klug.

While holding his main congregation on the east side of the Blue Ridge, several members and descendants from his "flock" eventually settled in the middle Shenandoah Valley. Klug often ventured into the Valley to administer the words of the gospel as well as perform baptisms and marriages. To many, it was the church that established policies by which to live and, inevitably, Klug was the head of that church and prime example for several members of the congregation.

Following the death of Johann Casper Stoever, Klug came to head the Hebron Evangelical Church in Culpeper County in 1739. Originally recruited by Stoever as a lay companion, Klug was exceptionally different in his ministry. He studied at Helmsted with the famous church historian and theologian Conrad Lorenz von Mosheim and was ordained at Danzig in 1736. Upon his arrival in Virginia, Klug quickly cultivated close relations with the Anglican establishment in Virginia and by 1752 pleaded for a "small allowance" which was granted.

While he did labor intensely to prevent the influence of the Moravians upon his flock, Klug did not live according to his predecessors' beliefs. Prior to Klug's arrival, dependency for survival had stemmed from European charity and insufficient salaries from congregational contributions.

Klug, however, was neither a pietist by training or inclination. Klug became so obsessed at attempting to impress and be recognized by the Anglican establishment that he soon became seriously involved as a major religious and cultural broker and intermediary between his German-speaking congregation and the wider world of

Virginia's planting society. As a result, he quickly learned to adopt the practice of planters and increase the wealth of his glebe by purchasing slaves. To Klug, it appeared that in adapting to the novelty of chattel slavery he had been provided with the North American answer to pastoral poverty.

In addition to embracing the institution of slavery, Klug began a practice of refined and sensuous taste. For his lavish efforts to continue to impress his friends in the Anglican ministry, he soon became seriously criticized by other members of the German established religious order. His efforts may have even drawn the attention of Lutheran Anton Wilhelm Bohme, who warned against this sort of newfound "false freedom," namely that of "self-willed" licentious behavior.

Bohme had established that true Christians of the new order would not act like these people, who resembled Old Testament Israelites who "wanted to possess lands, goods, and acres to divide among themselves." The Rev. Heinrich Melchior Muhlenberg was quick to recognize Klug as a large and imposing Prussian who enjoyed the regular income from his glebe land and slaves.

For his actions, Klug eventually fell out with many of his own congregations while still maintaining his well-established relations with his Anglican friends. Despite this, he continued to preach to Germanic and Anglican congregations alike until his death in 1764.

Ultimately, Klug became a prime example of what was on the horizon for this ethnic group. It had appeared that the language barrier and the remote location of the Germanic settlements had conspired together to ensure isolation from the influence of English-speaking society. However, while some Germanic settlements were well isolated (such as that seen in what would be known as the Page Valley), transactions with and influence by the English society was unavoidable. Then too, the adaptation of English society practices may have been looked upon favorably by many.

Muhlenberg's Revolutionary Inspiration to Valley Germans (1776)
Article of 10/5/2000

"There is a time to every purpose under heaven . . . a time of war, and a time of peace." With these inspiring words from Ecclesiastics, a Lutheran minister spurred many Valley Germans to arms in January 1776 at Woodstock, and supposedly in later weeks at both New Market and Rude's Hill.

John Peter Gabriel Muhlenberg was born the son of Henry Melchior Muhlenberg (organizer of the first Lutheran synod in America) in Trappe, Pennsylvania on October 1, 1747. Well educated, Muhlenberg first attended the Philadelphia Academy (University of Pennsylvania) before being sent to Germany as an apprentice to a merchant in Lubeck. Ill-treated, he ran away and joined an English regiment that saw service in the French and Indian War. By 1767 he had returned to Philadelphia where he was discharged from the regiment.

Seeking a direction in his life, Muhlenberg was encouraged by his father to study for the ministry and by 1771 accepted the call at a ministry in Woodstock, Virginia. Muhlenberg first traveled to England to be ordained in the Church of England. His work led him into politics, and he served in the House of Burgesses in 1774.

History reveals that in 1775 General George Washington requested that Muhlenberg raise a German regiment for service in the Continental Army. Part of his "recruitment tour" through the Shenandoah Valley may have inspired Virginia-Germans in the area later known as Page County.

Quickly raised to brigadier general, by the winter of 1777-78 at Valley Forge, Muhlenberg was in command of a brigade (in General Nathanael Greene's Division) that included the German Regiment of Pennsylvanians, as well as the 1st, 5th, 9th and 13th Virginia Infantry.

In the years that followed Muhlenberg served conspicuously in several battles and was noted for his administrative abilities. In 1783, Muhlenberg received a brevet major generalship.

After the war he returned to Pennsylvania and was elected to the Supreme Executive Council in 1784 and served as Pennsylvania's vice president from 1785 to 1788. He was elected to the First Congress (1788-1789) and served three terms in the U.S. House of Representatives (1789-91, 1793-95, 1799-1801).

Elected to the Senate in 1801, he resigned shortly thereafter to accept the appointment of supervisor of revenue for Philadelphia. He served in this post until his death on October 1, 1807.

Having quickly cross-referenced the list of men in Michael Reader's company with the *Historical Register of Virginians in the Revolution* (Gwathmey), there appears to have been actually relatively few who served in the Virginia regiments of Muhlenberg's Brigade from east of the Massanutten.

Additionally, as can be seen in reviewing Reader's list of men, a true accounting of all of those that served from this area with Muhlenberg's Brigade or other organizations may be more difficult to evaluate considering the various ways that the surnames were spelled in the muster rolls.

Interestingly, though certainly not German, the name "Kelly" was even distorted as "Celly" in Reader's list. If performing a personal assessment of Reader's list for your own family tree, be sure to remember that basic phonetics will probably be the key.

For example * Kuents = Koontz, Kepliner = Kiblinger, Overboker = Offenbacker, etc., etc.

Furthermore, it may be the case that Reader's Company was actually organized early and/or was a local defense of sorts. Many of the men are not listed in formal Virginia regiments of the Continental Army.

Early 19th Century Page County

The Legacies that Accompany Page County's Name
(1831)
Article of 1/11/2001

Governor John Page, for whom Page County was named, is likely forgotten by most in referring to the county. However, in his day the man accomplished much to justify the naming of a county in his honor.

Born at "Rosewell" in Gloucester County, Virginia on April 17, 1743, Page was a descendant of Colonel John Page, a Middlesex, England immigrant who settled in York County in 1655. Built on the land that the family had owned since the 1680s, "Rosewell" was constructed from 1725 to 1740 by Mann Page I, the son of Matthew and Mary Mann Page and the grandson of Colonel John Page. (Mann Page I was also the husband of Judith Carter, daughter of Robert "King" Carter" the Carter line also originating from Middlesex, England with Colonel John Carter). Though built to reflect the power and wealth of the Page family, upon the death of Mann Page I in 1730, he left the yet uncompleted mansion and accompanying debts to his son Mann Page II, father of Governor John Page. At the death of Mann Page II, "Rosewell" was left to John Page, the eldest son of Mann Page II and last of the family to actually reside in the home.

As for his career-life, John Page was naturally affiliated with many notables of the Revolutionary era including college classmate Thomas Jefferson. Graduating from the College of William and Mary in 1763, perhaps one of his earliest claims to fame brought him in the company and service of George Washington in an expedition against the French & Indians. Politically, Page first entered the stage as a delegate to the State constitutional convention in 1776. From 1776-1779 he served as Virginia's lieutenant governor (while Patrick Henry served as governor). Additionally, Page's political service included terms with the Virginia state legislature, the U.S. House of Representatives from 1789-97 ("at-large" from 1789-91, 10th District from 1791-93, 12th District from 1793-97) and finally as the sixteenth Governor (1802-1805) chosen by the Virginia State Legislature since Patrick Henry.

Governor John Page died in Richmond on October 11, 1808 and was interred in St. John's Churchyard.

While Page County stands as a memorial in theory to the man and patriot, people can also take interest in the fact that the Page family home of "Rosewell" is a major archaeological project in Colonial Williamsburg. Though relatively abandoned by the Page family after Governor Page's death and consumed by a three-day fire in 1916, the remains along with a few surviving outbuildings and several acres were turned over to the Gloucester Historical Society in 1979 - all of which still stand in close proximity of the Bruton Heights School (a former African-American school and now the home of the Colonial Williamsburg Foundation Center).

As a final note and interesting continuation of the "Page" family tradition, eight months after the establishment of Page County, in November 1831, Mann Page, "a black man, was returned to the court, examined and ordered to be certified as truly made." By being "truly made" it was established that in return for the sum of $600 to Philip Rudacille, Mann Page was officially freed from slavery. Though unlikely, in his *Short History of Page County*, Harry M. Strickler speculates that the "Colored Mann Page may have been a servant at 'Rosewell.'" The freed Mann Page will be the subject of yet another forthcoming article.

Early Geographic History and Roadways of Page County
(1831 – 1851)
Article of 12/4/1997

Formed by a division of lands from both eastern Shenandoah and northern Rockingham Counties, Page County came into existence in 1831. More closely resembling the cultural makeup of Shenandoah County due to most of descendants of German Palatine immigrants, Page County had remained a predominantly German speaking area well into the middle 1800's. By the time of the formation of the county, the residents had become more bilingual.

Not unlike the surrounding counties, Page too had become quite productive in farming, eventually leading to the reason that the counties of the Shenandoah Valley would become to be known as the "breadbasket of the Confederacy." In time the counties would abound in sawmills, merchant flour mills, grist mills, hemp mills, oil mills, tan yards and, for the abundance of iron ore available in the area, blast furnaces and forges.

The rich and fertile lands of Page County lay in the shadow of the Blue Ridge to the east while the Massanutten Mountain provides the western edge of the county. The main waterways of Page County were the South Fork of the Shenandoah River and the Hawksbill Creek. Before the Civil War, flatboats aided in the shipment of flour, meat, lumber and rocks from Port Republic, down the Shenandoah to Harper's Ferry, but was limited to available high waters. Also gracing the Page Valley were various springs.

The road system in Page consisted largely of the macadamized type being graded and rounded higher in the middle allowing for better runoff of rainwater. The "centerline" road was the Luray-Front Royal Turnpike, completed in 1851. When this road was formed it was "cleared 30 feet wide, constructed 18 feet wide (with) no grade over 4 degrees." The turnpike later connected with the Rockingham Turnpike. Being the main road in Page, in 1851, $20,000 was allotted for two bridges [the eventual Columbia and White House (covered) bridges] and $10,000 to "metal" portions of the pike between Front Royal and Luray.

Other important roads within the county would include the New

Market - Sperryville Turnpike that crossed the Massanutten or Luray Gap and Thornton's Gap. The New Market - Gordonsville Turnpike connected to the above-mentioned pike at an intersection at the eastern foot of the Massanutten and passed over Columbia Bridge at Alma, passing through Marksville and across the Blue Ridge through Fisher's Gap. Yet another pike crossed Milam's Gap across Tanner's Ridge near Marksville.

The village of Luray, actually founded in 1812, before the formation of Page County, is the county seat of Page. Page's Roman Revival courthouse, completed in 1833, still stands today on one of the highest points in the town. The building was designed and constructed by William B. Phillips and Malcolm F. Crawford who were formerly employed by Thomas Jefferson. Though threatened at different instances throughout history, the building is very much in its original form including the arcaded one-story wings.

In the Wake of Nat Turner: Controversy over Slavery in Page (1831 – 1842)
Article of 11/6/1997

By the time of Page's founding as a county, politically, the nation's representatives were very near to greater disagreements over the issues of slavery and states' rights. Slavery in the Shenandoah Valley, though low in size in comparison with several other Virginia counties, was on the decline. Page numbered lower percentage-wise than some surrounding counties such as Clarke, Warren and Augusta each numbering 50 and 20 percent respectively. Slave owning whites in Page numbered less than 19 percent.

Perhaps the start of the most controversial issues in Page County regarding slaves took place in 1831. Following the "Nat Turner Rebellion" during that summer in Southeastern Virginia, Page may have felt some degree of "after shocks." The events that followed may have either been a result of concern over the potential slave uprisings or the slaves in the area may have developed ideas of "rebellion" from the Nat Turner incident.

In Page County on November 10, 1831, "Joe," a slave owned by Mark Beasley, was accused to have plotted the murder of Vincent Wood and Jacob Hochman. Wood was a laborer living near Cedar Point. The end verdict of "not guilty" made it easy to believe that perhaps the white citizens may have become threatened by the recent Turner rebellion, and in fact, started on a "witch hunt." Nevertheless, Beasley was required to enter "into a recognizance in the sum of $2,000" to insure that "Joe" kept the peace for the following twelve months.

Fifteen days later another case was brought in front of the Page County court concerning a slave owned by Enos McKay known as "Dan." The charge in this event was that "Dan" had "willfully and maliciously" assaulted and beaten Mary McDaniel with the intent to kill her. Unlike the trial of "Joe," "Dan" had been witnessed in his assault upon Ms. McDaniel. Two such witnesses had been "Frankey" and "Rose," slaves apparently of the same household. After lengthy testimonies, "Dan" was found guilty. As a result he was to receive thirty lashes "upon his bare back to be well laid on."

Worse yet, or perhaps in the better interest of "Dan," he was to be banished from the United States altogether, with full reimbursement to be made to Mr. McKay for the loss of his "property."

In the years that followed, there were several slaves freed by their masters through self- purchase, including Mann Page. In his will of December 1831, Phillip Rudacille saw to the freedom of Page for $600 raised by his own labor to other people in the area. In turn, Mann Page turned over a great deal of personal property he had accumulated, to include livestock and his own crop of wheat, for the freedom of his wife Elizabeth. Furthermore, if enough money were left over, it would be applied to the freedom of his son, James. Again, this was one of many instances in the years following 1831 where slaves began to purchase their own freedom in Page.

Following 1831, there was clearly a distinct concern regarding the slave population in the county. As records show, as early as 1833, there had been formed a local militia for reaction against civil disturbances of any sort. Despite the formation of the militia, in both 1835 and 1836 fear of uprisings was still apparent. Because of such fears there were fines against owners of slaves for letting their "colored folks to run at large." A $10 fine per owner was assessed against seven citizens of Page in November 1836 for that exact infraction.

The last great "scare" in Page County apparently came with the murder of 29 year-old John Wesley Bell by his slaves, "Captain" and "Martin" on February 14, 1842. More of this event will follow in yet another article.

The Controversial 19th Century Murder of John Wesley Bell (1842)
Article of 11/20/1997

An incident in Page County that may have been inspired by the Nat Turner years earlier occurred on February 14, 1842. On that fateful day, 29 year-old John Wesley Bell was murdered by two of his slaves, "Captain" and "Martin."

Having been out about 250 yards from the Bell home, the slaves were busy cutting bushes along a branch. Apparently, Bell came out to the job and while speaking to "Captain" was struck by a blow from behind by "Martin." The ax-blow easily busted Bell's skull and killed him instantly.

At once setting to hide the evidence of the murder, "Captain" repositioned Bell's head into the stream so that the blood from the crime would be washed away. A larger problem was the cedar log that their master had fallen against and spattered with blood. Chopping away the bark of the log, the slaves piled it on the ground and concealed it under the brush. The snowfall the same night aided in disguising the bloodied chips. Eventually disposing the body in the river, the story that Bell had drowned was easily accepted by many until his remains were found. In turn the two slaves were arrested on suspicion of murder. When the snow melted away and exposed the crime scene "Martin" and "Captain" confessed but gave no motive.

The two Bell slaves were soon tried in the March court, presided over by Colonel Daniel Strickler, and found guilty. The sentence for the crime was that the two were to be "hanged by the neck until they are dead-dead- dead."

Ordered to carry out the sentence, Sheriff Daniel Blosser held the execution between 11 a.m. and 3 p.m. on April 8 on the Bixler Ferry Road in the first hollow after leaving Main Street in Luray. The account of the execution was published years later on August 12, 1898 in the *Page News*:

"... The prisoners were marched on foot from the jail with their hands tied behind them and ropes around their necks, lead by

Sheriff, Charles Flinn. The funeral sermon, half hour in length, was preached before the execution by Elder William C. Lauck. The preacher stood on the spring wagon and upon the same vehicle the condemned men. . . sitting on their own coffins waiting their death. When the sermon was concluded the preacher closed the book and without looking behind him hastily left the scene of the execution. When this was done, "Martin" and "Captain" were made to stand erect in the wagon while the sheriff and the deputy tied the ropes attached to their necks to the arm of the gallows and then the wagon was driven from beneath leaving the bodies swinging in the air. The tops of the surrounding trees were filled with people thick as blackbirds. . ."

A contradiction in the 1898 story is evident. If the two were sitting upon their coffins while they listened to the sermon, the two had apparently been under the impression that they were to be buried. However, according to the same account "Their bodies were never buried but were turned over to two Luray physicians who had bought them for cakes and beer of the Negroes themselves during their confinement in jail." Therefore, as can be expected, the 1898 story was probably exaggerated, having been written over fifty years later. In adding to the suspense of the hanging, the author may have added the idea that the two were sitting upon coffins waiting for their doom. Clearly, the story is subject to speculation.

A month following the execution, the Page court assessed the value of "Captain" and "Martin" as $914.28 that was accordingly paid to the Bell estate.

How the Slave Woman "Old Sill" Ran the Charles C. Dovel Household
(1820 – 1872)
Article of 3/18/1999

In the book entitled "The Families of Adam Beauregard Dovel" there is small account of one Dovel family and its interaction with a well respected and, obviously, outspoken slave woman named Drucilla or "Old Sill."

Born in 1806, Charles C. Dovel, in 1827, married Elizabeth Koontz, the daughter of Isaac and Susanna Kiblinger Koontz, Sr. Elizabeth and her new husband immediately made their home on her father's homestead in Alma. The son and son-in-law of slave-holders (fewer than three slaves each), Charles would own only two slaves, including "Old Sill" who was born around 1820 and had been left to him in 1832 by his father's will.

According to the Dovel book, the story pertaining to "Sill" was extracted from an undated clipping from an old *Page News & Courier* and was written by Jacob R. Seekford. While small in length, it is of interest in the further understanding of how one of Page County's over 1,000 slaves that resided in the county from 1840-1860 experienced life.

Seekford began: "Only a few slave owners living in this part of this county would have taken their slaves back after the war. Many of them were glad that the slaves were set free. I knew all of the old slaves of this county and the old masters and mistresses never let one suffer when they lived near their homes. I have seen as many as six of these old slaves, men and women, around one home when these big homes would have a big dinner." However, Seekford noted "the Koontz, Shulers and Dovels, who lived around Alma . . . were not fitting people to have slaves in many cases because they gave the slaves more privileges than they gave their own children. I never heard one of them that ever whipped a slave and they kept them more for pets than anything else."

Seekford went on to state that one slave in the Dovel household, "Sill", struck an imposing figure at "about 225 pounds" and had been "the complete boss of the Dovel home and ran things just to suit herself . . ." Showing how much the slave woman interacted with the family, Seekford continued that she was responsible for having named all of the Dovel children, including Drucilla, whom she named after herself. Interestingly, all of the girls' names closely resembled "Sill" including Priscilla and Cecilia.

When it came to disciplining the children, Seekford recalled that the children's own mother "never whipped one of them, but Old Sill laid the lash on them whenever she found it convenient." Seekford had once "heard one of the Dovel boys say that she whipped Russell Dovel with a switch when he was thirteen years old." Sill, on occasion, even found time to "get-after" her master Charles. "I have heard the late David Dovel tell about this women putting her hands in his father's coat collar and threatening to whip him" wrote Seekford. Furthermore, to show just how much she ruled the household affairs, Seekford remembered that "She also bossed and ran" Dovel's home distillery. "She looked after the selling of brandy, in fact she carried the key to the cellar where the liquor was kept."

Charles C. Dovel died in 1864, and, despite the emancipation and constant flow of Federal troops through Page County during the war, she did not leave the county until 1868. "She came back here [from Clarke County] in 1872" wrote Seekford, "and stayed about a year and spent all of her time with the Dovel children . . . She nursed old Daniel Koontz when he was sick and laid him out when he died."

"Sill" later returned to Clarke County where she died and was buried at the Old Stone Chapel.

A Forgotten People -- Page County's Antebellum Population of Free African-Americans
(1831 – 1861)
Article of 6/17/1999

Within the past year there has been a great deal of discussion over the institution of slavery and exactly what sort of impact it had on Page County. However, nothing has yet surfaced as to the "forgotten people" of Page County's antebellum years. Of the total African-American population in Page County in 1860, nearly one-third (394 of 1,244) were free. Additionally, many of the families of that number had been free since the first recorded census of Page County in 1840. While I don't have the space in one article to include all of my findings, I will take the time in this lead article to introduce some of the more interesting details I have found so far.

While not clearly indicated through county records, in all probability, these free African-Americans (the majority of which had not been listed as black, but rather as mulatto) had been slaves who had either acquired their own freedom through monies raised from having been hired during their lifetime, or had been freed by the wills (the subject of another upcoming article) of their very owners. Nevertheless, Mann Page, as having been freed by Philip Rudacille for payment for his own freedom in the amount of $600 in November 1831, was absolutely not the only one to find freedom from slavery within the boundaries of Page County prior to the Civil War.

Of the information gleaned from the early county records, there is much to be said, however, the census records reveal the most interesting information. From 1840 to 1850, there had been an increase in slaves and slaveholders. However, by 1860, the number of slaveholders had dropped below that of even 1840. Additionally, in that same year the number of slaves had dropped back to within sixty-one of the 1840 mark, showing that several had either been sold or freed.

Furthermore, by following a surname review of free blacks/mulattos from 1840 - 1860, much can be established. The count of surnames of the free African-Americans numbered over 21 in 1840. To that number 43 new surnames had been introduced by 1850 and another

33 by 1860, totaling at least 76 since 1840. The likelihood that migration of freed individuals to Page County transpired seems remote unless other family members actually resided in the county thereby drawing them to Page. Likewise, there had clearly been a trend for those that had been freed earlier on to remain in the county. Seventy-one percent of the surnames of the 1840 number still resided in Page as of 1860. However, out of those that had been introduced in 1850, only thirty-seven percent remained by 1860.

Of those living as single individuals dispersed among the white population of the county without any clear indication of other family in the home, there was a nearly equal number of free blacks/mulattos residing or working at the homes of slaveholders and non-slave-holders alike. Most resided or worked at the homes of farmers. Of those that resided with slaveholders, it is often presumed that other family members were still slaves in the same household. However, perhaps the most curious figure was that of the five census listed free black/mulatto children under the age of six that resided with non-slave-holding families - leaving no indication as to why they resided there.

Further research revealed that there were well over 30 free blacks/mulattos, as head of households, listed with occupations ranging from John Dixon as keeper of the furnace at Alma District #1 to those who held the occupations of laborer, blacksmith, forgeman, stone mason, cooper, carpenter, boatman, basket-maker, shoemaker, and tanner. The various homes of these people ranged from Overall (otherwise known as Milford) representing the northern-most area of the residences to the Shenandoah Iron Works as the southernmost point. The wealthiest ($850 in real estate) free individual was the 33 year-old mulatto trader Samuel Campbell, residing in Marksville.

Clarifying a Few Details in the Narrative of Bethany Veney
(1840s & 1850s)
Article of 8/24/2000

Some readers may recollect that in previous articles I have mentioned that Page County was among the three counties in the Shenandoah Valley with the lowest number of slaves. It is unlikely that numbers set in documented historical records will change, however, it is then certainly ironic to note that a former resident of Page County offers rare insight into her personal experiences as a slave.

The value of Veney's narrative is apparent. While *Weevils in the Wheat: Interviews with Virginia Ex-Slaves* (1976) and the WPA Records Group, Virginia Writers' Project files offer sketch-like recollections of slaves in Virginia, according to *Weevils'* annotated bibliography of slave narratives there are only 29 published narratives that cover the subject of slavery in Virginia between 1784 and 1865. Of that number, there are only three that deal with slavery in the Shenandoah Valley – two being from former Frederick County slaves, and one (Bethany Veney) from Page County. A review of the "Web" reveals that over 30 active sites offer links to one of three or four sites that offer the complete text of Bethany Veney's narrative. Additionally, a handful of university related sites hail Veney's narrative as essential reading when it comes to the history of slavery in the United States.

In addition to reading about the details of her life and experiences, it is also interesting to read into the Bethany Veney narrative for the mention of other Page County residents – specifically the families with whom Bethany Veney had the most contact – those her four owners. All of these families lived near Luray (the 49th District in 1850) and were simple farmers.

While Bethany's last (John Printz, Sr. – born 1807) and second to last (David McKay – born 1806) owners are mentioned in the narrative, it was her early history that offers much more intrigue. It appears uncertain if Bethany's first owner was truly James Fletcher of Pass Run. Taken into consideration as property and inventoried, Bethany and her sister Matilda were passed-on to Lucy (a "spinster" and daughter of James) Fletcher (born ca. 1801) as a "share."

Bethany's grandmother and Uncle Peter were given to Nasenath (also a daughter of James) Fletcher. Bethany recalled that Nasenath later married David Kibler (born ca. 1803 and a farmer with $2,500 in real estate in 1850), with whom all of them found a "home" shortly thereafter. However, the 1850 census records and county marriage records indicate that Kibler's spouse (as of August 1837) was Mary Ann Leavill (born ca. 1816) leaving a question as to whether Bethany's mother's owner was a Fletcher or Leavill. David, the son of Martin and Dorothy/"Polly" Kibler, died in 1873 of apoplexy.

It is worthwhile to note that as of the WPA Historical Inventory in Page County in the 1930s/1940s, David Kibler's former residence (3 ½ miles northeast of Luray) was said to have had one remaining slave cabin that was then being used as a smokehouse.

While not an owner of Bethany Veney, another key character in the narrative was Jonas Mannyfield (Menefee?), the owner of "Jerry," to whom Bethany was first married. However, a search of the 1850 census finds no Mannyfield (or other derivations of the name) listed, leaving the reader to remain curious as to where "from across the Blue Ridge" the Mannyfields came.

The last official purchase of Bethany Veney resulted in her freedom and subsequent move to New England prior to the Civil War.

A Review of the Family Profiles of the Antebellum African-American Population in Page County
(1860 – 1861)
Article of 9/2/1999

As mentioned in the previous article, out of the free black/mulatto male heads-of-household in Page County in 1860, over 30 had been listed with occupations and resided with family. In addition to that, there were another eight free households headed by four free black and four mulatto males without any occupations listed. However, what is more striking is the number of women that had been listed as the heads-of-household. Specifically, of that number, seventeen were shown as mulatto and five as black - the majority of these residing in the Massanutten Districts of Page. What is more interesting is the fact that the majority of these women were young, with children even under the age of 1, identifying the very possibility that their spouses were still held in slavery - not uncommon considering the fact that even Bethany Veney, while a slave, had married a freedman herself.

However, another aspect to examine is the fact that there were interracial relationships taking place in the Page Valley even before the foundation of the county in 1831. While it is generally assumed that the above shown women living alone with their children were the spouses of slaves, it can also be seen in some instances, (remembering that interracial marriages were illegal) that some of these women may have been the concubines of white men that did not reside with them. Only one white male, Haley Morris, was shown to reside with a mulatto woman and five mulatto children, ages one through nine, in 1860. Morris, a 29 year-old white laborer, resided in Shenandoah Iron Works, and, what is even more interesting, in May, 1863, enlisted in the "Page Grays" of Company H, 33rd Virginia Infantry. It is a possibility that he may have been conscripted/drafted, however, there is no evidence stating that possibility in his service record. No matter what the circumstances of his enlistment, on July 3, 1863, he was counted as one of the killed among those that fell in action on Culp's Hill at Gettysburg.

On a reverse note, there were at least five illegal "marriages" between mulatto men and white women. However, three out of those five relations included men with the surname of Campbell -

tracings to ancestors of earlier white Campbell men that settled in the county. The result of a few of these relationships brought about what the census taker recognized as, in some cases a mixture of both white and mulatto children.

Taking a step back into my personal ancestry, the census taker didn't always pay close attention to the job at hand. Specifically, in the case of Emily or Amelia Richards. Emily had been the former daughter of Reuben Cave, the Revolutionary War veteran, and, by the 1850 census, was the widow of Aquilla Richards - a former all-white household. However, in 1850 the census taker had mistakenly assumed that with the widow Richards (60) residing with the mulatto Jake Hughes (also age 60) in a primarily mulatto residential area (with the families of Hughes, Bundy, Berry, Marshall, etc. in the neighborhood), all of her children, except one, were also mulatto (granted this was the middle of summer). Perhaps Emily had found a romance with Mr. Hughes after the death of her husband, or perhaps he was a former slave of the Richards family. Nevertheless, the two oldest boys, Joseph (15) and Howard (6), might have been brought up in a multi-racial family and neighborhood. In 1861 the two boys joined the ranks of the Dixie Artillery. But then, with this as their background, were they fighting to preserve the institution of slavery or home and country in a second "War of Independence?"

American Civil War

Events & Personalities

A Former Page Citizen, Abraham Lincoln and the Winds of War
(1860 – 1861)
Article of 1/6/2000

While Abraham Lincoln had no direct connections with Page County, his ancestry did have roots in the Shenandoah Valley. In 1767, John Lincoln, the great-grandfather of President Abraham Lincoln, acquired 600 acres of land on Linville Creek in Rockingham County. Dying around 1789, he lies buried at the southwest corner of his land just north of present day Edom. One of John's children, Abraham L. Lincoln served as a captain of a Virginia Company during the American Revolution. Captain Lincoln's son and the father of the President, Thomas, was born in 1778 while the family resided in Rockingham County. However, four years later, Captain Abraham and his son made their trek to Kentucky. After settling on the "frontier", Thomas' father was killed by Indians. In 1809, Abraham, the second child of Thomas and Nancy Hanks Lincoln was born along Nolin Creek in Hardin County, Kentucky. Interestingly, Jacob, a younger brother of Captain Lincoln's, remained in Rockingham and was the progenitor of a line that produced a few of the Valley's Confederate soldiers.

In a letter dated August 9, 1860, one former resident of Page recalls having seen the president and his wife first-hand. It had been just eight years since George W. Kaufman, the son of Benjamin and Anna Kaufman, had "started from home for the first time." "I rode my Billy across the mountain to Newmarket, and Albert took him home, and this was the last I saw of Billy." By the time he drafted his letter to his sister Elizabeth and her husband James Robert Modesitt, George was making his living as a schoolteacher in Lincoln, Illinois.

"I was at Springfield yesterday" wrote Kaufman, "to a great Republican Convention, and saw a mighty Crowd of people there, there must have been sixty or eighty thousand . . ." at the "place of residence of Lincoln." "I went around to his house to see him, but

Mrs. Lincoln told us he was up stairs lying down, he was so much fatigued, from the Continual pressure of the people rushing to see him. . . but he is only a man, & looks very much like Nicholas W. Yager, as to form & color, but politically a much blacker Republican. He is a very fine, sociable fellow, but I can not vote for him, and I do not think Ills. Will go for him in November next. But of course some of the strongest abolition States will vote for him any how, but I suppose you have heard enough of him at this time, yet one thing remains that I want you to hear, and that is, I want to see him beaten in Nov. for President of these united States."

Less than a year later, on April 23, 1861, George wrote once again of the times that had changed. "I fear the mail will be stopped between here and Virginia, owing to the Secession of Va. & if so we will not hear from each other until peace is made between the two sections of the Country, and that in all probability be a number of years, now that the War has Commenced. You wrote to me about singing Mt. Morris, It is a splendid tune, I should like to hear you sing it again But God knows whether or not I ever will. Raising Volunteer Companys for War is all the talk here, 200 men started from Lincoln last Monday, & still they are raising more, things are indeed in a deplorable Condition, . . . I believe there will be a bloody time of it."

A Yankee Represented Page in the 1861 Secession Convention
(April 1861)
Article of 5/7/1998

Would anyone ever believe that the 1861 Secession Convention Representative for Page County came from an area just west of Albany, New York?! Peter Bock Borst was born in Schoharie County, New York on June 23, 1826. Likely the descendant of German Palatine immigrants, Borst came to Page County in 1847 and soon opened his law practice. Known as a man of "wonderful force of character," Borst devoted most of his life to his law practice and several aspects of Page County. Within a few short years of his arrival to Page, he met and married Isabella C. Almond on April 1, 1851.

The daughter of Mann Almond, Borst had instantly married into one of the most active families in the Page County courts. From their marriage would come four children, including Charles (ca. 1852), Elizabeth (ca. 1854), Cornelia (ca. 1856), and William (ca. 1858).

Soon after the arrival of son Charles, the popular Page County structure "Aventine" was constructed. Borst had designed the home when he was 20, without consulting any architects. All of the lumber that made up the beautiful home came from the Blue Ridge and had been seasoned for at least two years before being applied to the project. Built with no nails, the home was entirely "pinned and morticed." According to family stories, it was Peter's daughter Elizabeth, who later named the home for one of the seven hills of Rome. Later serving as the principal building of Luray College from 1925 - 1927, the home later moved "piece-by-piece" to make room for the Mimslyn in 1937.

With his office in the North wing of the courthouse, by 1860, Peter, having established himself as Commonwealth Attorney since 1852 had accumulated a great deal of property ($40,000 worth) and popularity within the county. Borst's inclination to increase his wealth is evident in the fact that he also owned a farm by the middle 1850's. Likewise, Borst had also built a three story tannery that would be later known as being "one of the most flourishing establishments in the county" in antebellum Luray.

With the election of republican President Abraham Lincoln in 1861, the Commonwealth of Virginia sat on the verge of joining sister southern states in secession. Page citizens found the best representative for the state's Secession Convention in Borst. In both of the votes on April 4 and 17 respectively, Borst voted for secession, helping to seal Virginia's role in the Confederacy.

Peter's presence in Page also lured two brothers from New York to the town prior to the Civil War. Both Addison D. Borst and John B. Borst would follow their brother's beliefs in the Confederacy and joined Co. K, 10th Virginia Infantry on June 2, 1861. As 2nd corporal, Addison would be captured with most of his company at Spotsylvania Court House on May 12, 1864 and was sent to Point Lookout and Elmira before being exchanged in October, 1864. Addison later married into Virginia's prominent Taliaferro family and resided in King George County in later years where he died.

Working as a tanner in his brother's business prior to the war, John was first brought into the service as 1st sergeant before being made commissary sergeant of the regiment in 1862. Paroled in 1865, John later attended several Confederate reunions, including the 1906 event in Culpeper.

Following his return to Luray, Borst resumed his practice as the Commonwealth's attorney for Page. Having been a representative to the Secession Convention however, Borst had been earmarked as a target of Federal aggression during the war. On July 22, 1862, under orders from General Steinwehr, an expedition under the command of Colonel William R. Lloyd entered the town of Luray. Easily taking Luray, Lloyd's force encamped on the high ground immediately south of Luray. The town was immediately placed under marshall law and Captain Abell, of the 6th Ohio acted the role of provost-marshal, with his company as the provost guard at the court house. Additionally, Peter Borst's home was seized, after his evacuation of the place, and used as a hospital, under charge of Surgeon Finch, also of the 6th Ohio.

Over a year later on December 22, 1863, a Federal raiding party entered Luray and broke up Harry Gilmor's camp equipage, destroyed large quantities of leather goods, and burned Britton's shops and Borst's tannery.

Following the war, Borst held the position as Commonwealth's Attorney until 1870, when due to the military (post-Civil War) appointment of Judge Hargest, Borst was without the office for one year. He resumed the post in 1871 however.

Borst became involved with other issues in the postwar as well, being the projector of the Shenandoah Valley Railroad and was largely interested in several other important lines. With the motto, "It is better to wear out than rest out," the latter part of his life was filled with labor.

On April 24, 1882, while in the service of legal matters at the Rust House, and in the presence of Judge Bird and several other lawyers, suddenly and noiselessly Borst fell back in his chair, and although a dozen hands were willing to go to his assistance he was dead from apoplexy, by the time they could lay him on the bed. Borst was laid to rest in Green Hill Cemetery. Isabella would survive her husband for several more years before passing in 1916 and being laid to rest next to Peter.

Thomas Jordan -- Page County's Earliest Accomplished Military Leader & Noted Journalist
(May 1861)
Article of 7/22/1999

A future "facile write, excellent manager, and loyal subordinate," Thomas Jordan was born the son of Gabriel and Elizabeth Ann Sibert Jordan on September 30, 1819 in the Page Valley, and became the only Confederate General produced from Page County. Educated first in Page County schools, Jordan matriculated at the United States Military Academy in the summer of 1836 and by 1840, graduated forty-first in his class which included future notables such as William T. Sherman (also one of his roommates), George Henry Thomas, and Richard S. Ewell. Commissioned as a brevet 2nd lieutenant, Jordan's first assignment was with the 3rd U.S. Infantry in the Florida Territory.

In the early years of his extensive military career, Jordan proved a colorful figure, serving in the Second and Third Seminole Wars and the Mexican War under both Zachary Taylor and Winfield Scott and in Pacific Northwest, where he served in the Steptoe War from 1857-58. During this same period of time, he also introduced steamboat navigation on the upper reaches of the Columbia River. Taking an extended leave of absence in 1860, then, Captain Jordan penned his first book entitled *The South, Its Products, Commerce, and Resources*.

In the wake of Virginia's secession, Jordan tendered his resignation in May 1861 and was commissioned as lieutenant colonel of Virginia troops. Ordered to Manassas Junction, he was promoted colonel and made adjutant general to General P.G.T. Beauregard's Confederate Army of the Potomac. Jordan would follow Beauregard extensively throughout the war usually as senior staff officer and adjutant general of various armies including the Army of Mississippi. Likewise, he would also have his brother, Francis Hubert Jordan (formerly of Page's Company D, 7th Virginia Cavalry) frequently assigned with him as a junior staff officer. Undoubtedly, the senior ranking Jordan also had an influence in the assignment of another younger brother, Macon (former captain of Co. D, 7th Va. Cav.), to General Henry Heth's staff in the east. Colonel Jordan was particularly noted for his exceptional coordination of Confederate reinforcements while he remained at army headquarters at the Wilmer McLean house during the First Battle of Manassas and for his coordination of troops at the Battle of Shiloh following the death of General Albert Sidney Johnson. For his role at Shiloh, he was promoted brigadier general in September 1862. Jordan was paroled at Greensboro, N.C. on May 1, 1865.

Following the war, Jordan was more noted for his work of the pen, including an article of the *Harper's Magazine* that attacked Jefferson Davis as "imperious, narrow, and lacking in administrative talents and statesmanship." In 1866, he edited the *Memphis Appeal* and in 1868, in collaboration with J.B. Pryor, penned his second book entitled *The Campaigns of Lieutenant-General N.B. Forrest*.

In 1869, Jordan became involved in the Cuban independence movement and in May, landed on the shores of Cuba at Mayari with three thousand men and weapons and ammunition for six thousand. Successively becoming the chief of staff and later, commander of forces in the rebellion against Spain, in 1870, he met and defeated a numerically superior army at Guaimaro. However with a price of $100,000 on his head, supplies nearly exhausted and strict enforcement of the neutrality laws by President Grant, Jordan reluctantly resigned his commission and escaped prosecution for his violation of the neutrality laws.

Upon his return to the United States, he became editor of the *Financial and Mining Record of New York* and championed the free coinage of silver. In 1887, he wrote the article "Notes of a Confederate Staff Officer at Shiloh" which was included in Volume I of *Battles and Leaders of the Civil War*. Jordan died on November 27, 1895, and was buried in Mount Hope Cemetery, near Hastings-on-the-Hudson.

Gallant Leaders of the "Page Volunteers"
Company K, 10th Virginia Infantry
(May 1861)
Article of 12/18/1997

In early May 1861, the "Page Volunteers" assembled under Captain William Townsend Young. The 57 year-old Young had established himself in Page County before the war as a successful merchant. The builder and owner of the fabulous "Calendine" estate, Young ran a general store and coach stop for the Burke Stage Line.

Dropped from the rolls the following spring, Young was succeeded by Rappahannock County born Richard Stewart Parks. Wounded in the right foot at McDowell in May, 1862, Parks later returned to duty until appointed the Enrolling Officer for Page County by order of the Secretary of War in 1863. Officially resigning as captain of Company K in 1864, Parks continued to make his life as an attorney in Luray. Serving as Attorney for the Commonwealth in Page in 1874 and in the Virginia House of Delegates from 1894 to 1900, Parks was known as a "striking character" and "an orator of no mean ability."

Parks was succeeded by the youngest of the "Page Volunteers" three captains and his own brother-in-law, David Coffman Grayson. The son of Page County Sheriff Benjamin Franklin Grayson, young David had also served as county sheriff. However, on the battlefield David Grayson had also made quite a name for himself.

In the post of 1st lieutenant at age 24, Grayson had been wounded at the battle of Cedar Mountain on August 9, 1862. Grayson took a number of months to recover from the wound he received in his right lung, finally returning to service in December. However, within five months of his return and within four weeks of his 25th birthday, Grayson was captured at the battle of Chancellorsville on May 3, 1863. Sent to Old Capitol Prison in Washington, D.C., David was soon exchanged and elected to the post of company captain on February 25, 1864. Once again however, the winds of war turned unfavorable during the following spring. Just over one year from the date of his last capture, Grayson was again captured on May 12, 1864 at the horrific battle of Spotsylvania Court House.

This time his prisoner-of-war status was to continue significantly longer.

Sent first to Fort Delaware, Delaware, Grayson saw a long series of transfers from several prisons that included Hilton Head, South Carolina and Fort Pulaski, Georgia before finally returning to Fort Delaware on March 12, 1865. During his life as a POW, Grayson acquired the unwanted destiny of becoming a member of the "Immortal Six Hundred" which consisted of Confederate officer POW's who were confined in the stockade on Morris Island, South Carolina, under fire of their own guns shelling that island. With Robert E. Lee's surrender in April and the inevitability that the war was no longer a cause for prolongation in June, Grayson selected to take the Oath of Allegiance on June 15, 1865 and was released to return to his citizen life.

All three former captains of the "Page Volunteers" departed their mortal lives in the order they departed command of the "Page Volunteers." Young on February 11, 1880; Parks on March 27, 1922; and Grayson on June 26, 1833. Likewise, all three decided to be laid to rest in the soil of the county they had defended in the War Between the States and are all buried within site of each other in the Green Hill Cemetery in Luray.

Marching with Stonewall - Leaders and Men of the 'Page Grays', Co. H, 33rd Virginia Infantry
(June 1861)
Article of 6/4/1998

On June 1, 1861, the "Page Grays" were enlisted of men from all over Page County. Officially mustered into the service of the Confederacy on June 18, the company was initially led by Captain William D. Rippetoe. A 25 year-old Methodist minister, Rippetoe had not been in Page County for too many years upon receiving the post. As of the 1860 census, Rippetoe and his 21 year old bride were in residence at James W. Modesitt's hotel in Luray.

The first of the four "solely" Page County companies, Rippetoe's company was designated as Company H, 33rd Virginia Infantry in what would become the famous "Stonewall" Brigade. Serving only briefly, Rippetoe would be succeeded by 30 year-old Ambrose Booten Shenk in November 1861. Shenk, a clerk and salesman in Luray, had been married for seven years by the time of Virginia's secession. Shenk's career in the Page Grays was cut short however, falling mortally wounded at the battle of Kernstown in March 1862. Mary Jones Shenk was left to care for two young children.

The third and final captain of the Page Grays was elected to the post on April 21, 1862. Captain Michael Shuler was to serve in his new post for at least two years. Born in Page County in 1844, Michael was the oldest son of John and Mary Ann Kite Shuler of Grove Hill. Michael had attended Roanoke College as a partial student from late 1860 to 1861, along with another native of Page, Benjamin Franklin Grove. Unlike Shuler however, Grove was a native of Luray and chose his service with the Dixie Artillery and later as a member of Mosby's 43rd Battalion Virginia Cavalry. A trusted leader to the end, Shuler would fall as a victim of the heated action at the Battle of the Wilderness in the afternoon of May 5, 1864.

Among the ranks of the Page Grays were several boys from the Hite family of Mill Creek. Daniel and Rebecca Hite saw witness to the enlistment of two of their sons in Rippetoe's company in June 1861, and two sons in the 97th Militia in July and August. A shoemaker, William F. Hite would be the first to enlist and was soon after elevated to the post of 1st lieutenant. Under his first trial of fire,

William was wounded on July 21, 1861 at Henry Hill during the First Battle of Manassas. Suffering from a wound to the lung, he died of complications due to typhoid four months later. David C. Hite, William's brother, having transferred and enlisted in the Page Grays in April, 1862, was also wounded at Second Manassas a year later, but recovered to join his remaining brother in the field. Nearly two years after William's wounding, 1st Sergeant John P. Hite was mortally wounded on Culp's Hill at Gettysburg during the heated fighting on July 3, 1863. Suffering for two more days, John died on July 5 and was buried by David two miles north of the Pennsylvania town. David, having taken the risk to remain behind with his dying brother, was captured and sent as a prisoner-of-war to Point Lookout, Maryland until March, 1864 when he was exchanged. Almost six months to the day of his exchange, David would be the last of his brothers to fall, being killed-in-action at Winchester on September 16, 1864.

Page County's Sole Artillery Battery –
the Dixie Artillery
(June 1861)
Article of 3/9/2000

By the latter part of June 1861, scores of Page's men had marched off with the first three units formed in the county at the outbreak of the Civil War. However, on June 21, the fourth and last company formed exclusively in the county and almost entirely of Page men was organized. Proclaimed the Dixie Battery or Dixie Artillery, the unit had ultimately been the brainchild of William Henry Chapman. Having recently left his studies, like most others, at the University of Virginia, Chapman sought out John Kaylor Booton to spearhead the effort. Booton himself had been the former commander of the little company of artillery that fired their two iron guns at 4th of July celebrations for a number of years.

Since funds for the organization of another company from the county were exhausted, Chapman tasked himself with convincing Booton to financially back the new unit. While Booton was initially reluctant to fund such an enterprise, after some persistence, Chapman succeeded in convincing the pre-war self-proclaimed inventor. In short order, a meeting was called at Honeyville for all interested men. By June 21, eighty-two men had enrolled for service in the battery.

Despite Booton's financial support, the company was extremely ill prepared for war. In need of horses, harnesses, and gun equipage, the men made due with little the battery had available. Not until after moving to Winchester was the battery made complete with new equipment by the order of General Joseph E. Johnston.

In November 1861, Booton resigned his post, having been elected as a member of the Virginia Legislature. In turn, Chapman was elected to battery command and would hold the position for the life of the company. William Crisp, father of the future U.S. Speaker of the House (who was at that time a member of the Page Volunteers or Company K, 10th Virginia Infantry), and William's brother, Samuel F. Chapman held the posts of senior 1st lieutenants.

Assigned to General James Longstreet's "wing" in the spring of

1862, the Dixie Artillery, alongside the famous battalion of Washington Artillery from New Orleans, marched in the Peninsula Campaign without seeing any action. However, on June 27, while held in reserve, the battery endured its first baptism of fire at Mechanicsville. Three days later, on Monday, June 30, Chapman's gunners made the battery's guns speak for the first time at the Battle of Frazier's Farm and according to the recollections of both Chapman brothers, the battery suffered "considerably." It would be nearly a month and a half before the Dixie Battery's guns would bark out again.

Before the close of the summer, as a direct participant in which its guns blazed, the Dixie Battery could add only three more actions to its list of battle honors – Rappahannock Station (August 23), 2nd Manassas (August 30), and Boteler's Ford on the Potomac (September 19). While not engaged, the company had also been present at the surrender of Harpers Ferry (September 15) and Sharpsburg/Antietam (September 17).

On October 4, 1862, as a result of the consolidation and reorganization of the artillery of the Army of Northern Virginia, the Dixie Battery was disbanded and the majority of the men remaining (46) were reassigned to the famous Purcell Artillery (Cayce's) of Richmond.

As for William and Samuel Chapman, larger famed loomed on the horizon as members of John S. Mosby's famous command. But that is another story and rest assured that the "Fighting Chapmans" will appear in their own glory in a forthcoming feature of Heritage and Heraldry.

Page County's Confederate Reserve & Militia Organizations
(1861 – 1865)
Article of 6/15/2000

While there were five constantly active Confederate units (two infantry companies, two cavalry companies and one artillery company) formed almost exclusively from Page County, there were also some units formed as a part of the Virginia militia (1861-1862) and reserves (1864-1865). These organizations were primarily organized of men that could not serve with the regular army units for whatever reason.

Originally enlisted from July 1 - July 7, 1861, the 97th Virginia Militia was primarily formed of Page County (though some companies indicate commanders from surrounding counties) men who had not already joined regular Virginia organizations. Twelve companies (A through M) composed this organization. The 97th Regiment was one of eight regiments and one smaller militia to make up the 7th Brigade under Brigadier General Gilbert Simrall Meem. Other regiments and organizations in the 7th Brigade included the 58th (Rockingham), 116th (Rockingham), 145th (Rockingham), Infantry Company Second Class Militia (Harrisonburg), 13th (Shenandoah Co.), 136th (Shenandoah Co.), 146th (Shenandoah Co.), 97th (Page), and the 149th (Warren) Regiments.

Commanded by Colonel Mann Spitler, the 97th was called into service by the Governor on July 13, 1861, to rendezvous at Strasburg, except for companies already ordered to Beverly. Available records give some indication that the organization may have been disbanded in April 1862 by order of General T.J. "Stonewall" Jackson. The likely reason behind this would have been the need to "activate" those men who were able-bodied and could serve in the regular regiments of Jackson's army. Some men formerly from the 97th can be found to have later served with such units as the 10th and 33rd Virginia Infantry Regiments.

Nearly two years later, on May 28, 1864, Captain Thomas Keyser formed Keyser's Boy Company of Reserves in Page County. Consisting of boys between the ages of 17 and 18, no record has been found of this company completing its organization and it is likely that the company was merged into the 1st Battalion Valley Reserves. All members of the company are shown to have enlisted on May 28, 1864 at Luray. However, it is likely that another "Boy Company" was formed prior to Keyser's organization. An unusual item to note is that while Keyser's company had been enlisted toward the latter part of May, several members of his company are shown as having joined the 62nd Virginia Infantry on May 4, 1864.

Just over two months later, on August 9, 1864, the 8th Battalion Virginia Reserves, commanded by Major W.A.J. Miller, was organized with four companies (A through D), as the 1st Battalion Valley Reserves. However, it was not officially recognized and designated as the 8th Battalion Virginia Reserves until February 27, 1865.

Company B was known as the Page Reserves and was formerly known as Company B, 1st Battalion Valley Reserves. Though organized in August 1864, enlistment's of several men from the Page Reserves goes back to May 28, 1864, possibly reflecting enlistments of Thomas Keyser's Boy Company.

In late 1864, the battalion was temporarily broken up and a remnant served in the 3rd (Chrisman's) Battalion Virginia Reserve, under Major George Chrisman. The 3rd appears to have been a temporary consolidation of various battalions then known as the Valley Reserves (the Page County men were in Company C of this organization with J.W. Modesitt as captain). Records indicate that the Valley Reserve may have been a "paper" organization composed of old men and boys, most of who never reported for actual service.

Captains of the Page Reserves included W.A.J. Miller (promoted to major) and James William Modesitt.

Page's Soldier-Farmers and Militia Dilemma in the Civil War
(August 1861)
Article of 4/6/2000

By the end of the summer of 1861, militia organizations from the Shenandoah Valley were in camp in the vicinity of Winchester. As such, several of the militiamen were facing a serious problem - time for seeding the wheat crop was at hand. These men had in fact signed on for service following the secession of Virginia, however, they had enlisted with the militia for a reason. They realized, that to sustain the regular army in the field, their role as farmers was equally important. However, General Joseph E. Johnston, commanding the Confederate Army of Virginia, continued to refuse the release these men to their farms. By the latter part of August, a letter enumerating the concerns of the officers and men of the 7th Brigade, Virginia Militia had been drafted and conveyed to both Governor John Letcher and President Jefferson Davis - a part of which follows:

We desire, first, to say that no portion of Virginia has been more loyal to the South and her interest than the militia of this valley; that we are among the first to send volunteers to the field of battle; that we have as great a number of volunteers in the field now in proportion to the strength of our militia as any portion of the State . . . We fully appreciate the condition of our country, and are willing to make any sacrifice necessary to advance the interest of the South and to secure our independence . . .

The valley of Virginia is a wheat-growing country, in which slave labor is scarce; consequently the larger portion of the labor must be performed by white men between the ages of eighteen and forty-five years. The time for seeding the wheat crop has arrived, and unless at least a considerable portion of the men now here can be returned to their homes to attend to putting that crop in the ground we will be unable to raise supplies sufficient for our own subsistence.

At first the letter appeared to receive little attention, leaving the militia officers to repeat their plea in yet another letter on August 31. By that time matters had worsened. The companies that were not actually from the Winchester area had become greatly annoyed with those companies that were from the area in that the latter had "....

failed to any great extent to respond to your call, and that instead of being ready to obey the call of the Governor promptly and coming forward to defend their own town, the very town that we are now defending, they are quietly pursuing their usual avocations." Finally, on September 9, large numbers of men (including those from Page) were temporarily released from service. With just enough time for sowing seed, the men were again called from their farms with the reactivation of the militia on November 4, 1861.

Heading the list of officer's names that had been affixed to the August 23 letter/petition to Governor Letcher and President Davis was Page County's own Mann Spitler. The colonel and commanding officer of the 97th Virginia Militia, Spitler had other objectives than farming. Born on May 21, 1825 at the family home of "White Hall" near Mill Creek in Page, Spitler had by 1861 been serving as a member of Virginia's House of Delegates for two years. Upon his return from service in the militia, Spitler succeeded Wright Gatewood of Shenandoah County and served on the Virginia State Senate representing Page and Shenandoah counties for the duration of the war.

An Early History of Page County's White House Bridge
(April 1862)
Article of 7/2/1998

Barely a decade old at the opening of the Civil War, the White House Bridge saw the passing of many soldiers in both Blue and Gray, advancing and retreating in the Shenandoah Valley. One such encounter, on April 19, 1862, saw the death of Private Charles C. Wheat. A member of Company D, 7th Virginia Cavalry, Wheat was shot and killed at the White House Bridge and Hamburg intersection by some of the advancing forces of General James Shields' army. Ultimately, the 19 year-old achieved the unwanted title of the first soldier known to have been killed in Page County. The exact details of the skirmish were not mentioned in the unit history of the 7th Virginia Cavalry, though they were operating in the area of Page and Rockingham County at the time. The incident, in fact, may have been the result of an attempted "bushwhacking."

Interestingly, Strickler's *A Short History of Page County* states that Judah Forrer and Dr. William H. Miller "were there at the time, but fled without injury." Forrer had just been discharged from the Dixie Artillery in January and it would be almost two years before he began riding with John S. Mosby's men. Miller, on the other hand, had been captured at Romney on October 26, 1861 and was confined at Camp Chase, Ohio during the affair. Furthermore, while Forrer's presence is possible, Dr. Miller was not sent to Vicksburg, Mississippi for exchange until August 25, 1862, making it impossible for him to be a witness to Wheat's death.

In 1926, Philip M. Kaufman recollected a springtime day on May 21, 1862 when "Stonewall" Jackson advanced on the bridge. Having marched through New Market and across the Massanutten at New Market Gap, Jackson reached the bridge and from what Kaufman recalled: "I was an eyewitness and, as far as I know, the only surviving one, not only of the crossing of General Jackson's army at the bridge at the White House. . . but also of Stonewall himself as he ran the gauntlet, with bared head, through the marching columns of his cheering 'foot cavalry'. His faded gray uniform with stars on the collar, his black beard and uncovered head, as he loped past the White House on Old Sorrel, are as fresh in my mind as on that day."

Within a couple of weeks of Kaufman's eyewitness encounter, the bridge again became a focal point. While at Strasburg, Jackson realized that Federal General James Shields might move through the Page Valley and across the Massanutten to close a trap with John C. Fremont's army striking from behind. In order to prevent the action and expedite his escape, Jackson made orders for the destruction of the White House and Columbia bridges in Page. Captain S.B. Coyner's Page men of Company D, 7th Virginia Cavalry were a natural selection to achieve the task. Sometime after 11 p.m. on June 1, Coyner's company made a quick trek toward Page and encountered "one of the most dreadful thunder storms" half way up the Massanutten. After a brief pause, the contingent pressed on under flashes of lightening that lit their way in the intense darkness. The bridges were "in flames by sunup." Coyner recalled that "the Yankees" later "pitched their tents and planted their cannon by the smoking ruins."

While the bridge had been destroyed, the ford at the White House had yet to see its last encounter between soldiers in the Civil War.

Bloodshed on the River –
A Little Known Civil War Action in Page
(May 1862)
Article of 10/9/1997

On the afternoon of May 7, as portions of "Stonewall" Jackson's army continued its screening action on the main body's march to McDowell, portions of the 6th Virginia Cavalry and one company of the 9th Louisiana Infantry stood posted on the east side of the Shenandoah River near Somerville and the Columbia Bridge in Page County. The Louisiana men were part of the famous "Wheat's Tigers" that were part of General Richard Taylor's Louisiana Brigade. Taylor was himself the son of President Zachary Taylor and perhaps a distant cousin to many Taylors who then resided in the county.

Poised near the river, the Confederates were attacked in the early afternoon as forward deployed pickets of the 13th Indiana Infantry opened fire. Hearing of firing, Brigadier General Jeremiah C. Sullivan, commanding the bluecoat brigade, ordered Colonel Robert S. Foster, commanding the 13th Indiana, to deploy with six companies to drive the Confederates back. Captain Wilson was to remain behind with four remaining companies of the 13th.

Taking six companies, Foster moved past Honeyville "about two and a half miles" and came upon the Confederates "advance guard" immediately in his front atop a hill. By this time, a company from the 7th Louisiana, under Major Davidson Penn, was moving in the direction of the action along the river. Deploying three companies on the sides of the road, Foster continued forward along the road with the other three companies.

Driving the Confederates through Somerville to Dogtown, Foster redeployed his infantry at Somerville. While five of the companies were positioned on the heights on the left of the road, companies B and I were placed near the remains of the burned Columbia Bridge "about two miles up the road, to the right of and distant about two and a half miles from Dogtown." A half hour rest that Foster allowed his men was shortly thereafter disturbed when a Captain Conger of Company B, 1st Vermont Cavalry rode in and reported to Foster. With no further resistance in his front and no loss of men,

Foster, the tinner-turned army officer, figured it best to call off the pursuit and return to camp to resume the attack upon the enemy the following morning. Conger's men would bring up the rear of the Hoosier companies. The skirmishers were quickly called back in and the march began back toward Honeyville.

After moving a short distance, the colonel called the column to a halt at Somerville where he called in the companies left on the heights and awaited the cavalry. In the pause, Foster received a dispatch from General Sullivan encouraging the break-off of the pursuit and heeding the colonel to "beware of a surprise." No sooner had the dispatch been received, when a courier from the Vermont men rode in bearing a message announcing that they were surrounded and needed his assistance. Frustrated that the Green Mountain state men had not followed as ordered, but had "gone some four miles up the river, and encountered the reserve of the enemy," Foster ordered the six companies of the 13th to "about face," and calling upon Captain Wilson to bring up the reserve companies, set off quickly toward the river.

Taking position on the heights above the road, and to the left of Somerville, most of the Indiana men engaged the Confederates at a distance of one hundred yards, and drove their skirmishers back two or three hundred yards on to their main body. Gripped for a half-hour in a "most terrific fire from the enemy," the Confederate force attempted to turn the Federal flank. Observing this, Captain Wilson was soon ordered to with the Federal reserve at "double-quick" to the left. With the Confederate threat countered, the Federal cavalry was able to escape by swimming the Shenandoah River.

The small engagement near Honeyville costs the Federal forces twenty-nine killed, wounded, captured, and missing, including the sergeant-major of the regiment. Colonel Foster reported that his number engaged included 180 men. The unnumbered Confederates who were captured were entirely from the 7th Louisiana Infantry.

One Yankee's Recollections of Marching through Page
(May 1862)
Article of 1/7/1999

On May 12, 1862, the 4th Ohio Infantry along with other elements of General James Shield's division made its way from New Market to Luray. One member of the Buckeye regiment took the opportunity to make note of his passage through the Luray Valley. Writing a series of reports for the *Cincinnati Daily Times* William C. Crippen assumed the pen name of "Invisible."

Upon crossing the Massanutten toward Luray, the Federal soldiers eagerly anticipated the "rich treat" of a view upon reaching the high point of the mountain. Crippen wrote that the site to be held was "one of the most cheering in this part of Virginia." As they made their way down the gap to Luray, Crippen noted that the "whole mountain glistened with bayonets, and the rumbling noise of the artillery and the immense baggage train, echoing and re-echoing, sounded like distant thunder." Twice along the route, the men of the 4th Ohio "stopped to refresh" themselves "at the dashing, splashing natural mountain fountains, as clear as crystal and almost as cold as ice."

Having marched along dusty roads in an unusually hot May climate, the column finally made "a long halt for rest on Cave Hill." According to Crippen, "all gladly sought the shelter of a forest strongly sprinkled with pine. Gen. Kimball and I made a pillow out of a knotty tree root and were lying there puffing our pipes and brushing off mosquitoes . . . ."

In passing through the town that was responsible for sending a large number of men off to war in Confederate gray, "Invisible" seemed surprised at the reception. At one point, the Ohio man was particularly moved by observing one "intelligent, well-dressed citizen sitting in front of his house." As a Yankee band struck up the strains of 'Hail Columbia,' he noticed that this man was "sensibly affected." Ultimately, the Page County gentleman was "very talkative" and was moved to pronounce:

"This is a great army sir. You come down on us like the locusts of Egypt and can destroy us if you choose. This is a dreadful state of affairs in our country, brothers against brothers and fathers against sons, but my conscious is clear. I fought secession, sir, fought it with all my might, but when my State went out of the Union I felt bound to go with her. I had queer feelings when I heard the national air today; I love the old flag and the Union. What a great army this is. If you have many such, you will soon overrun the whole South."

When the Page man was informed that there would be more brigades arriving the following day, he confessed that "the South may as well give up at once. . ." On continuing his sojourn through Luray, Crippen was also quick to note that judging from "various little incidents . . . . there is a good deal of smothered Union feeling in the town." Several people flocked to the streets and "gave bread and other edibles to the soldiers and would not take a cent as remuneration." At one house near the city one local lady was so excited at the Yankee arrival as to express her mood by waving "her cambric quite vigorously as the army passed." While greeted by a number of supporters, the Buckeye also remembered that "The genuine Secessionist, male and female, can be distinguished as soon as seen. They either have a hangdog look or attempt to speak defiance in their demeanor."

Price's Mill - Witness to the Last Days of the 1862 Valley Campaign
(June 1862)
Article of 8/10/2000

In the aftermath of the victories at Front Royal and Winchester, Gen. Thomas J. "Stonewall" Jackson's Army was suddenly in retreat.

While one Union army under Gen. John C. Fremont was bearing down from the North through Shenandoah County on the west side of the Massanutten Mountain, another (a "division" consisting of two brigades under Colonels Samuel S. Carroll and Erastus B. Tyler) under Gen. James Shields was pressing toward the Page Valley. If Shields could move quickly enough and strike across the Luray/New Market Gap to overtake Jackson's force, he and Fremont could unite and attack with a numerically superior force. Accordingly, Jackson made a rapid retreat along the Valley Pike (current U.S. Rt. 11) toward Harrisonburg.

In order to delay Shields' advance, Jackson ordered his cavalry commander, Col. Turner Ashby, to destroy both the White House and Columbia bridges in the Page Valley. In addition to the successful burning of the bridges by June 2, Shields' advance was also plagued by heavy rains that swelled the South Fork of the Shenandoah and turned the rough pikes through the Page Valley into a veritable quagmire. To make matters worse, the lack of supplies in Shields' army severely hampered morale – while all suffered from the lack of rations, many marched without shoes.

Ultimately, Shields was delayed for three days and was forced to abandon the plan of crossing the Massanutten and uniting with Fremont. By June 7, elements of Shields' army began moving toward Port Republic and crossed Naked Creek. The following day, elements of Shields' command, under Col. Carroll, came within a "breath" of capturing "Stonewall" at the town of Port Republic. However, the little effort was greatly overshadowed by the defeat of Fremont at Cross Keys on the same day.

On June 9, Shields' army was given a chance at Jackson's army, but also failed and was left to reel in retreat along the path by which it had advanced.

Ultimately, Shields' command suffered over 1,103 casualties. The 66th Ohio Infantry, which retreated to and made bivouac in the immediate area around Price's Mill on the evening of June 9, had suffered the second highest number of casualties of all the Union regiments at Port Republic, numbering well over 200 men killed, wounded, and captured or missing.

As Shields' defeated columns returned to march back through the streets of Luray, one member of the 66th Ohio recalled that "The female portion of the community seemed to enjoy our defeat – hugely! You could see them skipping from door to door happy as larks over the defeat of Shields' men." Shields' army remained in the area of Luray for only a few more days before retreating out of the Valley altogether via Front Royal.

While a later mill now stands near the site of the two previous Price's Mills, the first original mill was constructed by the Price family early in the 1800s. It is likely that the first mill was destroyed during the period known as the "Burning," when Union soldiers entered Page County and continued their devastation of the central Shenandoah Valley in October 1864. The mill was replaced after the war by another version.

"Captain" Joseph M. Price, the second generation of Price family mill operators and the owner of the mill at the time of the war, rests in the nearby cemetery overlooking what later became known as the Verbena Mills/Farms.

Page County and the Insult of Two General Orders
(July 1862)
Article of 9/3/1998

Remember those old family stories that told of hiding the hams underneath the floorboards, keeping the jewelry hidden away, and other necessary means to prevent the dreaded "Yankee's" from taking private property? In one incident, one of my distant grandmothers ran out to her clothesline and beat back a Yankee with a broom to keep him from stealing one of her better quilts. I recall several stories such as these that need to be preserved in family histories whenever possible. While 1864 brought the majority of the trouble, along with the "burnings," it was as early as the summer of 1862 when the atrocities commenced in earnest.

In July 1862, while Valley soldiers prepared for their next encounter with the enemy, General John Pope, now in command of the Federal Army of Virginia, issued two highly aggravating general orders that would impact Page County, and in fact, all Virginia citizens. General Order Number 5 directed the men of the army to "subsist upon the country." After giving vouchers for seized provisions, there was the guarantee that reimbursement would come following the war. The down side to the order was that the person making the claim had to give sufficient testimony that they had been loyal citizens to the United States since the date of the voucher. Many vouchers, even those who later testified, were not granted cash reimbursement. Furthermore, General Order Number 5 opened the Valley wide to seizures of grain, meat and crops. Pope's soldiers took the order as a license to pillage and steal. Virginia had become free fare for the Federals.

General Order Number 11 promised equal despair for the citizens of Virginia. In it, Pope's instructions were to "take up all active sympathizers, and either hold them as prisoners or put them beyond our lines. Handle that class without gloves, and take their property for public use." Capturing sympathizers or disloyal citizens was not clearly defined and left the majority of the population fair game to the order. If the citizen had been disloyal, but was willing to take the oath of allegiance, the citizen could "remain at their homes and pursue in good faith their accustomed avocations." According to issues of the summer's *New York Times* (July 31 and August 4, 1862 issues), Page County was quickly affected as all male citizens of Luray were rounded up by General Franz Sigel's men and placed in the court house for a time. Though none of the Luray inhabitants were sent South, General Robert Milroy, headquartered in Sperryville, enforced the order with more zeal in Rappahannock County. When 150 persons were brought to his headquarter, eleven persons refused to take an oath of allegiance to the United States. They in turn were summarily taken from their homes and sent out of "Federal lines."

But before I send the county into another fit of rage over times past, remember too that there were the compassionate Federals as well; those that took no pleasure in "inconveniencing" their "Virginia hosts." Still abiding by the philosophies that McClellan tried to maintain in the Peninsula and Seven Days battles of that summer, there were several Federal soldiers that simply preferred to fight the battles and leave the civilians alone. While the General Orders played havoc on the citizenry, another distant grandmother of mine, with sons serving for the Confederacy, washed Yankee uniforms and was paid for her trouble in gold. Little did the Federals realize however, that the money would probably pay for items meant for her son's comfort in the field and a prolonged war.

An Unwelcome Summer Expedition to Luray
(July 1862)
Article of 9/17/1998

On July 21, 1862, under the orders of General Baron von Steinwehr, an expedition to Luray was placed under the command of Colonel William R. Lloyd, of the 6th Ohio Cavalry. Within Lloyd's demi-brigade were the 73rd Pennsylvania, five companies of the 68th Pennsylvania [New York] Infantry, one section of Dieckmann's battery, all under Lieutenant Colonel Muhleck, of the 73rd; the 6th Ohio and mountain howitzers, under command of Major Steadman, and the 4th New York Mounted Rifles, under Lieutenant-Colonel Nazer.

By the following day, Lloyd's force held Luray and was encamped on the high ground immediately south of Luray. The town was immediately placed under Marshall law and Captain Abell, of the 6th Ohio acted the role of provost-marshal, with his company as the provost guard at the court house. Additionally, Peter Borst's home was seized, after his evacuation of the place, and used as a hospital, under charge of Surgeon Finch, also of the 6th Ohio.

At 5 a.m. on the following morning, Lloyd ordered reconnaissance made to the Columbia and White House bridges. Lieutenant-Colonel Muhleck was to take the first expedition to the site of the Columbia Bridge with six companies of the 73rd and four companies of the 6th Ohio, under Captain Barber, and the section of artillery. At the same hour, Lieutenant Colonel Nazer took four companies of the 4th New York, six companies of the 68th Infantry, and two mountain howitzers toward the White House.

Muhleck reached his destination without meeting resistance, but sent Captain Barber across with the cavalry to "scour the woods and roads for 2 miles south of the ford." With still no appearance of any Confederates, the party learned that there were "no indications that any scouts, patrols, or other parties of the enemy have crossed the ford for ten days."

Nazer's expedition would prove different. By 9 a.m. Nazer's men reached the White House Ford, also without meeting with resistance. However, upon reaching the ford, the Federals did encounter some "rebel cavalry, not more than 20," appearing on the opposite side of the river and "within rifle range." Having accompanied Muhleck's journey for about four miles, Lloyd decided to join Nazer's party moving on the White House Ford, and proceeded with his adjutant, Captain Richart, and a small escort of cavalry. Lloyd elaborated:

"... We learned that 15 rebel cavalry had crossed the ford yesterday morning and recrossed about 9 o'clock; that about 40 cavalry crossed the night of the 20th and recrossed about 2 the next morning. We know that this party rode through the town of Luray and back the same night, shouting for Jeff. Davis, but committing no other indiscretion..."

Reaching the ford shortly after Nazer's men had arrived there, Lloyd continued that "... A few shots were exchanged with the rebel cavalry, but a shot or two from the howitzers started their party back toward the gap." Concluding that the area around Luray was clear of any "rebel force of any description," Lloyd figured that the opposing force was no more than four or five companies that used Harrisonburg as their base of operations to New Market and into the Page Valley. Nevertheless, Lloyd would continue his stay in Luray for a while, establishing his own base of operations to send patrols "southward daily." It was just a hint of worse times to come on the Page home-front in the following month.

White's 'Comanches' included Leaders, Men of Grabill's Company E, 35th Battalion Virginia Cavalry
(July 1862)
Article of 6/18/1998

By the time that John Henry Grabill had enlisted his company on July 30, 1862, the Civil War was well into its second year. Not officially organized until September 9, 1862, it was another three months before the company was designated as Company E, 35th Battalion Virginia Cavalry on December 20, 1862. Grabill's Company was made up of men from both Page and Shenandoah counties. However, though many of the men may have been from Shenandoah at the time, several had ties either through marriage or ancestry in Page County.

Organized for service along the border, the 35th Battalion was destined to serve with the Army of Northern Virginia for long periods of time. This was a constant source of irritation, for they believed their destiny was as a raiding organization rather than regulars. However, this dissatisfaction did not prevent them from becoming good cavalrymen. Their wild charges with ear piercing yells often carried them into enemy lines, and prompted General Thomas Lafayette Rosser to give them the lasting name of the "Comanches."

When brigaded, they became an element of the famous Laurel Brigade. Commendations came from Brigadier Generals "Grumble" Jones, Thomas Rosser, and James Dearing, who led this brigade from 1862 to the end of the war. Through the mountains of Western Virginia they rode in General Jones' famous raid of 1863. The great cavalry battle of Brandy Station took the heaviest toll in men and horses suffered in any engagement. Among the men lost from Co. E were Isaac Newton Kibler, Marcus McInturff and Charles Triplett, killed; Franklin Clem, Charles B. Fristoe, Charles Giddings, and T. Honer, wounded; and Captain John Grabill, Isaiah Clem, George Duncan, Thomas J. Handright, John A. Pierson, Jacob F. Rudassiller, Thomas Rudassiller, William Walters, and James W. T. Warren captured.

On June 26, White's Battalion, reduced to no more than 200 men, was ordered to take the lead for an advance of General John B.

Gordon's infantry brigade on the little crossroads town of Gettysburg. As the battalion approached the quiet town, Page County native Lieutenant Harrison Monroe Strickler and Co. E, led the way, descending the grade to Marsh Creek. Immediately in their path was the Adam's County Federal Cavalry and the 26th Pennsylvania Emergency Regiment. With a blood curling scream, the Comanches, with Strickler and Co. E in the front, charged down upon the enemy, creating a route. With Private Albert Bowers riding "boot to boot" with Strickler, others in the charge included John W. Grove, Warfield Yates, Dallas Slusher, John H. Flinn, John Shenk, and John P. Mauck. In what might have been a bloody scenario, many of the Pennsylvanians fled the scene or threw down their arms asking for quarter.

Following the return from Gettysburg, Company E, the same company that had lead the way into the town, acted as the rearguard, and was among the last to cross the Potomac into Virginia.

The 35th continued the war in the years to come, fighting at the battle of the Wilderness, Trevillians Station, the "Beefsteak Raid," and in efforts to stop Sheridan's "barn burners" in the Shenandoah Valley. From Petersburg to High Bridge, the 35th acted as the rearguard to Lee's dying army. Refusing to surrender at Appomattox, the Cavalry rode out in a wild charge reminiscent of their earlier days.

The Grand 'Parade' and the Last Passage of Stonewall from the Valley
(November 1862)
Article of 12/21/2000

Given the chance to take a look at the four Civil War Trails markers recently placed in Page County one would realize that Jackson's last passage out of the Valley in November 1862 was given a sort of "double-duty" in two of those markers. While many may be aware of the significance of Jackson's last mortal glimpses of the Valley being upon Page County from near Franklin Cliffs in the vicinity of Fisher's Gap (see the Graves Chapel marker for this story), many may not be aware of a few other significant stories of the trek.

After several weeks in the vicinity of Winchester (in the wake of the battle of Sharpsburg/Antietam), Jackson's men marched up the snow-covered Valley and into Page en route to join Robert E. Lee in the defense of Fredericksburg. Jackson had only recently been promoted to lieutenant general and ultimately, was the commander of one of two of Lee's "wings." General James Longstreet commanded the other "wing."

By Monday, November 24, Jackson and his staff had made their way, with a large portion of his "wing" still in tow, to Page County. On that clear and crisp morning, the staff of the hero of Manassas took in the awe inspiring view of the Page Valley below, when, to the surprise of all, Jackson emerged from his tent with an amazing new look. The man that had only recently had his photograph taken in a less than noteworthy frock coat stood before his junior officers in a new coat given him by J.E.B. Stuart, a tall hat given by mapmaker Jedediah Hotchkiss, and a new captured sword given him by a cavalryman. As the men continued to gawk, Jackson announced: "Young gentlemen, this is no longer the headquarters of the Army of the Valley, but of the Second Corps of the Army of Northern Virginia."

In the days that followed, Jackson's Corps did not march toward Luray, but rather made its way from the gap in the Massanutten toward the former site of Columbia Bridge near Alma. From there, the approximately 38,000 men (including four divisions and 23 batteries of artillery) marched not along Rt. 340 as some may believe, but along the Honeyville Road toward Marksville, past Graves' Chapel and on to Fisher's Gap via the famous Red Gate Road.

To the Page County soldiers among Jackson's Corps, the march through the home county was a great opportunity for furloughs. Having secured "permission for the entire company to go home" on November 23, Captain Michael Shuler of the Page Grays did not rejoin his regiment until November 27 in Madison County.

Private John P. Louderback of the 10th Virginia Infantry determined to "go home and stay at home for several days" by November 23. Finding "all well at home" on November 24, like many civilian residents of the area, he went down to the site of Columbia Bridge to see "our regt Pass over."

Continuing to watch the "parade" of troops in the days that followed, at around noon on November 27, he finally witnessed "the rear of the Army pass along" with about "sixty prisoner with them."

In addition to the significance of "Stonewall's" exit of the Valley and the "birth" of the Second Corps, the four day event proved significant also for being the largest single assembly of soldiers to pass through Page County at any one time during the war.

The Stern Discipline of Stonewall Jackson and the Hard-Luck Page Grays
(February 1863)
Article of 5/20/1999

The execution of deserters during the Civil War was not uncommon but the Page Grays of Company H, 33rd Virginia Infantry held a remarkable record of execution sentences - the most of any single company in the 33rd Virginia and likely the highest of any single company in the entire Stonewall Brigade. Interestingly, the majority of all of these men had returned to the company voluntarily, faced their punishments, and fought in future battles - some being killed in battle and one dying as a prisoner-of-war in 1865.

At the "high tide" of the abundance of courts-martial in Stonewall Jackson's Second Corps in the winter of 1862-63, in addition to seven men sentenced to death, there were eleven others from the Page Grays sentenced to various other punishments including the laying on of between 25 to 39 lashes across a bare back.

Four of those that had been sentenced to execution were fortunate enough to have escaped on technicalities - the courts-martial recorder having improperly maintained a complete record of the courts. Gabrill L. Price, Andrew J. Knight and William Pence were not as fortunate. However, despite their sentences, brigade commander General E.F. Paxton, intervened, writing General Jackson on several points including the fact that the execution of three men from the same company and county might bear undesirable implications in discipline and morale. Instead, Paxton suggested to Jackson that the men be allowed to draw lots leaving only one to be executed. Not one for leniency, Jackson made his comments about the matter and routed the paperwork on to General Robert E. Lee who in turn made his recommendations. Though staff member Henry Kyd Douglas inaccurately stated in later years that on the day of execution the men were all pardoned by President Jefferson Davis, ultimately it appears that the decision for drawing lots was found agreeable. On that fateful day of February 28, 1863, William Pence, the thirty-one year-old laborer from Leakesville, was the unlucky man of the lot.

Map-maker Jedediah Hotchkiss recollected that the condemned man "wept bitterly, wishing to see his family." However, Mager William Steele, of the 48th Virginia Infantry, recollected much more. After the entire division had formed near the site of the execution in a deep hollow near Camp Winder "the condemned man leaning on the arms of two chaplains" was brought into view. Steele wrote: "we went up to the stake playing the Dead March . . . When we got to the place the men that were carrying the coffin put it down by the side of the stake and the condemned man sat upon it leaning against the stake. The preachers sang and prayed and then shook hands with him." When asked for his last statements, Pence stated he wished to see his brother, which was not honored. Again the condemned Page man was asked for a last statement to which he replied "No, nothing." When the order to fire was given Pence "threw up his hands and fell over. He did not speak after he was shot, he gasped for breath twice. His last words were 'O what will my poor wife do. . . .'" It was just over weeks since William's seventh wedding anniversary with his wife Rebecca.

On a final note, Andrew Jackson Campbell, a member of the Page Grays and one of the discoverers of the Luray Caverns barely escaped a court-martial of his own that winter. Having been absent without leave from November to December 1862, Campbell however, delivered a "satisfactory excuse" and went on to see the end of the war and the development of tourism in Luray.

A Sad Tale of Two Civil War Soldiers, Part 1
(March 1863)
Article of 5/4/2000

Have you ever been far away from home and loved ones in a strange and different place? Some who have been in the military can relate to the anguish of a soldier or sailor who has made long deployments. Then too, perhaps you had or have a child or sibling who was far away and you wondered how and where they were. Now, with that in mind, for just a moment, try to recall the coldest of days this past winter. With all of these thoughts collected, proceed to a point back in time over 136 years ago during the middle of the Civil War. You are a soldier from the Carolinas, here in the Page Valley, having been on campaign for nearly 2 years away from your home. If you were lucky, you might have been able, at some point, to obtain a furlough home. Though an odd sort of heaven-sent blessing – perhaps you would become ill or wounded – not too seriously, but just enough to secure that furlough home to see family and loved ones, just one more time. Perhaps it would be the last time.

In the winter of 1862-1863, thoughts of home may have been weighing heavily on the minds of two men that were making their way through Page County with their units. Both would fall seriously ill and die in and around the area of Marksville. Both would be buried in unmarked graves in the Graves' Chapel cemetery – forgotten except by those that laid them in the cold, hard ground of winter – forgotten except by their families that probably continued to grieve and wonder what had become of them.

Today, these graves can be clearly seen from the sidewalk leading to the front of Graves' Chapel. Two depressions in the earth that have remained unmarked and silent testimony to the final resting spots of two Carolina soldiers for over 136 years.

As early as February 1898, the graves received attention in the *Page Courier*. The article read:

"Mr. John W. Keyser, the Marksville correspondent of The *Courier* writes us that there are two unmarked graves of Confederate soldiers in Graves' Chapel cemetery, near that place. He knew the men well, and while no marble shafts mark their last resting place, the little mounds have ever been kept green. Mr. Keyser desires to make public these facts in the hope that they may reach some of the relatives and friends of the dead soldiers."

Over eight years later, the graves made another formal appearance in the media. Frederick T. Amiss, commander of the newly formed Summers-Koontz Camp Sons of Confederate Veterans, submitted an article that appeared in the December 1906 issue of *Confederate Veteran* and made an appeal to all those that knew of any unidentified graves of Confederate soldiers in Page County. The graves of the two Carolinians topped the list.

It was nearly 25 year later before more detailing information was revealed about the two mysterious unmarked graves in the Graves' Chapel cemetery. According to an article written for the June 12, 1931 issue of the *Page News & Courier*, a Stanley correspondent (Hobson) had asked Mr. J. H. Coffman for the names of the two soldiers that were buried in the cemetery years before. Then a resident of Westmont, N.J., Coffman was only too happy to reply.

A Sad Tale of Two Civil War Soldiers, Part 2
(March 1863)
Article of 5/18/2000

On June 5, 1931, Mr. Coffman provided his knowledge of the two silent graves in the Graves' Chapel cemetery:

"Now as I recall it, it was in March 1864, . . . I was informed that it was a North Carolina regiment came from east of the Blue Ridge crossing at Milam's Gap and rested over night . . .I think there had been a light snow which had melted, causing a small stream to flow, in which a dead man's feet were seen. This man of medium build and a blond was Sergeant Whistlberry, who evidently went to sleep on his leafy bed without complaining of any ills but died about 3 a.m. When it was reported that there was a dead man in the woods, my aged mother and I went to see him. I think this was about 10 a.m. the regiment had moved on, but two of his cousins had been detailed to give the body proper burial, and it was from them that I got my information. This was the one that is buried in the extreme Southeast corner of the cemetery, under the shade of a large red oak tree, that was the corner of the burial lot. The late Samuel M. Larkins made his coffin of poplar wood, stained red. Then with a jack plane the edges were taken off to create a finish. I think he was buried as well, or possibly a little better than most of the soldier dead. I think Mr. Larkin was allowed $5 for his work."

After a search of the Confederate military records, there has been no luck in identifying a Sergeant Whistleberry. However, the 1898 article may have provided enough details to identify the North Carolinian as Private Whortle Berry of the 1st Cherokee Regiment from North Carolina.

In speaking of the second Carolinian, Coffman wrote:

" . . . his name was Wm. F. Bruner. He was buried beside the first man and in the same manner, and also by Mr. Larkins. Bruner belonged to a Cavalry regiment . . . Graves' Chapel was used as a hospital . . . Bruner was of a dark complexion with jet black beard. I also saw him buried. He died in the church "hospital", on two of the short benches, used in the so-called amen corner, put together they made a very good bed."

After a review of the South Carolina records several months ago, I was able to positively identify Bruner. Having enlisted for the war on May 26, 1862 at Secessionville, S.C., Bruner served as a private in Co. D, 2nd South Carolina Cavalry ("Wassamassaw Cavalry") and was present on all rosters through November 1862. His record ends abruptly leaving no mention of death. However, unit records do positively show that the regiment made a trek from Raccoon Ford on the Rapidan River to New Market in March 1863. While there remains a question as to whether Coffman's recollections were precise to the year, there is no doubt that Bruner's company passed through the Page Valley.

Now, nearly 69 years since the last article about the silent graves, efforts are being made to obtain headstones from the Veterans Administration to finally give the men a proper monument. Not only will the headstones remember the soldiers, but they will also be acknowledged on the Civil War Trails marker that will be dedicated at the Graves' Chapel in November. It only took 134 years.

Some on the Retreat from Gettysburg Found Passage through Page
(July 1863)
Article of 1/25/2001

While not necessarily a direct result of the battle of Gettysburg and while General Lee wasn't among those that found passage through Page County in July 1863, there was an action near Front Royal that gave Page County a brief tie to the end and beginning of two major campaigns of the Civil War.

Nearly three weeks after the Pennsylvania battle, after having crossed the Potomac River into Virginia at Williamsport, Confederate troops from Lt. Gen. A.P. Hill's III Army Corps were in the vicinity of Manassas Gap. Wishing to both relieve the cavalry posted in that gap and to cut off the continued avenue of retreat, Union Gen. George G. Meade ordered Maj. Gen. William H. French (ironically of the Army of the Potomac's III Corps) to advance against the Confederates in that area.

On July 23, 1863, Brig. Gen. A.R. Wright's Brigade (under the command of Col. E.J. Walker of the 3rd Georgia Infantry) of Maj. Gen. Richard H. Anderson's Division was assigned to guard the flank of Hill's Corps. At daylight, the brigade marched 5 miles into Manassas Gap and was soon alerted of a possible Union cavalry force in their front. Taking position on a ridge that extended across the Gap, Colonel Walker detached the 3rd Georgia and ordered it forward about 1 mile to "Wapping Heights" overlooking the valley. At about 11 o'clock the enemy attacked all along the front in heavy line of battle. Although outnumbered, the 3rd Ga., with help from the strong position, held the Federals in check for several hours. Late in the day, Gen. Ewell formed the advanced lines of his corps and opened with several of his batteries on the enemy. Near dusk, the poorly coordinated Union assaults were abandoned. While Confederate forces withdrew into the Luray Valley that night, on the following day, the Union army occupied Front Royal.

The battle of "Wapping Heights" or Manassas Gap resulted in at least 21 killed and 84 wounded for the Federals. While Confederate losses were not ascertained, the overall casualties for the engagement was estimated at 440 total. Present with the II Corps,

Stonewall Jackson's former mapmaker, Jedediah Hotchkiss disputes this estimate stating, "we lost 45 killed and wounded."

Following the engagement, Hotchkiss also kept a careful account of the retreat into Page County. While Rodes halted at Milford on the 24th, some elements reached a point three miles beyond Milford. The following day, Hotchkiss was in the company of the force that made their way "up to Pass Run and fixed our headquarters near the Brick Church, Rodes being just below the Sperryville Road. Johnson [Maj. Gen. Ed "Allegheny" Johnson's Division] is encamped near the Luray and Front Royal, on Pass Run; Early [Maj. Gen. Jubal Early's Division] spends tonight at Mt. Jackson; Longstreet and A.P. Hill are in Culpeper." The following day, a Sunday, was spent comfortably still in Page County at the base of Thornton Gap in camp. Rev. Beverly Tucker Lacy preached at Headquarters in the morning. By that evening, Early's Division was moving across the Luray/New Market Gap into the Page Valley to join the balance of Ewell's Corps.

The following morning, Hotchkiss accompanied Rodes' and Johnson's Divisions as they crossed Thornton Gap. Early later marched across the Blue Ridge at either Fisher's or Milam's Gap. Thus passed the three days that tied the history of Page County with the conclusion of the Gettysburg Campaign. "Wapping Heights" is also associated with the beginning of the "Bristoe Campaign" that would not end until October.

Federal Cavalry and the December 1863 Raid on Luray
(December 1863)
Article of 4/20/2000

On the morning of December 21, 1863, Colonel Charles H. Smith, commanding the 2nd, 8th, and 16th Pennsylvania Cavalry and the 1st Maine Cavalry, set out from Bealeton Station on a trek to find the disposition of General Thomas L. Rosser's cavalry somewhere near Luray. Interestingly, Rosser's command, including a company of Page County men (the Massanutten Rangers of Co. D, 7th Virginia Cavalry), had itself just completed responding to rumors that a force of Federal cavalry was passing from Winchester to Staunton – actually a diversion from Federal Gen. W.W. Averell's descent upon the Virginia & Tennessee Railroad. After a grueling 72-hour march covering 230 miles, [from Fredericksburg to the Occoquon, Sangster's Station on the Orange & Alexandria Railroad, Upperville, Berry's Ferry, Front Royal, Luray, and Conrad's Store (Elkton)] Rosser joined forces under Gen. Jubal Early at Mt. Jackson on December 20. Having evaded one force of enemy cavalry, Rosser had also learned that the force he had been sent to the Valley to pursue had returned to Winchester.

Nevertheless, Smith and his troopers still believed Rosser to be in the vicinity of Luray and passed through Thornton Gap on December 22. As the Federal brigade descended into the Page Valley, it was fired upon by a few of Harry Gilmor's men (also having recently withdrawn to Page County) just after dusk, but the encounter lead to nothing but "more than a dozen shots." Smith's party reached a point just four miles from Luray that night.

On the following morning, with the 2nd Pennsylvania as a vanguard, the Federal expedition continued and was met by another "small picket force" that was "easily brushed away." When within sight of Luray, the Federals again encountered yet another group of about thirty men who were charged and driven through the town with a loss of at least two prisoners, and by evening, two deserters. After the pounding of hooves through the streets, Smith learned from a "reliable" source that Rosser had camped near the town two days before and had since taken "the 'grade' up the Page Valley, on the east side of the river in the direction of Madison, "thus putting itself between my command and the Confederate army, with the advantage of forty-eight hours' start." Believing the source to be true and with too much ground to make up, Smith came back into Luray and began to order detachments to investigate the town. Smith reported:

"At Luray, examined the post office, jail, &c., and learned that some conscripts had been removed on the news of our approach. Also discovered a large three-story building (Borst's tannery) used as an extensive manufactory of Confederate bridles, saddles, artillery harness, &c., well filled with leather, buckles, rings, tools, and everything requisite for such an establishment, together with a large supply of articles ready manufactured. Adjacent to this building was an extensive tannery, with vats filled with stock, and store-houses full of leather and raw material, all of which were completely destroyed by fire or otherwise."

In addition to Borst's tannery, the Federals had also destroyed Britton's shops and broken up Gilmor's camp equipage.

Now feeling threatened himself, Smith decided to withdraw from Luray, back through Thornton Gap. With the Valley clear of Federals once again, Rosser's men, including the Page County horsemen, were afforded the rare opportunity to receive furloughs and spend a wartime Christmas in their Valley homes. By the morning of December 31, the gray-clad horse soldiers were again on the move.

Though Page's VMI cadets Didn't Fight at New Market, They Did Distinguish Themselves in Service
Special Article that Appeared in the
"Page County Plus" Section
5/25/2000

Over 136 years ago the Battle of New Market raged across the Massanutten and concluded with a long-running tradition that would honor the boys of the corps that closed the gap in the General John C. Breckinridge's Confederate line.

Though most of Page's earliest matriculants (seven from 1843-1863) had attended classes under Professor T.J. (later "Stonewall") Jackson, there were none among the "New Market Cadets;" though over half did later "wear Confederate gray." Interestingly, Page's first three matriculants to the Institute (Willis Young Marye, Gabriel Jordan, and Hiram Jackson Strickler) would not see service during the Civil War.

Marye (the son of William Staige and Elizabeth Ruffner Marye) matriculated in 1843 but did not complete the curriculum at the Institute. Joining his brother in a venture to California, he immediately engaged in mining and remained in California through the Civil War.

In 1846, Gabriel Jordan, the son of Gabriel and Mary Betsy Seibert Jordan, entered the Institute and became the first Page Countian to graduate from VMI, numbering 13 in a class of 17, on July 4, 1850. Though a highly successful chief engineer in the construction of several southern rail lines, Jordan "tried very hard to get into the Confederate Army . . . but was requested to remain where he was being of more value where he was in keeping his line operating than he would be in the field fighting." Though he did not serve, three of Jordan's brothers held significant posts in the army.

Lastly, Hiram J. Strickler was one of a Page County trio (including William Overall Yager and Simeon Beauford Gibbons) to enter the Institute from 1848 - 1849.

The son of Abraham and Susanah Hollingsworth Strickler, Strickler was dropped from the Institute just short of graduation due to insubordinate conduct. With most of his education as a civil engineer complete, Strickler set out for the west, and in 1855 settled in Shawnee County, Kansas where he made a name for himself in that state's earliest history. However, prior to the war he married and "retired to his farm and devoted himself wholly to agricultural pursuits."

The Page Countians that remained among the list of VMI matriculants from 1849 - 1863 cast their lot for either Virginia or Texas during the Civil War.

The son of Nicholas Wesley and Christina Overall Yager, William O. Yager matriculated in 1848 and graduated 5th of 24 as a cadet lieutenant on July 4, 1852. Yager went on to continue his education and graduated from the University of Virginia Law School in 1854. Following his friend and former classmate Strickler to Kansas, Yager held several noteworthy posts in Tecumseh before the Civil War. By the opening of the war, he had removed to Texas where he was elected 1st lieutenant of state troops in 1861. Finding an assignment with the 1st Texas Cavalry, by 1864 Yager was elected as full colonel of the 1st Texas Cavalry. During the war (1863) he met and married Mary Elizabeth Rhodes in Seguin, Texas. Rhodes, the daughter of Alexander H. Rhodes, also claimed Page County roots.

Surviving the war, Yager became the county surveyor of Guadalupe County, Texas and was the principal of the Guadalupe Male Academy. By 1868 Yager returned to Page to become the hold top posts of several noteworthy Page County businesses to include the Page Woolen Mill, the Page County Bank, Luray Manufacturing Company, and the Page Valley Bank. Additionally, Yager kept busy in politics having served as a member of the Virginia House of Delegates and superintendent of Page County Schools. Yager died on January 20, 1904.

Being among the ranks of regimental commanders in "Stonewall" Jackson's Valley Army of 1862, Yager's matriculating partner, Simeon Gibbons, was to be held in high esteem as an early victim of the Civil War. The son of Samuel and Christina Miller Gibbons, Simeon graduated just behind classmate Yager as 7 of 24 in 1852. Beginning his post-graduate life as a teacher, Gibbons married

Fanny Shacklett in 1855 in Harrisonburg, where he made his home for the next few years. Taking a turn in life as a businessman and merchant in that town, Gibbons was also a member of the Board of Visitors of VMI until the opening of the Civil War.

Having maintained his military affiliation as a member of the Valley Guards, Gibbons served as captain of this organization "during the imprisonment and at the execution of John Brown, at Charles Town, in 1859. In the year that followed, the 4th Regiment Virginia Volunteers was formed from the men of the area and Gibbons chosen for command. This regiment was among the first to report to Harpers Ferry at the beginning of the war in 1861. Elected as colonel of the 10th Virginia Infantry, Gibbons served with distinction under General Joseph E. Johnston at 1st Manassas.

But, in the heat of battle at McDowell, Virginia on May 8, 1862, Gibbon's ever-fast rising star would come to an abrupt end. Though the Federal troops had been repulsed, Gibbons had received two fatal bullets. According to the history of the 10th Virginia Infantry: "His body was immediately carried toward the rear by members of the regiment. Gibbon's younger brother and acting aide, William S. Gibbons (VMI '63), rushed to his side but the colonel died just as he reached him. Gibbons died just seventeen days short of his 29th birthday."

The last of those to matriculate from Page County prior to the war were Colonel Gibbon's brother, William Stephens Gibbons and John Henry Lionberger. As matriculants intended for graduation in the class of 1863, both had just missed service with the cadets of New Market.

The son of John and Lavinia Seibert Lionberger, John Henry matriculated on July 28, 1859. With the corps of cadets just after the outbreak of the war, Lionberger marched to Richmond served as a drillmaster for forming Confederate regiments until June 1861. However, like many of corps, Lionberger left the Institute for active service soon after. Though he was listed as having enlisted with Page's own "Massanutten Rangers" of Company D, 7th Virginia Cavalry on June 1, 1861, records indicate that Lionberger was transferred to Page County's Dixie Artillery in July 1861.

Lionberger was listed as in command as captain of artillery at Romney, Virginia (now W.Va.) from September to October 1861, but not with the Dixie Artillery. By the spring of 1862, Lionberger was again in the ranks of the Massanutten Rangers and was present at the attempt to burn White House Bridge in April 1862. By March 1863, Lionberger had apparently found a home in Lee's Bodyguard or Company C, 39th Battalion Virginia Cavalry. He remained in the service of this organization, with others from Page County, until the end of the war.

After the Civil War and matters had somewhat settled at the Institute, Lionberger was honored with being listed as an honor graduate on July 2, 1869. Marrying Miss Laura Maguire, Lionberger left his wife and five children to mourn his early death (he was only 36) in 1879.

Though also listed as designated for the class of 1863, William S. Gibbons did not matriculate at VMI until July 21, 1860. Among the VMI drillmasters in Richmond in the summer of 1861, Gibbons was at first attached to the 1st Tennessee Infantry, but transferred to the 10th Virginia Infantry to serve as aide for his brother, Colonel Simeon Gibbons. Following the death of his brother, William continued service with the 10th Virginia as a private until he again transferred in May 1864 to Company C, 39th Battalion Virginia Cavalry to serve with classmate Lionberger. Captured at Hedgesville, Virginia (now W.Va.) As a scout on July 9, 1864, Gibbons was sent as a prisoner of war to Wheeling but was later transferred to Camp Chase, Ohio. Having been tried by a Federal court "three times on charges of being a spy" Gibbons "narrowly escaped death" and was exchanged on March 2, 1865. Gibbons career as a soldier apparently came to an end and he returned to his family's home in Rome, Georgia. However, in January 1866, he was arrested by U.S. authorities and with four other "young men, was carried to Atlanta and kept in confinement three weeks." The reason behind the arrest had evolved around the fact that a Confederate flag was owned by his family and had been used in a tableau in which the other four took part."

Like Lionberger, Gibbons was listed as an honor graduate of VMI in 1869. The light-haired, fair completed Gibbons served as a druggist from 1865 - 1872, when he moved to his farm near Rome, Georgia where he resided until his death in April 1931.

Ultimately, all of Page's early 19th century matriculants that passed through the famed halls of the "Institute" proved their worth to society, in both war and peace, whether it was on the battlefield or in public service.

Action at Overall May Have Prolonged the Civil War
(September 1864)
Article of 12/16/1999

Following the defeat of General Jubal Early's Confederate army by General Philip H. Sheridan at the Battle of Third Winchester, Confederate forces were quickly reassembled further to the south to prepare for a Federal attack. While Early regrouped his army at Fisher's Hill near Strasburg, Sheridan quickly dispatched General Alfred T.A. Torbert to take Colonel Wesley Merritt's 1st Division and join Colonel James H. Wilson's 3rd Division at Front Royal. From there, the combined Federal cavalry arm would move along the eastern side of the Massanutten through the Page Valley. If successful, Sheridan would strike Early's left flank with the bulk of his force while Torbert crossed the New Market/Luray Gap and surprised Early on the right.

Anticipating such a maneuver, Early had sent Fitz Lee's Division of cavalry, under Williams C. Wickham, up the Luray Valley. Clashing first with the Federals at Riverton on the Shenandoah River, then later on Gooney Run in Warren County on September 20, Wickham temporarily stalled Torbert's efforts.

By 2 a.m. on September 22, Merritt's and Wilson's divisions had merged to throw a full strength attack against Wickham. By then however, the Confederates had prepared a formidable defensive position at Milford (now Overall) that would prove impossible to attack. Among the group of Federal cavalry that had come upon the Confederate position was one of George Armstrong Custer's troopers who frustratingly scribbled in his diary, "Johnnys in a strong position."

Nonetheless, Wilson opened the action with artillery, which was soon joined by the crackle of Federal carbine fire. The Confederate forces soon responded in kind. While the rolling terrain rocked with a "ringing fire," Wickham rode off to consult with Early over the situation, leaving Colonel Thomas T. Munford to conduct the defense.

The fire continued for hours with little progress made by Torbert. However, late in the afternoon, he appeared to move against Colonel

William Payne's brigade, positioned closest to the river. Witnessing the effort, Munford asked his artillery commander, Major James Breathed, if he thought his guns were safe from capture. In response, a bold Breathed replied "If 'Billy' [Colonel Payne] can hold that bridge - and it looks like he is going to do it - I'll put a pile of cannister [sic] near my guns, and all h--l will never move me from this position."

Meanwhile, Munford realized the movement on Payne was a feinted attack, designed to distract from an effort to turn his right flank. In response, Munford sent a squadron of the 4th Virginia Cavalry to the support of the 2nd Virginia. Additionally, three buglers were sent to create a bluff of their own. When given the order, the buglers, spaced at good intervals, sounded the charge, and forced the Federals to abandon the maneuver.

Disgruntled, Torbert broke off the engagement and withdrew from the field. The following morning, Wickham withdrew from Milford while Torbert continued a withdrawal to Front Royal. Late in the afternoon however, the Federal commander learned of Sheridan's victory at Fisher's Hill. Quickly, he wheeled his cavalry back toward the Page Valley, catching up with Wickham's command near Luray. Driving the Confederates from the field near Yager's Mill, Torbert continued across the Massanutten toward New Market - but it was too late. Wickham had successfully held the line and effectively prevented what could have been the entire annihilation of Early's army. Furthermore, the effort, having prolonged the presence of Early in the Valley, may have prevented Sheridan's return to General Ulysses S. Grant's forces around Petersburg, and thereby delayed the end of the war.

An English Yankee and the Only Medal of Honor Earned on Page County Soil
(September 1864)
Article of 6/3/1999

In the wake of the tragedy that befell Jubal Early's Confederate Army at Fisher's Hill, cavalry action throughout the Valley and Page County became almost an everyday occurrence for several months in the fall of 1864. On one late September day, a clash of cavalry occurred just north of Luray in which one seemingly unlikely character would earn a Congressional Medal of Honor for his heroic actions on Page County soil.

An Englishman turned "Yank," Private Philip Baybutt was the son of an English merchant and native of Manchester, England. Listed by occupation as a teamster, 18 year-old Baybutt arrived in the United States in either late 1863 or early 1864. Enlisted by Colonel Charles R. Lowell, Jr. at Fall Creek, Massachusetts on February 25, 1864 (though another record shows him as joining at Vienna, Virginia), Baybutt would have the rare distinction to serve as one of the members Company A, 2nd Massachusetts Cavalry. Formerly known as the "California 100," the original group of 100 men had made their way from the Bear State and were initially attached to the Massachusetts cavalry regiment for service in the eastern theater. As one who enlisted in the company well after its initial organization, Baybutt was recruited to replenish the ranks of the depleted company. Additionally, if Baybutt had come seeking adventure, he had certainly enrolled in the right company as the 2nd Massachusetts would often find themselves in action against Mosby's famous band of rangers.

On September 24, 1864 however, Mosby was not the issue. Following the fight that had occurred at Milford (Overall), Colonel W.H.F. Payne's brigade of Confederate cavalry had fallen back to Luray as a result of the Federal withdrawal to Front Royal. Clearly seeing an opportunity, General George A. Custer, accompanied by Colonel Lowell, with two Federal Cavalry brigades (including Baybutt's regiment) and artillery advanced toward Luray. Somewhere between the county border and Luray, the clash of cavalry occurred. Badly outnumbered and outgunned, the Confederates were quickly overwhelmed, losing several men as prisoners. Additionally, sometime in the heated melee, Baybutt seized the regimental flag of the 6th Virginia Cavalry for which he was later (October 1864) awarded the Medal of Honor.

In all, by the close of the war, the 5' 2 1/2" Englishman participated in seven or eight battles and in excess of 50 skirmishes. Additionally, he had lost two horses killed-in-action and was himself wounded twice (once at Opequon Creek just ten days before the Luray fight) before suffering a hard fall from one of his horses while in the Shenandoah Valley.

Sometime following his discharge at Fairfax Court House on July 20, 1865, Private Baybutt returned to England and worked at his father's mercantile business. Married to Harriet Jones (listed as a 24 year-old "spinster" of Leicester) on December 26, 1872, the former Federal cavalryman and his wife would raise eight children.

In later years, Baybutt suffered a great deal from the fall from his horse during the war and applied for a veteran's pension from the United States in January 1904. Though he had at least three former comrades' written testimony as to the seriousness of the incident, his application was rejected in February 1906. Three years later, on April 17, 1909, the former hero of the little fight near Luray - now a 63 year-old shipping clerk, died from "exhaustion" in addition to other ailments experienced as a result of the war. In the wake of Philip's death, his wife of over thirty-years applied for a Union Veteran widow's pension and received an allowance of $8.00 per month by the United States. Ultimately, it was an ironic ending for a man that had been awarded the United States' highest military medal and had given loyal service in a war that was neither his own fight nor that of his country.

One Page County Confederate's Tale of the War, the "Burning" and Comrades
(October 1864)
Article of 7/13/2000

While the number of Page County men that flocked to join in the ranks of the Confederacy was above average for the size of the county, not all became a part of veteran's organizations and participated in post-war reunions. Enoch Van Buren "Mac" Kauffman was one of the few veterans that enjoyed the events with old comrades. In remembering the war he once stated that he "still . . . [held] it as the proudest memory of my life that I served under General Lee."

A member of Co. K, 10th Virginia Infantry (Page Volunteers), Kauffman was born November 6, 1840 in Page County, the son of Barney and Rebecca Mauck Kauffman. Enlisted on June 2, 1861, the 5'10", auburn haired, blue eyed young man was on his way to an experience that few would return from unscathed. A brother who served with him in the Page Volunteers, Joseph Franklin Kauffman, was killed at the 2nd Battle of Manassas on August 28, 1862.

By October 1862, Kauffman was elected as 2nd sergeant and became orderly sergeant for Captain David C. Grayson. Though captured during the following spring on May 4, 1863 at the battle of Chancellorsville, good fortune shined upon him rather quickly and he was exchanged within 6 days at City Point, Virginia.

Resuming service with his company, Kauffman evaded capture or wound at Spotsylvania Court House where most of the company was taken. However, on October 2, 1864, while assigned to a detail in Page, he was again captured. That same day, the Sheridan's raiders burned his mother's barn and his grandfather's mill, and had "all the horses, cattle, and hogs driven away." Kauffman wrote, "My brother [Philip M. Kauffman of Co. E, 35th Battalion Virginia Cavalry] and I were captured, and would have been put to death with other prisoners in retaliation for the death of two Federal soldiers near Luray except for the fortunate capture (for us) of the two men who had done the killing." After being held for almost a week, the brothers were sent to Point Lookout, Maryland. Philip was exchanged on March 28, 1865, but Enoch was not released until after taking the oath of allegiance on June 14, 1865.

Following his return to Page County, Kauffman soon headed west where he married Miss Sarah L. Slusher, of Hancock Creek, Illinois in 1868. A few years later he moved to Kansas and became the proprietor of the Sycamore Mineral Springs.

Kauffman attended the large reunion in Gettysburg, Pennsylvania after the turn of the century. He later wrote, "I will remember it as one of the best experiences of my life." During the encampment, Kauffman returned a bible to the friends of a man named Frost, who had been killed at Spotsylvania Court House, where he had found it. The bible also contained a photo that turned out to be that of Frost's mother.

"Mac" died at the home of one of his children on January 13, 1923 in Seneca, Kansas. Within days of Kauffman's death in 1923, Grayson paid tribute to him saying "He was as true as the needle to the magnet in his loyalty to principle and devotion to his friends and comrades, and when a clash of arms was imminent, he went forward with unfaltering step to meet whatever fate might befall him. He never wavered in his fidelity to the cause, and was always proud of the distinction of having been a Confederate soldier."

Page Execution: Marylanders Fall for Defying Barn-Burners, Part 1
(October 1864)
Article of 5/17/2001

No, it's not the Summers-Koontz Incident this time.

This incident stemmed from an episode at the Henry Pendleton Hershberger home "late on a Sunday afternoon," in October 1864.

Federal troops had been making the rounds in burning barns and mills and were closing in on the Hershberger family. The barn at the Kendrick farm and Willow Grove Mill were already on fire. Elizabeth Hershberger and six of her children watched terrified from the porch of the home anticipating the same for their barn. The husband had taken flight to the Blue Ridge to prevent the capture of a seventeen year-old son.

Though not a soldier, the fear was still prevalent that the boy would be taken as a prisoner of war regardless. The eldest son, John, was a member of Co. K, 10th Virginia Infantry and had been taken prisoner at Spotsylvania Court House in May.

As dusk approached, three Federal cavalrymen moved in on the Hershberger family and in a "loud and boisterous" manner claimed that they had come to burn their barn. However, if the family would pay them $30 or $40 in gold or silver, the barn would be spared.

Knowing that the barn would likely be burned anyway, Elizabeth refused the offer and likely did not have the money. Boasting of their last barn burning, the men appeared drunk to Mrs. Hershberger and demanded that she provide matches as they had run out.

Amazingly, about that same time, another band of horsemen was seen by the children approaching from the edge of the woods on the far side of their orchard. Meanwhile, the Yanks continued, apparently without worry, in a loud manner.

As the other set of horsemen closed in, they paused to hear the Federals give themselves away. Among the lot was Sgt. Frank Long of the Massanutten Rangers of Co. D, 7th Virginia Cavalry. Home from a wound received at Ream's Station, he and a fair group of other men that were at home had moved out that morning apparently with the hope of isolating some of the smaller bands of barn-burners and taking them on.

As Long and two other Confederate horsemen began to make their way down the Hershberger lane, the Federal horsemen near the gate immediately surrendered himself along with the horses of his comrades. Continuing on, Long and one other came upon the Federals at the house and demanded their surrender. Understandably defiant and willing to play his odds, one Federal cavalrymen drew his revolver and yelled, "I will surrender you!" Firing his pistol at almost point blank range at Long, the bullet whistled by Long without harming him.

The frightened mother quickly hurried her children in the house and slammed the door before the next exchange of shots followed. Not knowing the end result of the scrap in the yard, the family remained in the house throughout the evening, and feared that a report would be made to Federal headquarters in Luray and that another patrol would soon follow.

Sometime after dark another band of local men, frequently connected to Confederate activity, came to the house and asked for supper. Upon putting their horses in the barn, they stumbled upon a dead Federal in the yard, took him down near the bottomland not far from the creek and hastily buried him, placing fodder atop the grave to prevent suspicion should other Federals see the grave.[1]

The third Federal had apparently made his way back to the main Federal force and reported the incident. Some sort of repercussions now seemed certain. More to follow . . .

Page Execution: Marylanders Fall for Defying Barn-Burners, Part 2
(October 1864)
Article of 5/31/2001

When last we left the Hershbergers, fear was moving through the family for concern over the dead Federal cavalryman that now lay buried nearby in a shallow grave. As the visiting local men, who had carefully concealed the grave of the soldier, finished their supper, they reassured Mrs. Hershberger that they would remain nearby during the night to keep an eye out for what may happen.

Federal cavalry did not arrive until the next day. Finding the grave of the soldier, the troop gathered information from Mrs. Hershberger and felt confident in her honesty, holding no blame to the family except for leaving the body in the open without properly seeing to him. "Courteous" to her from that moment, the Federals still swore die straits to the Confederate assailants.

Meanwhile nearby, having evaded wound or capture throughout the war, Enoch Van Buren "Mac" Kauffman (Page Volunteers of Co. K, 10th Va. Infantry) was at home with his brother Phillip M. Kauffman (Co. E, 35th Battalion Va. Cavalry) when Federal cavalry came to burn the family barn. Sometime in this event, both brothers were found and captured (October 2, 1864) and stood as very good candidates for revenge over the dead Federal cavalryman. As a fortunate turn of fate, the young men were spared because of the actions of two Marylanders from Company C, 1st Maryland Cavalry of Major T. Sturgis Davis' command.

Three days following the capture of the Kauffman brothers, these Marylanders clashed with Federal cavalry in the Page Valley. It was said of Confederate trooper Churchill Crittenden that he emptied every load in his pistol and wounded "a Yankee lieutenant very severely" before being taken. Confederate John J. Hartigan accompanied Crittenden in the affair. Having been detailed to procure provisions for their company in the county. "Whilst getting their supplies at a farm-house," wrote W.W. Goldsborough, author of "The Maryland Line," a large party of the enemy came suddenly upon them. They attempted to escape, and a running fight ensued, which resulted in the death of two or three of the enemy and the wounding of Crittenden severely, and the capture of both himself and Hartigan."

A Crittenden family newsletter in 1912 gave further details of what followed. After having been brought to Colonel William H. Powell, commanding the Federals from near Luray, the men were taken through a mock trial and ordered to be executed. Prior to the execution, both men asked for pen and paper to draft farewell letters, but were refused the opportunity; Crittenden to his mother and Hartigan to his "young wife."

The family newsletter continued: "At noon Crittenden and Hartigan were set before a firing party of twenty-five and told to run for their lives. Hartigan ran and fell, pierced by many bullets. Crittenden stood with folded arms, facing his executioners. Again the order to fire was given, but not a trigger was pulled. The Union officer in command then addressed his men saying he would repeat the order once more; they were soldiers and must obey, and should any man fail to respect the command, he should suffer the penalty of death himself for his disobedience."

"During this harangue Crittenden seated himself on a rock, calmly looking at the squad and awaiting his end. Then he rose. "Ready! Aim! Fire!" rang out the third command. A line of leveled rifles greeted him as he rose and faced them. Down dropped twenty-four silent rifles, their owners unwilling to harm the quiet man before them. One alone of the twenty-five pressed a trigger. A single flash, a little smoke, a sharp report, and Churchill Crittenden's life blood flowed for the cause he loved."

Page Execution: Marylanders Fall for Defying Barn-Burners:
The Conclusion
(October 1864)
Article of 6/7/2001

On October 17, 1864, the Richmond *Examiner* called the execution of the Marylanders an "atrocity" and declared "The reason assigned for shooting them was that some of their men (the Federals) were shot while burning barns."

According to W.W. Goldsborough, "The facts were all carefully traced out, and verified by the statement of the citizen at whose house the two young men were first attacked, and near which they fought and were captured; by the statement of the citizen, some two miles to the rear, near whose house they were buried, not by the men who killed them, but by the pitying farmer, and by the evidence rendered by the opened graves of the poor men."

Apparently, the men had been temporarily buried "by the last farmer who had given them supplies" in Page County and later relocated. It was also said that upon opening the graves, comrades made "vows" to "avenge their deaths -- and were avenged, though Powell escaped."

John James Hartigan lies today in the Lutheran Reformed Church cemetery in New Market. As for Crittenden, according to the family newsletter, "Col. Lawrence Kip, son of the bishop of California, and then serving in the Northern army, hearing of the tragic death of his boyhood friend, visited the spot and caused notice to be telegraphed Churchill's father. Relatives secured the body and sent it to Richmond, where it now lies in Shockoe Hill Cemetery."

Interestingly, only Hartigan appears to have been a true Marylander -- though again, nothing has been found to yet confirm this. Having enlisted in Co. G, 13th Virginia Infantry early on and having been wounded in action at Munson's Hill on August 27, 1861, Hartigan was later discharged as a "non-resident."

On September 7, 1862, he enlisted with Co. C, 1st Md. Cav. at New Market. Hartigan had served with good service throughout the war. In February 1864 he was allowed to go to Augusta County to secure a new horse for his former mount had been rendered unserviceable.

Churchill Crittenden offers a much more detailed life. The son of Alexander Parker Crittenden, grandson of Judge Thomas Turpin Crittenden of Kentucky, and the great grandson of Major John Crittenden of the Revolutionary Army (from New Kent County, Va.), Churchill was born in Texas on May 17, 1840. Interestingly, Churchill's mother came from a line of Rhode Islanders. In 1851, his father moved his family to California. A. P. Crittenden had pioneered to California across the plains from Texas, in the winter of 1848 and 1849.

Churchill was attending Hobart College in Indiana when the Civil War began. Seeking permission to enlist from his father in San Francisco, Churchill served as a volunteer aide-de-camp to General James J. Archer from June 1862 until he joined the 1st Maryland Cavalry on August 4, 1862 while in Richmond.

Not unlike Hartigan, Crittenden's service record was commendable. On June 12, 1863, Crittenden's horse was killed in action near Winchester, Va. for which he was reimbursed $450. Obviously recognized for his keen military ability, in April 1864, he was detailed to the Mississippi for four months to "organize a band for special service." Returning to the Valley, he was furloughed for 60 days from July 24, 1864, meaning that when the execution took place, he had not been back very long from the respite.

As is known from a previous article (July 13, 2000), the brothers Kauffman survived prisoner-of-war camp after evading execution and lived long after the war.

Page County Confederates Dispatched at Rude's Hill
(Summers-Koontz Execution)
(June 1865)
Special Article of 8/13/1998

By late April 1865, the life of Emma Jane Shuler had turned in a positive direction for the first time in four years. Just short of her nineteenth birthday, the eldest surviving daughter of John and Mary Ann Kite Shuler had certainly had her fill of war and tragedy. A year before, Emma and her family had received news of the death of her oldest brother Michael. He was a captain in the Page Grays and served in that capacity until May 5, 1864 when he was killed in action, at age 20, during the battle of the Wilderness.

Knowing the hazards of duty for her brother, Emma had also kept a watchful eye on another young man's well being.

In the years preceding the war, sweet Emma had grown fond of Isaac Newton Koontz. Just more than a year older than Emma, Newton was the son of Isaac Newton and Anna Keyser Koontz. He enlisted just after his 17th birthday, chose the cavalry as his branch and served with distinction with Company D of the 7th Virginia. Severely wounded once in 1864, Koontz returned to close out his service in the war with what remained of his regiment.

On May 22, over a month after Robert E. Lee surrendered the majority of his remaining army at Appomattox and with Emma yearning for his return home, Newton joined a small band of former comrades from the 7th Virginia who set out for Mount Jackson, where Federal troops were headquartered, to receive their paroles. In addition to Newton Koontz, the party also included Capt. George Washington Summers, Pvt. Jacob D. Koontz and Pvt. Andrew Jackson Kite. Standing at six feet, with light hair and blue eyes, the striking Summers enlisted at the opening of the war and rose quickly through the ranks.

A lieutenant in 1862, within two years Summers was made the last captain of the Massanutten Rangers of Co. D. "Jake" Koontz, a first cousin to Newton, had served with the company since January 1863. A three-year veteran, Jackson Kite was a cousin of Emma. He was the oldest and the only married man in the group.

No one knows what crossed their minds as the band of four rode out of Page that warm day in May. Perhaps, after witnessing four years of war and destruction, they may have greatly resented that Federal troops still occupied the Valley. To make matters worse, the men still carried their side arms on that day, even as they sought their paroles.

The passage across the Massanutten and down the Valley Pike took the party past a group of Federals escorting ex-Governor John Letcher. After passing this contingent, the Page men stumbled into about a half dozen straggling members of Co. H, 22nd New York Cavalry.

The words exchanged between the ex-Confederates and the Rochester cavalrymen are lost to history, but in the end, the Page men demanded that the Bluecoats dismount and surrender their horses. A resentful Federal lieutenant drew his revolver only to be met by the return gesture from one of the ex-Confederate cavalrymen. As both pulled their triggers, the weapons only produced a "pop" of the caps, leaving the other Page men with the advantage of having their weapons drawn first. The New Yorkers reluctantly surrendered their mounts.

Realizing they had committed an illegal act of guerilla warfare, the Page men returned to their homes between Alma and Grove Hill until the matter could be sorted out. Upon learning of the incident, Summers' father, also named George, chastised the boys severely and convinced them to give themselves up, then organized a group of respected citizens to pleas before the provost on the boys' behalf.

The next day, the group, along with several citizens, resumed the trek across the Massanutten and entered the camp of the 192nd Ohio Volunteer Infantry at Rude's Hill. The elder Summers recalled that Col. Francis W. Butterfield, the post commander, "courteously" received them. After explaining at great length the purpose of the "mission," the elder Summers and Butterfield agreed that if the property were returned, the men would receive no punishment. As evidence the matter was settled, Butterfield issued receipts to the ex-Confederates.

That matter should have ended there, but on Sunday soon after the incident, a run-in took place in Monger's Church just across the river from Somerville in Page County, not far from the Summers' family home. The elder Summers later recalled that William Tharp, a local Union sympathizer, "became very much enraged" during an argument with some of the boys involved in the incident. Tharp apparently was unaware that the matter had been resolved with the federal commander and cried out, "You had better return those horses stolen from the Yankees!" The argument escalated into an episode that nearly ended in fisticuffs, and Tharp swore revenge for his mistreatment.

No one knows if Tharp carried through with his threat, and if he did, no record of it was made in the books of the 192nd OVI. But coincidentally, Col. Butterfield went on a furlough that same week, leaving Lt. Col. Cyrus Hussey in command.

Again, it is unknown whether Hussey disagreed with his commanding officer's handling of the run-in with the Page County Confederates, or whether Tharp convinced him that justice was not yet done. But, on Monday, June 26, 1865, Hussey issued Special Order No. 3 to Capt. Lycurgus D. Lusk, commanding officer of Company H, 22nd New York Cavalry, to "proceed to Luray Valley at 9 p.m. and there arrest and execute severally and all without delay whatsoever, the following named men who had been guilty of attacking U.S. troops and stealing horses since the surrender." The four young men's names were underlined several times in red ink.

Early on the morning of June 27, the Federal detachment reached the vicinity of the homes of Summers and Daniel Koontz (Jake's father) and proceeded to encircle the residences, located near what is now Strole Farm Road in the Grove Hill area. Jackson Kite and Jake Koontz evaded the Federals, and George Summers also made an attempt to steal away, but was convinced by his father, who did not know the fate that awaited his son, to give himself up. Newton Koontz was arrested at Daniel Koontz's house and arrived soon after at the Summers home with his captors.

Before arriving however, the Koontz party had stopped briefly at Kite's Mill near Columbia Ford. Recognizing a passerby, Koontz asked permission of the lieutenant in charge to draft a quick note to his family and wrote his Emma:

"I was arrested this morning before daylight at Uncle Daniel Koontz's in bed . . . . I hope dearest Emma you will bear up under this well as you can, and doubt not but that God will allow me to return to you. He will not allow such innocence to be bereft of its happiness . . . Should it be my sad lot to suffer death, I shall endeavor to die a brave man, and a gentlemen."

The elder Summers tried in vain to explain the agreement made with Col. Butterfield and showed the receipts for the returned items, but Lusk remained steadfast, stating he knew nothing of the transaction.

Arriving at the foot of the Massanutten on the Shenandoah County side sometime in the afternoon, Koontz and Summers were finally informed of their fate, told that there would be no trial and allowed to request last rites by a local minister, Socrates Henkel, who, unfortunately, never arrived.

Koontz and Summers continued to plead for their lives, and Captain Lusk himself began to question his orders. He finally decided to delay the execution and ride ahead to camp to see what could be done. Shortly after the captain left, another detachment was sent out by Hussey to do the job Lusk had failed to do – to execute the two men immediately. Within 100 yards of the Federal camp, the new party met the prisoners and their escorts and carried out their orders.

Summers and Koontz were given a few minutes to pen their last farewells to their families. Summers note was simple:

"My Dear Father, Mother, Sisters, and Brothers: Very much to my surprise, we must soon leave this world to try the realities of an unknown one, but I pray God that he may receive my poor, sinful soul. Would to God that I had died upon the battlefield in defense of my dear native South! But it has been otherwise ordered. I submit to my fate. Pray for me and try to meet me in heaven. I feel as though God will forgive my sins. Don't grieve after me . . . .."

Newton Koontz had time to draft two notes. One went to his family while the other was written specifically for his "Darling Emma." To her he wrote:

"Oh, how can I write you? Affliction is bearing me down . . . They are now ready to shoot me. Oh Emma, dearest in the world to me, how can I leave you but I must. Oh, I have heard you too often say that it would kill you to hear of my death. But dearest Emma take it as you can . . . . I wish to be buried with this ring on my finger. Emma, my respect to your father and mother whom I have loved as such, but no more."

At 7:30 p.m., the men fell before the firing squad. On the morning of June 28, the elder Summers arrived at Rude's Hill at 11 a.m., only to find his son and Newton laid out on the ground with "stones for pillows." Grief-stricken, Summers wrote in later years, "To those that spoke evil and treated me unkindly, I returned many kind acts."

Years after the tragic incident, a lonely white monument was erected at the site of the execution. Still standing today, it reads simply: "Capt. George W. Summers and Sgt. Newton Koontz, Company D, 7th VA Cavalry, were here executed on June 27, 1865, by order of Lt. Col. Huzzy [sic] 192 O.V.M.I., without the privilege of any kind of trial, they having been arrested at their homes in Page County, brought here and shot."

The grave of Capt. Summers lies quietly today on a hill in a grove of cedars near Grove Hill. Sgt. Newton Koontz rests peacefully in a family lot near Alma. Jackson Kite and Jake Koontz were never caught and lived past the turn of the century.

Emma Jane Shuler outlived them all. She died in 1912.

Last Letters of Sergeant Isaac Newton Koontz

New Market,
June 27, 1865

My Darling Emma: -

Oh how can I write to you? Affliction is bearing me down! But I will write you a few lines. They are now ready to shoot me. Oh Emma, dearest in the world to me, how can I leave you but I must. Oh I have heard you too often say it would kill you to hear of my death.

But dearest Emma take it as easy as you can,. I will endeavor to die as easy as I can. Emma I have loved you dearer than life its self and I feel as if I could die for you were you in my fix. Emma I want you to attend my burying. I wish to be buried with this ring on my finger, Emma my respect to your father and mother whom I have loved as such, no more, but yours in death, I.N. KOONTZ. P.S. Try and meet me in heaven where I hope to go.

Near New Market,
June 27, 1865.

My Dear Father, Brothers, Sisters, Nephews, Niece, Black ones and family,

I write to bid you all farewell in this world, hoping to meet you all in a better and happier world. I have been bandaged and tied to be shot, but have sent for Parson Henkel, I feel easier than I did at first, I think God is working a change upon me. Remember dead ones that this world is all a shadow, only a moment in life, and death ever lasting. Prepare to meet me in heaven every one of you, I will close. Divide my property among you only consider it though as dust, and lay not the value of your lives on riches. Do not let our deaths grieve you, take it easy. I wish to be buried beside my dear mother. No more, good bye forever.

Your darling, I.N. KOONTZ
My love to all my friends.

Who was the Man behind the Summers-Koontz Execution?
(June 1865)
Article of 3/8/2001

Some may recall the story of the Summers-Koontz execution; whether having read it in an article, a book, or on the highway marker in front of Page County High School. Basically, you likely know the Page County men involved, but do you know the man responsible for the execution?

According to a modern biographer, Lt. Col. Cyrus Hussey was "a stern and righteous man . . . Hussey was a Quaker before the war." However, "he had lost his pacifism but not his self-righteousness [and] that was probably a dangerous combination when he was occupying territory rather than invading it. He apparently never did have a sense of humor."

Born in Highland County, Ohio on 4 November 1838, Hussey was the second youngest of ten children. Interestingly, Cyrus' father, Stephen, was born in Orange County, N.C. in 1793 – the Hussey family later migrated to Ohio. A schoolteacher prior to the war, Hussey was married to Rebecca Hodson in 1858. Quaker records show that Rebecca was disowned by the Clear Creek Monthly Meeting for joining the Methodist Episcopal Church in 7/10/1858. In 8/11/1860 Cyrus was disowned as well for his 12/24/1859 marriage to Rebecca, who was no longer a Quaker and for joining the Methodist Episcopal Church himself.

On September 9, 1861, Hussey enlisted in the 48th Ohio Infantry. Clearly, the death of his 5 month-old daughter, just three days later, must have made an impact on his outlook on life.

During his four years with the 48th OVI he rose from private to captain (2/6/1863) of Company A. According to his biographer, Cyrus Hussey held a great deal of suspicion "of anyone who spoke of the Union in a disloyal way. He refused to sign a recommendation for promotion of Corp. Mitkalf A. Bell (Co. F) to 2nd lieutenant because Bell had made disloyal statements."

Hussey experienced action first at the battle of Shiloh (where Page County native Gen. Thomas Jordan served as Gen. Beauregard's right-hand staff officer) and was a veteran of the siege of Corinth, the capture of Arkansas Post, and the Vicksburg Campaign (the regiment was at Port Gibson and Champion's Hill). Hussey was detached in Columbus, Ohio for the Ohio Draft Rendezvous when his entire regiment was captured during the Red River Expedition in April 1864.

With the handful of men remaining from the old 48th, the regiment was merged with the 83rd OVI and Hussey was mustered out as a supernumerary officer in December 1864. However, four months later, on April 30, 1865, Hussey was appointed as Lt. Col. of the newly formed 192nd Ohio Volunteer Infantry. He remained with this regiment until mustered out in September 1865. A web-biography mentions little about the controversial execution.

Interestingly, Hussey had two brothers -- an older brother, Joshua, also served as a member of the 48th Ohio; the other, William, was killed by Apache Indians in January 1863.

Hussey's life shortly after the war brought the veteran little relief from gloom, losing his first wife to consumption in 1870. Six years later, Hussey remarried and had two sons. Nearly 70 years old, Hussey was serving as an agent for the Aerie Insurance Company in Toledo, Ohio when he applied for his veteran's pension in 1904. Despite surviving war and disease and the trials of time, the former officer responsible for the execution of two Page County men suffered a concussion from a car accident and died on October 23, 1926.

More on Hussey (including a photo and a good portion of his diaries up through 1863) can be read from the web site of the 48th Ohio at:

http://www.48ovvi.org/oh48hussey.html

Miscellaneous Stories Relating to Page Co. in the Civil War

County had Not-So-Pleasant Prisoner-of-War Experience
Article of 3/12/1998

Prison life, in both the North and South, has often been either exaggerated or sugar-coated in order to substantiate the denials that came out of the war. However, it is often said that "history speaks for itself." Neither side was prepared for prisoners-of-war. However, by the close of the war over 410, 000 soldiers, North and South, had been imprisoned in various POW Camps; nearly one-eighth of those that had served in the entire war.

From available records it can be estimated that over 1,350 men served from Page County in the Confederacy during the war including those that served in the regular volunteer units, reserves, militia and other various units formed outside of Page. Of that number, approximately 950 men were frequently "on-the-line" with active regular volunteers. Even from this number we cannot yet (but give me time) give a fair assessment of those that served strictly from Page County as a number of men in the units that were formed in Page County actually came from other counties or states. Nevertheless, after all "ciphering" has been completed, approximately 170 (eighteen percent) Page men found themselves on the wrong side of the fence when the battles were over. Of that number, fortunately less than one percent of the Page men died of disease while in the camps. By comparison, the overall death rate average of the POW camps stood at thirteen percent.

After capture they were sent to three of the four winds (excluding, of course, that "southerly wind"); including POW camps in Illinois, Libby Prison (it was converted from holding Federal POW's to Confederate POW's at war's end) in Richmond, and the infamous "Helmira" or Elmira prison camp in New York state. More than 75 of Page's POW's found their way into Elmira.

While conditions for POW's in any war are typically poor, Civil War prisons were extraordinarily inhumane. It was worse in that Americans were mistreating Americans. While conditions at Camp Sumter/Andersonville were appalling, supplies and manpower were more readily available to the POW camps in the North to rectify poor conditions; sanitary and otherwise. After all, the manpower in the Northern armies represented only a fraction of what was available, continuing to support the theory that the North fought the war with one arm tied behind their back.

Not unlike Andersonville, while at Elmira, prisoners were continually insulted and belittled by the guards. To add insult to injury, tickets were sold to Northern citizens to take a look into the Elmira prison camp from observation towers. In an account by one prisoner, mention was even made of a "sweat-box" as a means of discipline in Elmira. Ultimately, Elmira could be fairly compared as the Andersonville of the North, sustaining the highest mortality rate of the POW camps in the North.

Does the article sound biased? I'll remain somber but pleasantly neutral and straddling the fence in this argument and state that I have indirect ancestors that lie buried today near the confines of the camps that once held them at Andersonville, Elmira and Point Lookout.

Excellent sources are becoming more readily available on this darker side of the war including one of the newer books on the subject entitled *Portals to Hell*, by Lonnie R. Speer. A much older book worth reviewing, when it comes to at least three Page County POW's, is entitled *The Immortal Six Hundred*. Web sites are also becoming available including the Elmira Prison Camp On-Line Library which can be reached at: <a href="http://www.innova.net/~vsix/elmiradoc1.htm"> http://www.innova.net/~vsix/elmiradoc1.htm.

Did Page County African-Americans Serve for the Confederacy?
Article of 11/2/2000

At a quick glance, it is difficult to answer the above question with any certainty. However, historians are currently involved in a great deal of work to answer the larger question. There are currently three significant published studies that help to confirm that African-Americans did serve for the Confederacy - and not necessarily under duress.

It is however Irvin L. Jordan Jr.'s examination of Black Virginians that is the most intriguing. The Associate Curator of Technical Services, Special Collections Department, University of Virginia, Jordan, an African-American, is also a cum laude graduate of Norfolk State University and was a three-time recipient of the Floyd W. Crawford Award for Distinguished Historical Scholarship. He also holds a Master of Arts from Old Dominion University. For a number of years he has thoroughly examined the role of Virginia's African-Americans in the Civil War leading to the publication of Black Confederates, *Afro-Yankees: The History of the African American Experience in Civil War Virginia.*

Jordan's essay, "Different Drummers: Black Virginians As Confederate Loyalists," opens with an examination of an incident in Scottsville. On December 2, 1859, the same day that John Brown hung from the gallows, "blacks led by a slave named Ben hanged him (John Brown) in effigy as an 'old murderer, horse thief and traitor' and proclaimed their willingness to use pikes to defend their owners against abolitionists." Another remarkable incident took place in Culpeper County where a black resident proclaimed "If old Lincoln does put his foot on old Farginny I can raise a regiment of [negroes]." It does not begin or end with the proclamations that Jordan has unearthed, as he also points out that "One hundred thirty-years later, an African-American scholar observed: When you eliminate the black Confederate soldier, you've eliminated the history of the South . . . [We] share a common heritage with white Southerners who recall that era. We shared in the plantation scheme of things as well as the forces that fought to keep them."

For years Black historians have often rejected the authenticity of

Confederate blacks. However, the facts are being made clear that Black Confederate patriotism took many forms from slaves devoted to their owners, to free blacks who donated money and labor, to blacks who diligently supervised the plantation in the absence of their owners. While several "faithful" body servants did make up a large number of Black Confederates, there was a significant number that were either took up arms or otherwise volunteered for the South and staunchly worked on its behalf. Jordan cites numerous references that indicate that approximately 15 percent of Virginia's slaves and 25 percent of its free blacks supported the Confederacy.

While it may take some time to clarify whether any African-Americans from Page served in Confederate gray, in the meantime these noteworthy efforts are worth an examination. In one paragraph Jordan quotes Stephen Vincent Benet in saying that "It is worthy to assemble facts to put truth in the face of legend . . . to investigate impartially, to throw new light on an old problem." Jordan adds that "While the names of thousands of prominent and little known white Confederate civilians, soldiers and politicians are writ large on the pages of history, ignored are the black men and women without whom the nascent Confederacy could not have mobilized."

Why did Page Take a Stand?
Seeking an Answer to the Confederate Question
Article of 11/16/2000

For quite some time, I have been collecting data that may offer help in answering the question regarding the intentions of Page County Confederates (in excess of 1,000 men) as they went off to war. Many believe that the Confederate cause was focused on the preservation of slavery. Then too, there are many that take the stand that it was defense of states rights and defense of the home from Northern aggression. Quite actually there were several factors that played into the ultimate formula for war. But before we begin, remember first that we have the mind-set of 20th/21st century individuals and it is simply not that of individuals in the midst of war in the 19th century.

Over the past several months, I have dug deep into several different resources in order to get a better perspective of Page's stand with the Confederacy. However, there are some peculiar points to bring out regarding the county's support for secession and the "Confederate cause."

First of all, county records show that slavery existed in the county and slaves were a key issue to the ultimate militarization of the county thirty years prior to the American Civil War. In the wake of Nat Turner's efforts in the Tidewater region in 1831, county records indicate that the county reacted upon fear when it established a "policing force" and militia.

Moving ahead on "fast-forward" to 1861, the question is posed as to whether or not slavery had remained the primary issue for military mobilization. From 1840 to 1860, slavery in the county had gone on a roller-coaster ride, increasing from 791 slaves and 189 owners in 1840 to 957 slaves and 230 owners in 1850. However, in the last decade before secession, that number had actually dropped to 850 slaves and 184 owners in 1860. Slavery was, by the numbers, actually on a decline in Page County on the eve of the war.

Ironically, Peter Bock Borst, a New Yorker by birth and only a most recent resident of Page County, represented Page in the 1860 secession convention. Borst was a son-in-law of the prominent slaveholder, Mann Almond. Obviously, Almond's seven slaves were not an earth-shattering number, but he apparently had an influence on Borst's purchase of one slave by 1860 and the hiring of 4 others. Despite this, Borst's actions in the convention were not as a "hot-head" secessionist. His first vote on April 4, 1861 was actually against secession (although I've seen one source that disputes this). On April 17 however, just five days after the bombardment of Ft. Sumter and two days after Abraham Lincoln's call for 75,000 troops, his opinion had changed, like several others, and he voted for secession. Again, however, less than a week later, a referendum vote was made by the citizens in Page County. As a whole, Page nearly swayed against secession with a peoples' vote of 520 for and 430 against. The Ordinance had passed with an extremely narrow margin.

Furthermore, considering that the county had 184 slaveholders in 1860 (and hesitantly assuming that all of them had voted and voted for secession) that left at least 336 who had been "influenced" either by slaveholder's or by Lincoln's call for troops to put down the "insurrection" that was "too powerful to be suppressed by the ordinary course of judicial proceedings." The act was, to many in the South, an act of tyrannical proportions equal to that of King George III on the eve of the American Revolution 86 years before. To many Southerners, and quite likely many Page County citizens, a second war for American Independence was at hand.

A forthcoming article will be more in-depth in examining the social status of Page's officers and soldiers.

The Return of Union Soldiers to Page . . . After the War: Part 1
Article of 2/8/2001

Even in the wake of defeat at the Battle of Port Republic did Federal soldiers find some sort of comfort in the beauty of the Page Valley in June 1862. A member of the 14th Indiana Infantry wrote his "dear wife" while near Luray or what he referred to as "Beulahland":

"Luray is a small town 25 miles south of the Manassas Gap RR in the Blue Ridge range of the Mountains. Our camp today is in a beautiful grassy field, in the midst of magnificent scenery. Within three miles of us, the tall peaks of the Blue Ridge rise away up above the clouds, for the clouds literally hid the summits of many of them. Close by runs a fine stream of pure mountain water, affording an excellent place for dirty soldiers to bathe. I confess that such scenery has peculiar attractions for me, and sometimes in viewing it I almost forget that these lofty hills hide a hostile foe in their bosom, only a few miles away."

Interestingly, several "boys in blue" found a liking to Page County either while in the war or after the war during the railroad boom. In all, over two-dozen former Union soldiers found a home in Page by the close of the 19th century. One particularly interesting man, and senior ranking of all of the bluecoats to find home in Page, was Captain Robert Russell of Co. G, 66th Ohio Infantry. He, like the 14th Indiana Infantry author, was in Page in the wake of the Battle of Port Republic and something may have struck a cord.

Born in 1837, Robert Hill Russell was the son of Valentine and Margaret Hill Russell. While Margaret was a native Ohioan, Valentine had been born in Loudoun County, Virginia in 1814 - giving Robert a tie to the Old Dominion. At age 24, Robert Russell enlisted in the 66th Ohio in Champaign County, Ohio on October 4, 1861. Russell's first true exposure to the horrors of war was in the wake of the Battle of Kernstown in March 1862 when he and the bulk of the 66th were assigned on burial detail for Union and Confederate soldiers alike. By May 1863 Russell had risen rapidly through the ranks and was appointed as captain commanding Company G. At the Battle of Gettysburg, during the contest for possession of Culp's Hill, Russell's regiment faced many veterans from the Shenandoah Valley's famous Stonewall Brigade, which included the men of Co. H, 33rd Virginia Infantry (the "Page Grays").

By the late 1863, the "white stars" of the second division of the 12th Corps of the Army of the Potomac (to which the 66th belonged) was transferred to the war in Tennessee. On November 25, 1863 at the Battle of Lookout Mountain, Captain Russell, while performing a reconnoitering of the Confederate line, had a tremendous fall nine or ten feet before landing on his face, slamming his head backward, causing a sprain to his neck and upper back. While he was fortunate enough not to break his neck, his injury did cause him the loss of four front teeth and would later plague him greatly later in life. A few months later, on the outskirts of Atlanta on July 20, 1864, Russell was prostrated by sunstroke, but refused to leave the line as Confederates advanced on their position on Peachtree Creek. Nine days later Russell's poor luck continued when he was shot in the instep by a Confederate sharpshooter and was finally forced to an officer's hospital, ironically enough, at Lookout Mountain.

The Return of Union Soldiers to Page ... After the War: Part 2
Article of 2/22/2001

After Captain Russell returned to his regiment and participated in Gen. William T. Sherman's famous - or infamous, depending on your viewpoint - "March to the Sea," his three-year term of service expired Dec. 28, 1864, and he was subsequently discharged. Instead of returning immediately to Ohio, Russell opted to remain in Savannah for a few weeks and went into the grocery business (he had just received "mustering-out" pay) with a German resident of the city.

Though in warmer latitudes, Russell was not quite prepared for a cold winter and, by February 1865, opted to go ahead and return to familiar surroundings and warmer clothing in Ohio. By 1867, Russell seems to have left Ohio and ended up in Rohrersville, Md. where, on Feb. 27, he married Almira J. Rohrer.

Russell's return to Page County may be the greater mystery. There may be the chance that he found Page captivating during his passage through the county in 1862. However, with the enlistment of a Francis P. Cave in August 1862, there are a few more questions to be addressed. There are records that show Cave as a pre-war Page County resident - though he does not appear in any of the census records prior to that time.

However, as did many of Page County's families prior to the Civil War, he may have been the son of a Page County resident who departed for Ohio (in addition to Ohio, other families seem to have moved to areas in Indiana and Missouri among other states).

The "Ohio theory" seems the possible. There were at least five Page County Cave family members to have served for the Commonwealth during the Civil War and, had Francis been from the county, surely his return as a former resident-turned Union soldier would have been found most difficult. But more on the strange tie with the Cave family later.

By the 1870 Page County census, Robert H. Russell (listed as a farmer) and his wife Almira were living in Springfield, in the same house as Jeremiah H. and Malinda Rohrer (both old enough to have been Almira's parents). The final curious link to the Cave family was that Lucy Virginia Cave (age 15) was also residing in the home in addition to a Mr. Benjamin M. McCullough (age 21).

Interestingly, one of Russell's residences in Page County was the famous Bell family home - which no longer stands. As some will recall, it was near there nearly 20 years prior to the war that John Wesley Bell was murdered by two of his slaves.

As a resident of Page County, Russell appears to have been rather successful. Russell's final resting-place can be found in Green Hill Cemetery alongside his wife.

Other former Union soldiers in Page County included John T. Baker, James Wade Laconia, Charles H. Carman, Washington Isaac, Benjamin House, Joseph M. Manning and several others, mostly hailing from Pennsylvania, Indiana, New York and Ohio.

A 'Clasping of Hands' - the 1881 Luray Reunion
Article of 5/3/2001

Not all Civil War reunions in Luray were limited to local Confederate veterans. In a meeting in Carlisle, Pa. on June 7, 1881, the Captain Colwell Post No. 201 of the Grand Army of the Republic (G.A.R.) made preparations for an excursion to the awe-inspiring Luray Cave. But more importantly, Union veterans felt an ideal opportunity to "have a general hand-shaking and expression of good feeling" with former foe.

An article was placed in the *Page Courier and Virginia Advertiser* that stated: "It has been sixteen years of peace and national prosperity has been fully long enough to cure all the heart-burns and bitterness engendered by the unholy and unnatural strife."

Though the proclamation was highly optimistic on the part of the Union veterans, within 12 days of sending invitations for a reunion to "prominent men of Page County," a warm and friendly response was returned by local Confederate veterans.

When the G.A.R. Camp arrived in Luray at the Shenandoah Valley Railroad Depot on July 21 (the 20th anniversary of the First Battle of Manassas), Confederate veterans were drawn up in military form in two files, with an evergreen arch on their right bearing the inscription: "In Union there is Strength."

The G.A.R. Post then took position about 12 paces in a line facing the Confederate veterans. Between the two lines of ex-foes was planted a United States flag. With an opening address by Mayor H.J. Smoot, the reunion was officially opened.

Addresses by veterans Captain Francis H. Jordan, Jr. (Co. D, 7th Virginia Cavalry and Gen. Thomas Jordan's staff) and Andrew Broaddus (Co. C, 39th Battalion Virginia Cavalry) followed. Near the end of his speech, Broaddus emphasized the meaning of the evergreen arch and bore-up proudly in the remembrance of service by the Confederate veterans: "Cowards bear malice - it is the part of the brave to forgive, and he, who deaf to his country's call, refused to bear his breast to the leaden storm of bullets, is the last to smoke the calumet of peace."

The playing of the Star Spangled Banner followed and introduced speeches by Judge R.M. Henderson and Captain W.E. Miller (Co. H, 3rd Pennsylvania Cavalry). With words of fraternal reunion" completed, and amid a roar of cheers, the two lines of men stepped forward and "clasped each other by the hands." The *Carlisle Herald and Mirror* reported: "During this part of the exercises many eyes were dim with tears of joy mingled with tears of sadness at the recollection of the dark days of war."

The procession of men and guests then moved onto the large dining hall of the Luray Cave and Hotel Company, "where a fine collation was served." The dinner cards upon the tables bore devices of clasped hands, with the word "Re-Union," and under this "Pennsylvania, July 21, 1881, Virginia."

When it came time to board the train again, "many were the regrets when the engineer whistled 'up brakes,' and all felt they must leave. "Cheer after cheer went up as the train moved off from the station."

With such a warm reception received in Luray, the Union veterans agreed to invite the Page County Confederate veterans to Carlisle for a reunion on Sept. 28. "The citizens (of Carlisle) promptly furnished the money for the needed expenses." More than 200 veterans made the train ride with their families from Luray for a similar round of speeches and hospitality.

The Original Summers-Koontz Memorial of 1893
Article of 4/1/1999

First let me take the opportunity to thank everyone who supported the Summers-Koontz Roadside Marker effort made over the past year. The goal for raising the $1,100 in funds has been met and the process for approval is now underway. Ironically, the same time that my letter and proposal was submitted to Richmond, another was submitted by Coiner Rosen of New Market for a marker regarding the same event. While his marker will be located near the site of the execution, the funds raised over the past year will be for a marker in Page County which will be located, pending the approval of the Virginia Department of Transportation, somewhere between Page County High School and Newport along Route 340. Both roadside markers are tentatively scheduled for dedication on June 27, 1999 (the 134th anniversary of the tragic event) - at non-conflicting hours that day.

In 1893 a similar effort was made by Thomas Jackson Adams of Quicksburg, Virginia. However, instead of a roadside marker, the goal was set for a marble monolith, which still stands at Rude's Hill today.

Adams, a native of Frederick County, was a former member of Company K, 23rd Virginia Cavalry, postwar postmaster of Quicksburg and member of the Turner Ashby Camp, United Confederate Veterans. An important fund raiser in several monuments in the Shenandoah Valley, Adams had hoped that the site at Rude's Hill would "often visited by those who admire courage and fortitude, and the tragic deaths of Capt. Summers and Sergt. Koontz will long live in the memories of our citizens and deserve to be recited in song and story, - to show what atrocities our people suffered in war, and how heroically these men met their untimely fate."

Unlike the cost of the cast aluminum roadside marker sought after in today's fund raising efforts, Adam's goal was for a marble monument. But time and prices have changed significantly. The marble monument, though probably much more expensive when purchased today, represented "a cost of about $175, at a low estimate." The marble monument was to replace the wooden pillar that had been erected on the spot soon after the execution of the men in 1865. Adam's 1893 one ton marker was constructed of five pieces and made of Italian marble. The base is 28 X 28 inches and 6 inches in height, with a plinth, 22 X 22 inches and 8 inches in height. The die is 16 X 16 inches and 19 inches in height and bears different inscriptions on its east, north and south faces. The lettering being done by Mr. Walter M. Cox of Quicksburg, whose father was a Confederate soldier. The die is surmounted by a column 30 inches in circumference and 5 ½ feet in height, terminating in a cone. Though it once was highly polished and "beautifully proportioned," the monument has grown gray with time. The entire structure is still surrounded by the original - though rusting - iron fence, consisting of 4 posts of solid iron, 3 inches square, sunk deep into the ground, connected with 8 rods bolted together. The iron work having been done by Mr. John H. Myers, also of Quicksburg. Henkel & Co. Publishers of New Market provided the complimentary printing for the programs for the dedication.

Contributors to the 1893 monument included several Confederate veterans. From the 7th Virginia Cavalry were Col. Richard H. Dulaney, Erasmus Nicewarner, William H. Olinger, William A. Pence, and Lt. John H. Connel and Benjamin D. Guice (both of Capt. Summer's Co. D); 1st Va. Cav.: Thomas L. Williamson; 10th Va. Infantry: Philip W. Magruder; 12th Va. Cav.: John T. Colston, Henry W. Glaize, Alonzo F. Grandstaff, R.M. Lantz, John C. Ruby, O. Shirley; 18th Va. Cav.: Dr. Isaac N. Baker; 23rd Va. Cav.: Col. Charles T. O'Ferrall, Capt. Thomas J. Adams, Bowman, John E. Hopkins; Captain Rice's 8th Star Artillery: George W. Koontz, Capt. Berryman Z. Price, Jacob H. Woods; Stonewall Brigade: William E. Russell; civilians: M. Bantz, John W. Clinedinst, Miss Sallie Glaize, David Kingree, Gideon Koiner, Mag Moore, David & Cass Moyers, Miss Nannie Quick, Jacob W. Rice, N.W. Shuler (relative of Sgt. Koontz), Charles B. Stiegel, and the Honorable M.L. Walton.

Page County's Civil War Claims Amounted to Only One Percent
Article of 12/17/1998

The American Civil War cost Americans, not only a great deal in lives, but also an incredible amount in personal financial loss. In the early 1870's Congress created a channel through which pro-Union Southerners could apply for reimbursements for some of the losses caused as a result of the war. The Southern Claims Commission handled these claims and remained flexible in that it extended the deadline for application several times before finally closing acceptance in March 1880. In all, 22,298 cases were filed by individual family groups, churches and businesses claiming a total of $60,258,150 in damages and losses. However, after reviewing all applications, only one-third (7,092) of the claims filed were accepted.

Recently I had the opportunity to sift through a book entitled *Southern Loyalists in the Civil War: The Southern Claims Commission* (by Gary B. Mills. Genealogical Publishing Co., Inc., Baltimore, Md., 1994). Interestingly, out of the 45 applications from Page County, only 1% were accepted. The typical Page claimant was from Luray, 40 years of age (as of 1860), and held the occupation of a farmer.

Of the total number of applicants from Page County, 33 claims were listed as "Disallowed" and seven were listed as "Barred." Several of these claimants were ex-Confederate soldiers.

Of the claims "Allowed," all but one had been filed in 1874. Reuben Kite filed in 1877. Two of the claimants (John Dogans & Martin Ellis) were from Luray and the remaining three from Grove Hill (Kite), Leakesville (Joseph Painter, Sr.) and Massanutten (Benjamin Strickler). If Dogans is the same John A. Dugans that was listed as a free mulatto living in Luray with his family in 1860, no occupational data is available. Ellis was a 48 year old farmer with $825 in Real Estate and had a son that served in the 97th Virginia Militia. Kite was a 34 year-old farmer with $6,000 in Real Estate with no known (at present writing) direct affiliations with Confederate soldiers. Painter was a 42 year-old farmer with $350 in Real Estate. Strickler was a 55 year old farmer with $4,665 in Real

Estate and a son in the 7th Virginia Cavalry.

From the claim applications filed from Page County, (especially considering the number with Confederate soldier affiliations) it appears that either the public was poorly informed as to the policies regarding the acceptable criteria or ignored them in the hope of receiving government money in a financially difficult post-war period. While some of the claimants may have in fact been "loyalists," with the above being taken into consideration, filing a claim with the Southern Claims Commission in no way indicated that the claimant had been loyal to the United States during the Civil War.

If you review the book, find a familiar name and wish to order a copy of the claim file, obtaining copies of these files may not be as simple as a one day trip to the National Archives. For "Allowed" claims - provide a full citation to:

Civil Reference Branch (NNRC) National Archives 8th & Pennsylvania Ave., NW Washington, D.C. 20408

If the claim was "Barred" or "Disallowed" consult NARA microfiche M1407 "Barred and Disallowed Case Files of the Southern Claims Commission, 1871-1880. First consult the NARA's Descriptive Pamphlet M1407 for a table that provides exact fiche numbers that can be purchased. This pamphlet is available without charge and is available from:

Publication Services Branch National Archives Building 8th & Pennsylvania Ave., N.W. Washington, D.C. 20408

Former Page Confederate Served as Speaker of U.S. House
Article of 9/16/1999

While the surname of Crisp defiantly isn't among the long scroll of names from Page County, one family of Crisp did play a part in the county's early history. Just prior to the secession of Virginia, the family of William H. Crisp moved to take up residence in Luray. Crisp, a native of Sheffield, England, had immigrated to the United States in 1845 and originally settled in Ellaville, Georgia. William and his wife were most noted for their roles as Shakespearean actors who started several theaters and toured throughout the South.

As the war opened, the father, and two sons; Harry and Charles, enlisted. Two of the three joined units organized in Page County. William served with the Dixie Artillery and was appointed 1st lieutenant. Harry joined with Company F (Muhlenburg Rifles of Shenandoah County), 10th Virginia Infantry, and deserted in the summer of 1862. He later died in Chicago, Illinois sometime after the war.

Perhaps the most famous of all three was Charles Frederick Crisp. Born January 29, 1845 in Sheffield, England, he enlisted in Company K (Page Volunteers), 10th Virginia Infantry as 4th corporal. Reduced to the rank of private at the company's reorganization in April 1862, he also went absent without leave for over a month during that same summer. However, his reasons for the absence were apparently justified as he was elected as 3rd lieutenant on June 9, 1863. Eventually captured at the battle of the Wilderness, Charles became one of the "Immortal Six Hundred" Confederate officers who were incarcerated in the stockade on Morris Island, South Carolina, under fire from their own guns (unknowingly to the Confederates that fired on the stockade) that shelled the island. Released June 16, 1865 after taking an oath of allegiance, Crisp returned to Page County only briefly before setting out on a larger political venture.

Using the post-war to prepare for a career in law, Crisp was admitted to the Georgia bar in 1866 and beginning in 1872 served as that states solicitor general and then as a superior court judge. In 1882, he resigned from the bench to run as a Democrat for the U.S. House of Representatives, easily winning election to the 48th

Congress. While in this capacity, Crisp participated in the most significant legislative battles at the time. According to one source, "his knowledge of parliamentary rules, his skill in disputation, and his commanding physical presence marked him as a leading Democrat. Playing a major role in the passage of the Interstate Commerce Act of 1887 and a strong supporter of the Sherman Silver Purchase Act of 1890, Crisp was remembered also for using his powers by bringing the Committee on Rules into the Speaker's domain. This committee was especially important as it, being under Democratic direction, virtually dictated the legislative business of the House.

In 1896 Crisp announced his candidacy for the senate seat of the retiring John Brown Gordon (former famous Confederate General) the same seat which had been formerly held by Alexander Hamilton Stephens - more popularly remembered as the Vice President of the Confederate States. Crisp easily won the primaries during that fall because of the free-silver inflationists domination in Georgia. However, Crisp's health soon failed and on October 23, 1896, one week before his confirmation to the post and the general assembly convened, he died in Atlanta, Georgia.

While much of the same information regarding Crisp's political life is conveyed in *The Encyclopedia of the United States Congress* (1995), more information can be found on Crisp in *Reminiscences of Famous Georgians* (1908) and the 1954 *Georgia Review* article "Charles F. Crisp: Speaker of the House.

James Huffman's
'Ups and Downs of a Confederate Soldier'
Article of 11/4/1999

Books pertaining directly to Page County soldiers in the Civil War are few and far between. The first (and I think only) book ever solely published about and by a Page County Confederate was James Huffman's *Ups and Downs of a Confederate Soldier*. It was only at the urgings of his son, Oscar C. Huffman, that James agreed to write a memoir. However, before initiating the project James thought it absolutely necessary to have an automobile in order to drive around to the battlefields and sites throughout Virginia. So, at age 72, James began the great task of recording not only his Civil War experiences, but also his life before and after the war. A veteran of Company I, 10th Virginia Infantry, James was one of several of Page County's Naked Creek residents that slipped into Rockingham County and enlisted in the mostly Rockingham County manned company. James fought in all the principal engagements of the war in the East except Gettysburg, was captured in 1864 at Spotsylvania Courthouse, and was held a prisoner at Point Lookout and Elmira. Though he completed the task, James never saw the work go to publication and died on April 14, 1922. James was laid to rest in the Confederate Section of the Arlington National Cemetery.

Seventeen years after the death of James Huffman, his son Oscar, then President of the Continental Can Company, Inc., submitted the manuscript to the editors of *Atlantic Monthly* and received a response desiring that a portion of it be published in their publication. Oscar agreed and the article "Prisoner of War – A Confederate Soldier's Story" was published in the April 1939 issue. Later that year, the same editor remarked that the manuscript "showed considerable natural literary ability" and proposed that Oscar publish the entire manuscript in a book that would be entitle *Ups and Downs of a Confederate Soldier*. The title deriving its name from James' father's "Up and Down sawmill" – the same mill that James began to work on at age 8.

Finally going to press in 1940, *Ups and Downs of a Confederate Soldier* was published through William E. Rudge's Sons Press in New York. Limited to 400 copies, the book was 175 pages in length and was bound in blue buckram with a paper cover label. The volume was also illustrated with several impressive tipped-in photos.

Today, the work is a rare find. Finding one in good quality and under $100 is an extreme challenge. Fortunately, several months ago, I lucked-into a volume for my personal collection. While it may be unusual to say this since I have an extreme interest in Page's veterans in the Civil War, I am rather partial to the first chapter (pages 6 – 29) that detail Huffman's youth and experiences in Alma and on Naked Creek. Bringing a rare sense of nostalgia into his writings, Huffman's memories of youth are quite impressive and recall humorous accounts. In the first few sentences of the book, James recalls his father, Ambrose, selling the Huffman homestead near Alma Bridge to Charles C. Dovel in 1845 (when James was but five and a half years old). Then too, James particularly loved to take trips with his father across the river to Isaac Long's – "I was delighted to go for he always gave me a good slice of honey bread." There are also warm recollections regarding swimming in the famous "Deep Hole" (perhaps the same place that was once referred to as "Blue Hole") in Naked Creek.

"But I know My Great-Great-Granddaddy Served in the Civil War"
Article of 1/29/1998

In search of a Confederate ancestor for personal reasons or for membership in organizations such as the United Daughters of the Confederacy or the Sons of Confederate Veterans? First there are several books that have been written as a part of the Virginia Regimental Histories Series published by H.E. Howard, Inc. All of the units formed in Page County have been covered in books written or are on the verge of publication. The units organized in Page County included Company D, 7th Virginia Cavalry; Company K, 10th Virginia Infantry; Company H, 33rd Virginia Infantry; Company E, 35th Battalion Virginia Cavalry; Captain William Henry Chapman's Dixie Artillery, the 97th Virginia Militia, and Captain Peter J. Keyser's "Boy Company."

The benefit of these books is that the rosters of the units have been nearly entirely transcribed, the only exception usually being the pay records. Furthermore, these books will also provide maps, photos (in some instances) and a unit history of some depth. Readers will note that some books are of greater length than others due to the availability of actual letters and diaries of the veterans of the units being available to the authors when writing these books. Unlike the advertisements often seen for "capsule histories" that usually costs about $20 each, at $19.95 each the regimentals provide much more information for the buck.

But while the regimental series is a great source for information on your particular veteran's service with the unit, do not however rely upon the book to give a full genealogical tree as it was not the focus of these books. Another source for information is found in a book entitled *Page County Men in Gray*. This book list the names of the men alphabetically, gives the unit in which they served and in some cases parental information, the names of the spouse and/or the names of some of the children.

Spratt apparently also took the opportunity to scan some cemetery books for Page County to give birth and death dates of the veterans. There is an added benefit to this book in that it provides a handy cross-reference guide for further research into the regimentals.

However, do not "put all of your eggs in one basket" with Spratt's book and become disappointed when you do not find your ancestor's name that you KNOW served in the war. In his work he did cover units organized in Page County and individual soldiers that served from Page in other units. But a big disappointment with his book is the fact that he did not go through the Virginia pension records for Page County Confederate veterans. Furthermore, upon close examination, Spratt has missed a considerably large number of men who served in the units formed within Page County and yet were positively identified in the Virginia Regimental Histories Series.

Upon personal examination of the Virginia Confederate pension records a number of years ago, I found the names of over 80 men who resided in the county at the outbreak of the war and served in companies formed outside the county that were missed entirely by Spratt's work.

I even found one of my own ancestors who served with Keyser's "Boy Company" and later enlisted with 2nd Company M, 62nd Virginia Infantry. Upon close examination of Spratt's book, however, I did not find his name, although he was descended from a family who had been in Page County since its formation, resided there before, during and after the war and even died here.

Sources Abound for Information on Local Civil War Ancestors
Article of 2/5/1998

"So where do I start?" I started with a family story. First I found out that a great-great grandfather had served in the war. From there I figured out the exact family tree back to this ancestor and then I was off to the Virginia State Library (now known as the Library of Virginia) in Richmond. Others can start with Harry Strickler's *Short History of Page County* and go from the incomplete lists of veterans published therein. Today, with the aid of the books in the Virginia Regimental Histories Series and, in some instances, Spratt's book (*Page County, Virginia Men in Gray*), one can "quick reference" and find a bonanza of information in seconds.

For those who cannot find the ancestor they KNOW to have served in the war, either in the regimentals or in Spratt's book, go first to the Library of Virginia, then to the National Archives in Washington, D.C. or my personal web site for Page County Confederate veterans (http://www.geocities.com/Heartland/Hills/1850/pagecoconfeds.html).

From the Library of Virginia or National Archives you can begin with the Combined Service Records of Confederate veterans available on microfilm. First check the cross-reference microfilm for Virginia soldiers, at Washington there is one for all Confederate soldiers from all states including Virginia. Then, after you have found the name you were searching for you can go to the microfilm of the particular unit in which he served and find your veteran and his specific record.

If your in Richmond and have found your ancestor's microfilm record, I highly recommend a search of the Confederate pension records. Whether he survived the war or not, there may at least be a record for his widow that would give either vital statistics information otherwise unavailable from the service record.

In the case of Union soldiers one would need to go to Washington and check the cross-reference of Federal soldiers in the war. There at Washington, one too can find a pension record for a Union veteran.

In addition to all of this, within one or two years and as the grand finale to the Virginia Regimental Histories Series there will be a set of books (now estimated to be a three-volume set) that will include all of the names of all of the veterans of all of units from Virginia who served the Confederacy. Therefore, by referencing this set of books one would be able to quickly reference the particular name and then find the unit-specific book in which the ancestor's military record can be found.

For those who look into the regimentals and, though they find their ancestor's military record, find there is no photo, there is still a way to rectify the situation. Each book is limited to 1,000 copies in its first edition, but when the book goes into a second or third edition (limited to 200 copies each), new photos and new vital information provided by readers can be added.

If you are one of those people who are concerned that there are letters or diaries that have yet to find their place in history in these books, or there is no photo of your ancestor in the books, whether a wartime or a postwar photograph, you can send a copy to the publisher of the series for future publication. The address is H.E. Howard, Inc., Rt. 2, Box 496 H, Appomattox, Virginia 24522. Please reference the unit and name of the veteran for easier placement of the information or photo.

Daughters of the Confederacy in Page County
Article of 5/21/1998

Originally organized on January 16, 1901, the Luray Chapter, United Daughters of the Confederacy was initially a small chapter consisting of just five members. With membership dues placed at fifty cents, the chapter's earliest ledger of September 7, 1901 noted that for the first year there was three dollars and eighty cents listed on hand. Expenses for the year tallied at one dollar for use of a chapel where the chartering ceremony was held, Confederate songbooks at fifty cents each, and two dollars for the designated delegate to attend a meeting in New Orleans.

Charter members of the first organization included Miss Caroline Long, Mrs. Herbert Barbee, Miss Louise Catherine Dickson, Miss Mary Ida Hargrove, Miss Lena Gertrude Stover, Miss Frances Yager Rhodes, Mrs. Eliza Wharton Lowry, Miss A.A. Davis, and Miss A.J. Davis.

With membership numbers increased to eleven in 1903, the chapter contributed seven dollars and fifty cents to the J.E.B. Stuart Monument Fund. During the year the chapter also gave considerable effort toward the Confederate Reunion and Memorial Day on June 25, spending five dollars and eleven cents toward purchasing flags (with which they added bouquets of flowers) to decorate the graves of the dead. Likewise, several living veterans and widows received monetary gifts at Christmas.

In the years that followed membership continued to grow and in keeping with its desire to be an active, vital organization, the chapter continued to contribute to the Stuart Monument Fund as well as marking veterans' graves with iron crosses (few of these markers remain on the graves today). In 1905 membership reached peak at 22 women. However, soon after the ranks began to significantly decline. Despite the lack of growth, those few members continued to keep the memory of their Confederate ancestors alive and contributed to the Manassas Monument, Camp Chase, the Daughters' Building in Richmond, and to needy Confederate veterans. By 1913 however, with only two members still on the rolls, the chapter was disbanded.

Following the Centennial of the Civil War, on August 3, 1968, Luray Chapter #436, of the United Daughters of the Confederacy was reactivated with Mrs. L. Wallis Alves, Mrs. Dewey R. Wood, and Mrs. I. Clifton Warner present. Ultimately, twelve daughters received certificates for membership including one transfer from the Warren Rifles Chapter. As honorary Real Daughter and original member of the 1901 chapter, Mrs. Lena Stover Bostick also honored the chapter's new member ranks. In time, other Real Daughters and original 1901 chapter members were honored including Ms. Anita Grove and Mrs. J. Gill Grove. Officers of the chapter included Mrs. Thomas C. Jennings as president; Mrs. Dorothy H. Judd, 1st vice-president; Mrs. Raymond Bauserman, 2nd vice-president; Mrs. Lynn Black, 3rd vice-president; Mrs. R.R. Huffman, recording secretary; Miss Virginia Martin, treasurer; Miss Helen Kibler, registrar; Miss M.J.W. White, historian; and Mrs. Lester Hoak, recorder of crosses. Other members included Mrs. R.B. Long, Mrs. A.S. Modisett, Mrs. Frank Kite, Miss Jean Jennings, and Miss Anita Grove.

In the years since its reorganization, the Luray Chapter has been involved in numerous activities including purchasing markers for members' Confederate ancestors' graves; contributions to the Vietnam Fund, Lee Chapel & mausoleum; bestowal of World War I Cross of Military Service; donation of eight lap robes (afghans) and two pairs of crutch pads for amputees of the Vietnam War at the Veterans' Hospital; remembrance of the Confederate dead on special days with flowers and flags; and numerous volunteer activities.

Early Confederate Veteran & Descendant Organizations in Page
Article of 3/4/1999

While one of my columns this year covered the local United Daughters of the Confederacy Chapter which is still in existence, I found my way through old copies of the *Confederate Veteran Magazine* (1890's - 1930's) to find more about other organizations that existed in Page County at the beginning of the century. After scouring the three volume index for all entries related to Page County, Page Valley, Luray, etc., I found over 50 entries - most dealing with the old veterans of the county.

The Rosser-Gibbons Camp No. 89, United Confederate Veterans, was apparently the first recorded organization of ex-Confederates in the county. Named for Page County native Colonel Simeon B. Gibbons (one time commander of the 10th Virginia Infantry killed at the Battle of McDowell) and General Thomas L. Rosser (former commander of the Laurel Brigade), the camp was initially mentioned in the July 1898 issue as having been organized in Luray, with sixty-seven members. Former Captain Richard S. Parks was elected commander; Samuel N. Judd, James W.T. Warren, and Paul Miller, Lieutenants; William E. Grayson, Adjutant; John S. Hershberger, Sergeant-Major; Thomas E. Schwartz, Treasurer; Dr. Thomas B. Amiss, Surgeon. A photo of the June 17, 1924 reunion for the camp has been included in previous issues of the *Page News & Courier*. The photo included 26 Confederate veterans supporting a last National flag of the Confederacy (with camp identification) and James Wade Laconia of Pennsylvania wielding a U.S. flag. As the lone "Yankee" veteran in the photo, Laconia seemed to be enjoying ribbing the old Rebels.

Through 1931, various Page County Confederate veterans were mentioned in obituaries or small articles. The obituaries included those of Robert C. Bragonier, Ambrose C. Huffman, James A. Melton (all in 1905); Tilman S. Weaver (1909); Joseph Groves (1910); Erasmus L. Bell (1920); Isaac N. Kibler, Richard S. Parks, M. Warfield Yates, and William H. Rogers (1922); Theodore H. Lauck and Enoch V. Kauffman (1923); Silas K. Wright, Martin V.B. Gander, George K. Fitch, James W. McCoy, Charles E. Beidler, and Henry C. Shenk (1926); James A. Matthews, John S.

Hershberger, John P. Grove, and John W. Stover (1927); W. Peter Broy (1928); and lastly, Harrison M. Strickler (1929). Enoch V. Kauffman and David C. Grayson often wrote the tributes to their slowly thinning ranks of veterans in gray.

The first mention of a Sons of Confederate Veterans Camp in Page County was made in the December 1906 issue - though leaving a question as to when the organization had formed. The Summers-Koontz Camp #490, S.C.V. included F.T. Amiss as commander and A.A. Grove as lieutenant commander. The number and names of other members is uncertain. Named for the two men killed in the postwar incident (another previous article) the camp was only mentioned three times in all of the issues. The camp's last note of existence was in November 1914.

The long gray line of Page's Confederate veterans has passed on well over fifty years ago. Likewise, the original "sons" from the Summers-Koontz Camp have all likely joined the fathers that they honored (though I await a roster). The exact date that the S.C.V. Camp last held a meeting is uncertain, but presumed to have been prior to 1920. Today, those in Page that continue the legacy of honoring their Confederate heritage belong to different camps including the Waller Tazewell Patton Camp in Greene County.

Anyone with ANY information regarding the Rosser-Gibbons Camp or the Summers-Koontz Camp is encouraged to contact me in order to more accurately document the respective histories of the two organizations.

The Winnie Davis Cottage (Luray Orphanage)
Article of 2/18/1999

When recently going through old copies of the *Confederate Veteran* Magazine, I came upon various items of interest relating to Page County history that bore merit in repeating. One item that resurfaced regarded the Winnie Davis Cottage which was also recognized as the Luray Orphanage.

The idea for the cottage memorializing the daughter of Jefferson Davis was planned in 1899 and was to be devoted specifically for the care of the orphans of Confederate soldiers and their descendants. Conceived by Rev. Dr. H.M. Wharton of Baltimore, the idea was endorsed by Mrs. Jefferson Davis who wrote; "I accord permission to name the Confederate cottage after my child with pride and pleasure. If there is anything good in a name, I think God will bless this if only to hold the memory of my good and noble child, and your great and successful efforts to serve the cause of humanity. I am much gratified by your desire to honor my daughter's name, and send you every good wish for your success."

Former Confederate General John B. Gordon also endorsed the project. Then the commander of the United Confederate Veterans, Gordon wrote Dr. Wharton:

"My Dear Doctor: I am rejoiced to know that you are still carrying on your heart and shoulders the 'home for orphans.' Your last movement to erect a cottage bearing the name of the beloved 'Daughter of the Confederacy,' within whose walls are to be nurtured and prepared for useful lives Confederate orphans, will find encouragement and support from every true son and daughter of our section. God bless you in your truly noble work! Is the prayer of your comrade and friend, J.B. Gordon."

Within months nearly $10,000 of the necessary $25,000 was raised for the project which was to be built on the "Whosoever Farm," near Luray. The "functional memorial" was to contain "paintings, photographs, and such Confederate relics as can be gathered, and where will be preserved the names of all contributors to this fund." Within weeks of the appearance of the article in the magazine, Dr. J. William Jones, the co-sponsor of the project and Chaplain General of the United Confederate Veterans, was to begin delivering lectures in order to raise funds for the orphanage, the first stop being Columbus, Mississippi.

In a note to the magazine, Dr. Jones wrote: "Surely our Confederate veterans, the Sons of Veterans, the Daughters of the Confederacy, and our people generally will esteem it a privilege to contribute to the erection of this appropriate and noble monument to the 'Daughter of the Confederacy,' to be located in the beautiful Valley of Virginia, whose clear streams murmur the praises and whose mountain gorges echo the glories of Ashby and Stuart and Jackson and Lee and the barefooted heroes of the rank and file who followed these great leaders to an immortality of fame."

One young lady who was brought from Baltimore by Dr. Wharton to live at the orphanage was a Miss Bessie Booth. Booth later married Mr. Charles Burner who was the son of Hamilton Vincent Burner (a veteran of Company D, 7th Virginia Cavalry of Page County). Orphaned in her early life, Mrs. Burner's unfortunate life was yet to be marred in 1917 when she was and her children were murdered by Will Nichols.

Interestingly, Strickler's *A Short History of Page County* mentioned that the orphanage was discontinued by 1900. According to Strickler, the farm was located "east of Luray on the Lee Highway . . . . and is opposite Benton Smith. In referring to Wharton, Strickler wrote that he had been the pastor of the Brantly Baptist Church of Baltimore, and an eloquent speaker of great ability." If anyone has more information to share regarding the Winnie Davis Cottage, please contact me.

Surnames & Genealogical Research Tools

The Origins of the Aleshire/Aleshite/Elscheit Family
Article of 5/6/1999

While it has puzzled me for sometime, recent revelations have begun to make the origins of the Aleshire family that much clearer. As the research of others has become available, it appears that the overall immigrant ancestor of the Aleshire family was Conrad Elscheit of Niederhonnefeld, Prussia, Germany. Conrad had married Maria Catharina Goessel (the daughter of Christopher Goessel of Hardert) in Rengsdorf, Rheinland, Prussia, Germany on September 29 1747. Niederhonnefeld, Rengsdorf, Hardert and a small town by the name of Ehlscheid are all located in West Central Germany, within a short distance of the border of Belgium.

Conrad Elscheit is believed to have been the same Conrad Ellscheid who arrived in Philadelphia from Rotterdam on August 21, 1750. Over time the family name was anglicized to what is now more commonly recognized as ALESHIRE. The tracks of the newly emigrated family were made even more clear from an obituary of John Conrad Aleshire, a son of Conrad Elscheit, in 1849 found in Philadelphia, Pennsylvania's *Saturday Courier*.

Apparently after their arrival in North America, the family settled on the Monongahela near Fort Redstone, now Brownsville, in Pennsylvania. "This being the extreme frontier settlement at that time, they soon found it necessary in consequence of their unprotected situation and the frequent depredation of the hostile Indians, to retire farther into the interior. Accordingly, they sunk a pit, into which they put all their implements of husbandry and other articles inconvenient to remove in this hasty retreat, and converting it into a lettuce bed to divert the attention of the Indians, they retired to Cedar Creek, in Frederick, now Shenandoah County. Even after relocating, the "The settlements were being still annoyed by the Indians. They erected forts or block houses to which they retired for safety on any demonstration of hostilities. In the spring of 1756 . . ." when John Conrad Aleshire was "but a few months old, a party of hostile Indians made their appearance in the settlement and murdered several members of a family named Painter, a neighbor of Aleshire's family made a precipitate retreat, but in their haste, entirely neglected the infant who was sleeping in his cradle, until they had nearly reached the fort. His sister returned determined to peril her life for his safety, and cautiously approaching the house, entered through the window, succeeded in getting her infant brother in her arms and bore him in triumph to the fort. She had scarcely left the house, ere the demoniac sound of the savage war-whoop rent the air and told how narrow was the escape from their blood thirsting vengeance."

In the years that followed, the Aleshire family continued to grow and at least eight children were born to Conrad and Maria Catherina. Two of the children, Henry P. Aleshire, Sr. and John Conrad Aleshire, left a number of heirs in what became known as Page County. Likewise, in addition to Henry and John C., at least three other siblings served in the Revolutionary War. Leaving a detailed pension of his service, Henry served as a corporal in the 4th Virginia Regiment. John Conrad served as a sergeant and from the appearance of his obituary, upheld a remarkable record of service.

According to his obituary, John Conrad Aleshire participated in Washington's crossing of the Delaware and the follow-on battle of Trenton. " He continued in the army during three tours and was in several of the hardest contested battles. For a time, he retired from the field, but was not inactive in furthering the common cause. His frequent sallies against the Tories caused them much discomfiture and his name among them struck terror in their ranks . . . In the closing scene, near to the side of the father of his country, he stood before Yorktown."

Origins of the Broyles Family in Page County
Article of 10/19/2000

The patriarch immigrant, Johannes Breyhel, was christened the son of Conrad and Margaretha Schelling Breyhel on May 1, 1679 in Dusslingen, Wuerttemberg (just south of Tuebingen in present day Germany). Fifty years later, Breyhel was living 50 miles to the south in Oetisheim, where on November 6, 1703, he married Ursula Ruop, the daughter of a local gravedigger. Fourteen years later, Johannes, his wife, and several children joined approximately twenty other families aboard the ship *Scott* in immigration from the German Palatinate. Like an earlier group, this second group of German colonists was sponsored by Virginia Governor Alexander Spotswood. In return for payment of passage, the German families were to be indentured to the governor for seven years and were joined together with the twelve other German families that were settled in 1714 at what became known as Germanna in Orange, then a part of Essex, County.

In 1724, the Rev. Hugh Jones published a description of the Germanna colony in his Present State of Virginia. In it he stated: "Beyond Governor Spotswood's furnace above the Falls of the Rappahannock River, within view of the vast mountains, he has founded a town, called Germanna from the Germans sent over by Queen Anne, who are now removed up further. He has servants and workmen at most handicraft trades, and he is building a church, courthouse, and dwelling house for himself; and with his servants and negroes he has cleared plantations about it, proposing great encouragement for people to come and settle in that uninhabited part of the world, lately divided into a county, that is Spotsylvania."

The Breyhel family, along with most of the colonists of 1717 and yet a third group of colonist of 1719, remained at Germanna until about 1727. For the three years preceding, many families had been "proving" their importations in the Spotsylvania County Court "in order to take up lands under the Head-right Act." Relocating to the Robertson River section of Madison County. It was while also there that the German immigrants founded the Hebron Lutheran Church. It was also at this time that there was a change in the Breyhel name. Johannes/John's son Jacob (Hans Jacob) became the progenitor of the BROYLES family, and son Conrad was progenitor of the

BRILES family. It was from Hans that the Page Valley Broyles family descended.

Hans Jacob had been born in Germany in 1705 and had thus been one of the few fortunate children to survive to adulthood. About 1727, Hans married Maria Catherine Fleischmann. One of their sons, Zacharias (named for Maria's Germanna immigrant father) married Delilah Clore in the early 1760s. Like Zachariah, Delilah was also a child of Germanna children (Peter Clore and Barbara Yaeger). In the succeeding generations, the Broyles family remained in the Madison-Culpeper County area and by the middle 1800s had begun to marry into English surname families. As early as the 1840s, branches of the Broyles family began entering Page County from Madison County. The earliest marriage of a Broyles in the county is shown in 1848. However, succeeding generations from Madison entered Page in the third quarter of the 1800s to marry and reside here.

There is a great website for those interested in the Broyles family lines - http://homepages.rootsweb.com/~george/index.html#Index and several fantastic publications available about the settlers of old Germanna from the Memorial Foundation of the Germanna Colonies in Virginia, Inc. Their address is P.O. Box 693, Culpeper, Virginia 22701-0693.

Patriarch of the Cave family in Page County
Article of 9/18/1997

Researching an ancestor who served in the Revolutionary War can be exciting and rewarding. Often, a researcher will use their find to join the Daughters or Sons of the American Revolution just to name a few organizations. However, what do you do with your new found ancestor once you find them?

There are some fine published resources to aid a person and eventually lead to the microfilm record of the unit in which the ancestor served in the Revolution. The microfilm record, available at the National Archives in Washington, D.C. will usually disclose where your ancestor enlisted and follow the course of his service until his enlistment expired, he was wounded or killed.

But before you leave the Archives there is one more rock left unturned - the pension records. While a search in the pension files may be fruitless, there are exceptions. Regretfully, not every soldier who served or widow who had a spouse who served applied for the pension.

A prime example of success in researching the pension records is evident with the record of Reuben Cave, a private in the 2nd Virginia State Regiment in the Revolutionary War and the patriarch of the Cave families that reside in Page County today. In the records of the pension, Cave revealed a great deal more than just service in the war but also shed light on his prewar and postwar years as well as some viewpoints on certain political events that took place in his life.

As a testimony to his life, Cave at age 94 in 1832, had his story transcribed as a part of the evidence that he had served in the war.

Born about 1738, Cave gave no indication to whom his parents were, leaving yet another family mystery. Prior to the outbreak of the war he had been a resident of Spotsylvania County and recalled living for over two years at the residence of Mr. William Hutchinson, to whom he was bound. Following the end of his term of servitude with Hutchinson, Cave began work as an overseer for Andrew Manson, Frank Coleman, and others up until the year of

1776. Following the events that opened the war with Great Britain, Cave, then about 38 years old, decided to join in the efforts for independence.

Traveling to Orange County, Reuben Cave enlisted at the home of Captain Roland Thomas, about twelve miles from where he then lived. Signing as a member of Captain George Stubblefield's company for a three year term, Cave soon joined other soldiers in a march to Williamsburg to be trained under French Captain William Clummer. Though Clummer was an artillery officer, the company of men was trained for infantry. From Williamsburg, the company marched to Yorktown where they remained for two months before joining other elements of the Continental Army at Valley Forge.

Cave's review of his military service after training is brief but interesting, taking him from the time that he learned of the capture of the Hessian troops at Phillip's Mills to his time spent in winter quarters on half-rations. Cave was at the storming of Mud Point or Fort Mifflin under Captain Muehlhaney, and recalled taking possession of the fort "at the point of the bayonet." Sometime after this the regiment was ordered to Virginia to reinforce General "Mad" Anthony Wayne against Lord Cornwallis, then to Guilford Courthouse, North Carolina. But before reaching Guilford, Cave's enlistment expired and he received his discharge.

The Other Residents of the Ruffner House – the Chapman family
Article of 7/19/2001

What a great lead to a ghost story . . . but that's not what this is about. In fact, the house, already so incredibly rich in history, can also claim a link to a pair of brothers who shared close company with the "Gray Ghost."

Though they were not born in the house, the Ruffner place was the boyhood home of both Mosby's second in command, and one of the his company commanders.

A native of Madison County, William Allen Chapman was a grandson of Brevet Maj. Gen. Edmund Pendleton Gaines, (Gaines is clearly a subject worthy of a series of articles).

William married Elizabeth Forrer, daughter of Samuel and Catherine F. Ebersole Forrer, in Page County in 1837. It was around this time that the Forrer family owned the "Willow Grove" farm and mill. Almost exactly nine months from the date of their marriage, William and Elizabeth's first child, Samuel Forrer Chapman was born. William Henry Chapman would follow in 1840, then Edmund Gaines in 1842.

Shortly after, Chapman purchased the first tract at the Ruffner place. Six years later Chapman purchased a second tract, including the farm and large brick mansion. The births of at least three daughters and four sons would follow while in residence at the former Ruffner residence.

Of the sons, only three served in the Civil War – Samuel, William and Edmund.

By the opening of the war, Samuel had attended Columbia University and was listed as a minister. Enlisting first in Co. B, 17th Virginia Infantry, Samuel transferred to serve with his brother William in the Dixie Artillery in October 1861. Elected to lieutenant, Sam continued service with the Dixie Artillery until it was disbanded in October 1862. He was among the list of young lieutenants recommended for another battery, though his destiny would remain closely tied to that of his brother William.

Edmund had started the war with the Page Volunteers of Co. K, 10th Virginia Infantry. Transferring to the command of his brothers in May 1862, Edmund served with the Dixie Artillery until the unit was disbanded in October 1862, and subsequently served with the Purcell Artillery, was promoted to corporal and likely closed the war with the organization.

William's military star shone the brightest of all. A student at the University of Virginia at the opening of the war, he enlisted in the Southern Guards – a group of students from U.Va. Chapman returned home after Governor John Letcher urged the guards to return to their homes and "help organize and drill companies for the defense of the state."

On arriving in Page, young William began drilling the Page Volunteers and Page Grays. Chapman declined an opportunity to serve as an officer in the Grays with hopes of forming an artillery battery of his own. An opportunity arose when John Kaylor Booton organized the Dixie Artillery at Honeyville. By June 1861, Chapman was mustering as a lieutenant. With Booton's decision to serve as a member of the Virginia State Legislature in October, Chapman was voted to captain.

Little did he know that in almost exactly one year, the battery, short of horses and equipment, would be disbanded. Stationed as the enrolling officer in Fauquier County in February 1863, Chapman found an opportunity for assignment to John S. Mosby's command, later the 43rd Battalion Virginia Cavalry. By the spring of 1863, the brothers Chapman, both Samuel and William, were together again in action at Miskel's Farm with Mosby's command.

The exploits of the "Fighting Chapmans" were extensive and well recorded and some of the men that followed them, especially in Company C, hailed from Page County. Not only did the brothers find plenty of action under Mosby during the war, but also brides from the heart of Mosby country.

Page's Fighting Chapman brothers - Postwar Life
Article of 8/2/2001

While the combat exploits of the brothers Chapman can be found among a good grouping of books on Mosby's Rangers, a bit of romance was not out of the question in the midst of war. After less than a year with Mosby's command and less than a year of courtship, on February 25, 1864, William Henry Chapman married Josephine H. Jeffries near Delaplane, Virginia. She was the daughter of James Eustace and Esther Foote Jeffries.

There is a tale of the wedding taking place quickly in order to avoid a Federal patrol that was descending upon the marriage site. A Chapman family story recalled that during the war, Federal troops tried to capture her and Col. Mosby's wife to put them on the railroad trains to prevent Mosby's men from capturing and destroying them. The attempts to capture them never succeeded.

Five months after William and Josephine tied the knot; Sam Chapman married Eliza Rebecca Elgin, the only daughter of S. Gustavius and Catherine Lewis Smith Elgin at Marshall, Fauquier County, Virginia.

Following two years of action packed service with Mosby's Rangers, Sam and William Chapman continued to make their mark in society. Sam, a graduate of Columbia University, was said to have, during the war, "embraced combat as if it were an article of faith." Mosby himself proclaimed that Sam was "the only man he ever saw who really enjoyed fighting, and who generally went into the fray with his hat in one hand and banging away with his revolver with the other."

Following the war, Sam continued as a minister in Virginia and later went on to serve as chaplain with the 4th Immune Regiment in the Spanish American War. Settling in Covington in Alleghany County, Sam became well known as the "father of public schools" in that county and became the first superintendent of public schools. On May 21, 1919, Samuel Forrer Chapman, aged 80, died in Covington and was buried in Cedar Grove Cemetery.

Of William Chapman, one mother of a Ranger complimented him in saying: "It seemed to me he knew everything." At the end of the war, following Lee's surrender at Appomattox, it was William that offered the surrender of Mosby's men to Gen. Winfield Scott Hancock. Complimenting Mosby's right hand, Hancock described Chapman as "important as Mosby." William's postwar career was much more covered by the papers. He apparently never completed his college work started at the University of Virginia before the war. However, for his previous senior status in the 43rd Battalion Virginia Cavalry and his continuing ties with his former commander, Chapman found an interesting lifestyle in the postwar years.

In 1873, William was appointed by direction of President U.S. Grant to the railway mail service. Five years later, President Rutherford B. Hayes offered an appointment to Col. Mosby to "clean up" the "great amount of 'moonshining'. . . in Florida." Mosby declined the position, but in turn recommended William Chapman, then a resident of Alexandria, Virginia. Chapman accepted.

Though he returned unscathed from his adventures in Florida, during a raid near Huntsville, Alabama, William was shot through the wrist by a moonshiner. Years later, William received yet another wound while trying to catch a fleeing moonshiner from the U.S. Court in Atlanta. William remained with the Internal Revenue Service for over 20 years, not retiring until the Civil Service Annuity Pension became effective in 1920. The last of the service members to be appointed in July 1878, William's tours of service included Atlanta, Milton and Greensboro, N.C., New York, Tennessee, St. Louis, San Francisco, Salt Lake City, Pennsylvania, and Virginia.

On September 13, 1929, nearly 90 years of age, the old warrior died at his home at 840 West Market Street in Greensboro and was buried in Green Hill Cemetery in that city. Interestingly, his father, William A., is buried in Green Hill Cemetery in Luray.

The Irish Dorraugh-Dorrough-Derrough Family of Page
Article of 3/22/2001

Though a week behind in wishing the Irish descendants in Page a Happy St. Patrick's Day, I'll make up for it by focusing on one of the Irish surnames of Page – the Dorraugh family.

Seemingly, the first traceable Dorraugh in Page County is William M. Dorraugh who was born around 1811. William's first "blip" in Page County appears with his marriage to Sarah Ham on April 27, 1837. He then disappears until the 1850 census. Despite his diligence as the county census-taker that year, a listing for his family cannot be found.

During that same year, the only surnames close to "Dorraugh/Dorrough/Derrough" in Virginia are listed primarily in counties that would later be part of West Virginia. The closest spelling is that of a "Darragh" in Ohio County.

In the 1860 census, William M.'s family appears with the surname of Derrough in Grove Hill, District #1. From the records provided that year, William seems to have been doing rather well as a farmer/miller with $3,730 in real estate. Death records of two of his children in the late 1850s seem to zoom-in even further on the exact site of his residence - likely Poplar Mills near Somerville (later Ingham Station).

William and Sarah had at least nine children. Interestingly, the five oldest (born between 1837-1847) survived childhood, while the last four (1850-1857) seemed less fortunate. At the opening of the Civil War, both sons, James Hiram and Elijah Russell served with the "Massanutten Rangers" of Co. D, 7th Virginia Cavalry. Interestingly, Mary, Sarah and Rachael, all married veterans of that same company.

Oddly, the Dorraugh family is elusive in county census records after the war. Apart from showing up in 1860, the family does not reappear until 1880. By then, William M. had apparently died (he was listed as being the informant of the birth of one of his grandchildren in 1866) and his wife Sarah was living with son-in-law and daughter (Samuel B. & Mary Ann Davis) at Shenandoah.

So, where did the surname come from? One web page(http://home.att.net/~SMDRDD/RDD.html) states that "The Dorough surname is Scottish and Irish in origin and is a derivative of the Scottish name Darroch. Darroch is a sept of the clan McDonald of the Isle.

In 1794 the Lord Lyon King of Arms officially registered "Duncan Darroch of ourock, chief of this ancient name, the patronymic of which is MacIliriach," showing that Iliriach was the progenitor of this sept.

The name has its meaning based in the Gaelic Dubh Dara which is "Black Oak" . . . there are those who argue that the term Scotch-Irish does not apply to the McDonald Clan because the clan was in Ireland long before the plantations.

English land records for the plantations do list "Native Irish" who were given land. Among this list were the MacDonalds. This list also contains Irish with variations of the name Dorough assigned land. The name Dorough in Ireland has long been associated with county Antrim and Down."

The same web page also gives us a possible clue for our Page County line. There was one William Derrough listed as having served in the War of 1812 in the 19th Regiment (Ambler's) Virginia Militia – perhaps the father of William M. Dorrough?

The Dovel Family & an Introduction to the Terror Experienced by the French Huguenots
Article of 4/15/1999

The Dovel Family is one of various families from Page to come forth from the religious controversy that spread over France during the 16th century. What caused the great exodus from France is not clearly known by many but tells of a dark and gruesome religious event in European and World history.

By definition, Huguenots were French Protestants of the 16th and 17th centuries. The phrase also has roots stemming from French, specifically - "influenced by the gate of Roi-Hugon, where the Protestants of Tours assembled at night." However, the controversy that included this Protestant group of people stemmed from a power struggle for control of the French court. Not only had there been a distinct rivalry between France and Spain for the control of Flanders, but there had also been a bloody noblemen's war in existence between Catholics and persecuted Huguenots for ten years. On August 20, 1572, Catherine de Medicis, the pro-Spanish mother of France's Catholic King Charles IX, had engineered an attempt on the life of his powerful Protestant aide, admiral Gaspard de Coligny, who was advocating war on Spain. A badly wounded Coligny warned the king about his mother. King Henry of Navarre, a Protestant who had just married Charles' sister Margot and came in line for succession to the French throne, demanded that Coligny's attackers be punished. Catherine de Medicis then ordered a massacre of Protestants during which Coligny would be finished off. Her powerful allies, including the duke of Guise, stormed Coligny's home, slit his throat and dumped his body in the house's yard. Church bells pealed, calling Catholic militia to arms. The killings went out of control.

On the night of August 23, 1572, Roman Catholic militia wielding knives and swords fanned out through Paris, dragging Protestants from their homes and slitting their throats in an reign of terror. By the following morning thousands of bodies lay silent on the streets of the French capital. However, the exact final death toll of the notorious St. Bartholomew's Day massacre still remains a mystery to this day and is estimated from between 1,000 to 10,000 in Paris, and 2,000 to 100,000 throughout all of France.

Twenty-two years later the "wars of religion" flared again. Henry of Navarre, after besieging the French capital, declared in a famous quip: "Paris is well worth a mass." He converted to Catholicism and was crowned king of France. His Edict of Nantes in 1598 granted the Huguenots toleration and civil rights. He was assassinated 12 years later in an anti-Protestant plot. King Louis XIV, attempting to forcibly convert Protestants, revoked the Edict of Nantes almost a century later.

Many Huguenots went to hide in remote mountain villages of southern France. An estimated 400,000 went into exile, taking their industrial skills mainly to Britain, the Netherlands, Germany and Switzerland. Persecution of Protestants ended in 1764, and the 1789 French Revolution made them fully-fledged citizens, granting citizenship to the descendants of exiled Huguenots who returned.

Born ca. 1728, David Dovel, Sr. was a son of one of the Huguenot families that migrated to England following the revocation of the Edict of Nantes by Louis XIV. Later, with his brother William, the Dovel line made its way to the new world and arrived in North America in 1745. While David and his heirs settled in the area around Alma in Page County, it is not clearly known as to the disposition of William.

The Early Hillyard/Hilliard/Hilliards Family Lines
Article of 2/19/1998

The earliest patriarch traceable for the Hilliard/Hilliards families of Page County is Amos Hilyard. Born April 3, 1760, Amos' state or country of origin is uncertain. His first appearance in record in Virginia was in Berkeley County, Virginia (now West Virginia) in 1784 with the birth of his son, Jacob. Though his first wife's name remains a mystery, children from that first union other than Jacob included Amos Jr., John, and Mathias. By 1788, now a resident of Rockingham County, Amos, Sr. was shown as enlisting in Captain Josiah Harrison's Militia Company #9. Within another nine years, Amos would be a widower and married for a second time in 1797 to Susan McFarland.

From Amos' second marriage there were at least two additional children including James and Jesse. After residing for a long time in Rockingham County, Amos and son Mathias relocated to Barbour County, Virginia (now West Virginia) in 1843. Amos died on April 26, 1850, at the age of 90. He is buried on the land that the family settled in 1843 at the Hillyard Cemetery in Weaver, West Virginia.

The one son of Amos, Sr. who is of concern to most of the Page County lines today was Jacob Hilliard. Like his father, Jacob was nomadic for several years prior to finally settling in Page County. Married first to Elizabeth Taylor on September 29, 1803 in Frederick County, Jacob had at least seven children including Jacob Taylor, Grafton, John T., Mathias, Nancy Ann, and two other daughters.

Drafted in Captain Price McCormick's and Richardson's Company at Winchester during the War of 1812, Jacob served as a private in the 4th Virginia Militia in the defenses at Point Comfort in Norfolk for at least three months of a six month term before the war ended. Honorably discharged in either Pocohantas or Norfolk, Jacob's final records described him as about 5'10", with black hair, blue eyes, and light complexion.

Like his father before him, Jacob was left a widower in the middle of his life in 1835. From many of these Hilliards, the family lines of Winchester and Frederick County sprang forth.

By 1840, Jacob had relocated to Rockingham County, near his brother Mathias. However, the stay in Rockingham was only brief, for on May 30, 1842, he had returned to Frederick County once again and married Phoebe Elliott. Here the growing family remained temporarily with the new union producing sons Jacob (Jake) Theodore and Charles Robert. By 1847, the family again returned to Rockingham County where Jacob applied for bounty land and received 40 acres for his service in the War of 1812.

Residing near the Rockingham-Page county line, Phoebe bore Jacob's last son, William Christopher, in 1852. With the family growing still, Jacob disposed of his land in 1855 and reapplied for another section of bounty land in Page County. Whether he received a grant from his second application is unclear, however, in 1860 Jacob, Phoebe and the three remaining sons were residing in Warren County near the Bentonville Post Office.

Occupied as a shoemaker and farmer since 1850, Jacob and his family finally settled in Page County by 1864. In the early part of spring 1864, Jacob's health began to fail horribly. Jacob passed away sometime between April 9 - May 21, 1864. Though the exact site is uncertain, he is believed buried somewhere in the Sam Comer Cemetery in Stanley.

Five Brides, a Witch and a Deadly Curse
(re: Charles Robert Hilliard)
Article of 4/5/2001

No, it's not Halloween, but in the tradition of Appalachian folk stories, it would seem that any time is a good time for eerie tales. Anyone familiar with the old *Foxfire* series (see Volume #2 for some good ghost stories from the hill country) would agree. Additionally, when I come up with an idea for a story, it's hard to keep it on hold for the appropriate season.

When I first heard this story growing up, it gave me a spook. But I didn't really understand that the affected persons were my great-great grandparents. As I got a little older and I came to understand the relationship, but became skeptical, and being an historian, I had to look some things up. With a little bit of research I was able to place some names and dates to the story and add a bit to its validity.

Then too, I've learned over the years that nearly every Hilliard cousin I know can also tell the tale bringing me to believe that there must be something to the story.

The year was 1886, and, in all likelihood, the place was somewhere in the vicinity of Steam Hollow in Page County. Forty-two year old Charles Robert Hilliard and his wife, Margaret Elizabeth [Eaton], had a grand family of seven boys. One of which was by Charles Robert's first wife, Martha Susan Monger, who had died in 1871. The youngest of the lot was not yet one-year old.

As the story goes, one day, an elderly lady came to visit Margaret. Whether the exchange between the lady and Margaret was neutral, peaceful or heated, the meeting concluded with the old woman taking great-great grandma's tobacco pouch. The next day or so, Margaret became deathly ill – so ill that the family called for the local doctor.

After the doctor examined her, he must have drawn some unnatural conclusion and stated that he knew what had taken place and that he would see that "witch in hell by morning."

The story goes on to show that Margaret died from the "curse" put upon her by way of the tobacco pouch. The story also leaves us to believe that the witch met a similar fate soon thereafter.

Leaving Charles Robert with seven to care for on his own - naturally, by November of 1887, he was married again, for the third time. Oddly, Charles Robert must have felt as if some curse continued to plague him. When his first wife died (married 1870), they had not even been married two years. He had been married (married 1872) to Margaret for fourteen years. His third wife, Ella Nauman, (married 1887) died after less than six years of marriage. A fourth wife, Sarah Elizabeth Breeden, (married 1894) died after less than two years.

Finally, his fifth wife, Bessie Comer, broke the mold - barely! At the wedding, it is recalled, that after Bessie got into the carriage, the team was spooked and took-off. The team and carriage were stopped and, fortunately, Bessie's life was spared. When asked what he would have done if she had been killed, rumor has it that he replied, "I would have moved on to number six."

Thirty-three years his younger, Bessie was married (1896) to Charles Robert for forty years before he died at ninety-one years old, only four days after their anniversary in 1936.

Margaret Elizabeth Eaton was born in 1849 to Thomas Eaton (of Eaton Hollow in Rockingham County) and Amanda Shifflett. Though the two were not married, they had a large family of at least nine children. Margaret was likely the oldest or second oldest of the lot. Thomas was the son of William and Nancy Eaton, perhaps the descendant of an early (18th century)Baptist minister to the Shenandoah Valley. Amanda was the daughter of Edmond and Millie Wyant Shifflett.

There now, that wasn't too scary was it . . .?

Current Genealogical Work Regarding Michael and Mary Kiser
Article of 4/23/1998

Michael Kiser, his wife Mary, and their ten children came to the Shenandoah Valley about 1783. Initially purchasing 455 acres of land along the south fork of the Shenandoah River, the family settled in what was then Rockingham County. At best contemporary estimates, the current location is in the bend of the river directly to the west of Grove Hill in the Shenandoah Iron Works District of southern Page County.

Married between 1757 and 1760 in southeastern Pennsylvania, Kiser and his wife were children of recent German immigrants. Michael's father was Valentine Keiser, possibly the same Valentine Keiser who, with his wife Agnes, arrived in Philadelphia on 17 August 1729 aboard the English ship *Mortenhouse*. Mary's parents are believed to have been Jacob Lingel and Anna Ursula Banckard, who arrived in Philadelphia a few years later on 26 September 1737 on the English ship *St. Andrews Galley*. Both families settled in the area that is now near northern Montgomery and southern Lehigh Counties in southeastern Pennsylvania.

Recently identified through a birth and baptism certificate written in the 1820's for the family of Christian Strole and his wife Elizabeth Kiser (daughter of Michael and Mary Kiser), Mary has been identified as an Eppert instead of the previously believed Lingel. The document proves that Elizabeth was born in Berks County, Pennsylvania in 1769, lists the names of all of the children of Michael and Mary Kiser, and identifies Michael's father as Valentine.

After their marriage, Michael and Mary lived in Heidelberg Township, Berks County, Pennsylvania. In 1763, they moved again to Cumru Township, Berks County. All of their ten children (five daughters and five sons) were probably born in Berks County. Michael served in the American Revolution in Capt. Philip Krick's 8th Company, 4th Battalion, Pennsylvania Line. His name appears on a list of fines assessed in the years 1777-1778 for being absent from muster or drill.

In 1783 Michael Kiser sold his farmland (234 acres) and moved his family to Rockingham County, Virginia. At the time of their departure from Pennsylvania in 1783, only their oldest son Valentine was married. He and his new wife Catherine Stiehl accompanied Michael and Mary Kiser and their other nine children to their new home about 150 miles to the southwest in Virginia. Some of the Lingel family had moved there in the 1770s. Michael and Mary would remain in Rockingham County for the rest of their lives. He died in 1798; she in 1805.

Many of their descendants lived in present-day Page and Rockingham Counties, although most of the descendants carrying the Kiser surname (and its variations) moved elsewhere. Of the 2568 known descendants in the first four generations (children through great-great-grandchildren), the most common surnames were Kiser (Kizer, Keiser, Keyser) (551), Kite (330), Strole (184), Foltz (90), Coiner (Koiner) (81), Dovel (80), Spotts (74), Huffman (68), and Shuler (58).

A study of this family shows how the population of post-Revolutionary America increased so quickly. Michael Kiser and Mary Lingel had 10 children, 92 grandchildren, 521 great-grandchildren, and 1945 great-great-grandchildren. Since the youngest of this fourth generation were born after the year 1900, there may be some alive today.

An excellent resource for the Kiser/Keyser/Kayser family has been created by Mark B. Arslan (e-mail address: arslanm@ibm.net) and now exists on the internet. Access to this site can be gained at URL: http://www.geocities.com/Heartland/Hills/6359/kiser/kiser.html

Discovering the Roots of the Page County Nauman Families
Article of 4/9/1998

On August 21, 1750 the ship *Anderson* arrived in Philadelphia from Germany with 86 passengers. Among the large number of recent immigrants were Johannes and John Gottlieb Nauman of Hanover. Germany. Once debarked from the ship, the new settlers took their oath of allegiance to the English crown before embarking on the ultimate challenge of heading for land on the frontier. Settling initially in Pennsylvania, John Gottlieb and his wife had several children including Thomas and John Christian Nauman.

Stories from the other lines of Naumans collaborate the information of the 1750 Nauman arrival in Pennsylvania. Though only two brothers were recorded as arriving in Philadelphia, there was also a third brother, Christian Nauman, that arrived on the *Brotherhood* on November 3, 1750 from Rotterdam and Cowes in England. From this confusion of Johannes, Johns and Christians, there leaves room for possible variation in family lineage, though inevitably ending in the same line of blood brothers that came from Hanover. Christian, who had arrived on the *Brotherhood,* was said to have gone south and never heard from again, leaving the possibility that it was him rather than the above stated John Christian that was the progenitor of Page County families, with a son, John Christian Nauman, Jr. as the husband of Christina Stoneberger.

While this may remain a uncertain link for a short time to come, there is one certainty of the Nauman family that remained in Germany. Apparently there was yet another brother, Emil Nauman, that remained and was reputed as telling his children never to go to America, "because he had brothers who went to America and he never heard of them afterward, the wild beasts must have killed them." Ultimately however, a grandson, also named Johannes Gottlieb Nauman, later settled in 1853 in Iowa.

Nevertheless, around 1774 - 1775, Thomas and one of the above stated John Christian Naumans, like many other Swiss and German settlers, made their way to the area of land that later became Page County. Thomas settled in the Valley only briefly before moving on to Ohio. John Christian found happiness in the valley and made permanent settlement. Between 1777 - 1778, John, now a school master and farmer, married Christina Stoneberger, the supposed daughter of Frederick Stoneberger.

From the union of John and Christina there were several children including Elizabeth, John Christian, Jr., Catherine, David, Eva, Mary, Barbara, Benjamin Harrison, Hannah, and Christina. In 1795, John played a part in the foundation of St. Luke's Lutheran Church at Alma as a trustee, along with Daniel Snyder. Deeded the property by Frederick Stoneberger and Mathias Friermood, the church was originally located on Stony Run near Stanley before a new log structure was built in 1801. This church was later abandoned and moved to Alma.

Sometime around 1835, both John and his Christina passed away, buried on their land in roughly marked graves, "a large white oak tree" shading the spot where they were laid. Of the number of children produced from the marriage, over half or their heirs later relocated to Ohio or Missouri. In time, the irony of history would bring the family at odds with each other in the Civil War. Though no documentation or proof exists that any family members clashed on the battlefield, several family members did serve on opposite sides during the war.

The Trek of the Nicholson Family –
Whitehaven, England to Virginia to the Valley
Article of 7/1/1999

Early portrayals of Madison County's Nicholson family show them as an illiterate, "back-woods" sort of people that were removed from the property that became the Shenandoah National Park. However, recent research and archeology being conducted in that county by the Colonial Williamsburg Foundation is proving quite the contrary. Most prominent in that area east of the Blue Ridge, many of the family eventually found their way across the mountains and into Page County (my own Nicholson lines did this around 1880). Some contemporary Page County residents with both the surnames of Nicholson and Nichols are the remnants of that line.

At the very earliest, the Nicholson family roots can be traced to Thomas Nicholson. Listed as mariner from Whitehaven, Cumberland County, England, Nicholson came to Virginia around 1732 and bought 1,000 acres in Spotsylvania County (the area that would later become Madison and Rappahannock counties) "near the great fork of the Rappahannock River."

While the original tract of land was sold by 1750 and in the wake of the progenitor's demise, John Nicholson, son of Thomas, remained in the area until he purchased 327 acres on the Hughes River near the mouth of what would later become known as "Nicholson Hollow" in 1797. He later bought an additional 170 to add to the "family homestead." In time, John's sons bought portions of that land as homes for their own families. Thomas' and John's descendants remained in this area until the relocation.

In October 1886, sixteen year-old George Freeman Pollock - the founder of "Skyline"- ventured out to explore the area around Stony Man. In his wanderings, he came upon the area known as Free State Hollow. Pollock's memoirs distinctly gave the impression that it was an area in its most primitive state with residents to meet the same description. A "center of the moonshine business . . . Very few of the dwellers in Free State Hollow had ever been to the town of Luray, the women and children and most of the men had never even seen a locomotive and there was no reading or writing, the people being absolutely illiterate. Old Man Nicholson was the 'granddaddy' of the entire clan and for that reason Free State Hollow was also called Nicholson Hollow."

Likewise, in 1933, in their sociological study known as "Hollow Folk", journalist Thomas Henry and University of Chicago sociologist Mandel Sherman supported Pollock's findings, perhaps justifying the relocation of the family from the area upon the establishment of the park. They described the residents sheltered in tiny mud-plastered log cabins . . . an "unlettered folk a primitive agriculture," in communities which were "almost entirely cut off from the current of American life."

As mentioned earlier, the Colonial Williamsburg Foundation has taken on the project of doing archeological work in the area of Nicholson Hollow, as well as Corbin and Weakley Hollows. In their diggings, and as opposed to Pollock's descriptions, the findings show that the residents were quite in step with the times and "residents did, in fact, wear shoes, cured their sore throats not only with cherry tree bark but with patent medicines, . . . ate their meals off of a variety of imported and domestic ceramics, listened to records on the phonograph, slept in fancy brass beds . . . . owned the same types of goods which are found on archaeological sites of the same era throughout the United States–many no doubt originating from the Sears and Roebuck Company." As the author of this article and descendant myself from the same Nicholson line, I have clear evidence in my own possession in family papers from the time that support the same findings.

For further reading of interest regarding the archeology being conducted, visit the Foundation's web site at: http://www.history.org/cwf/argy/argyshen.htm.

Thomas Purdom and His Role in the American Revolution
Article of 8/6/1998

Born around 1751, Thomas Purdom was a future forefather of Page County Purdom/Purdham family lines. Years into his life and prior to the foundation of Page County, Purdom made claim for what was due to him for his service in the American Revolution. In response to the Congressional act of March 18, 1818 allowing Revolutionary War pensions, Purdom made his application on August 8, 1820. Reflecting back upon his youth, Purdom recalled that he enlisted for eighteen months in the 2nd Virginia Regiment in June, 1780. Initially under the command of a Captain Harrison and Lieutenant Colonel John Green of Culpeper (actually of the 1st Virginia Regiment), Purdom would transfer to a Captain Williams's Company.

From the arrival in or near the future capital city of Virginia, Thomas Purdom's service is traced mostly out of Virginia. Though he makes no detailed log of his exact travels (unlike the Cave pension), it is possible that he was among the 1,400 militia recently recruited from the western counties of Virginia that reinforced General Horatio Gates prior to the battle of Camden, South Carolina on August 16, 1780. After the green troops were thrown into battle with little or no training, the result was disastrous as many of the troops had thrown down their arms and fled upon being exposed to the musketry. However, due to the high influx of British activity in Virginia during that same time-frame, many Virginia troops were held in the Old Dominion in lieu of being sent south. There were in fact a series of invasions through late March 1781 along the James River, in the Richmond-Petersburg area, and into the Chesapeake Bay and Portsmouth, Virginia. Where Purdom was at during this time remains to be found. It is possible that his actual service record at the National Archives could shed some light.

What is certain is that Purdom was with General Nathanael Greene's troops in the 1781 Southern Campaigns. General George Washington, needing improvement in activities in the South, selected Greene, the former Continental Army's quartermaster, as the commander-in-chief of the Southern Department. Upon being placed in command, Greene quickly initiated action against the British. In the months that would follow Greene's assignment, the

British were engaged by elements of Greene's army at Cowpens, S.C., Guilford Courthouse, N.C., and Hobkirk's Hill, S.C.

Determined to gain an edge against British Lord Rawdon, Greene struck westward against Fort Ninety-Six while Rawdon reorganized in Charleston, S.C. Originally an important backwoods treading post, by 1781, Ninety-Six was the site of an impressive star-shaped, earthen fortification. While involved in the siege of the fortification, Purdom sustained a severe wound " "through the body by a bayonet." Typically, this sort of wound would be certain death for a soldier, especially in the 18th century. However, while the details simply aren't available, Purdom survived and lived to be discharged in Salisbury, North Carolina in January 1782.

For his service, Purdom was awarded a pension of $8.00 per month on April 24, 1822, retroactive to the date of his application on August 8, 1820.

Now a National Historic Site of the Department of the Interior, Fort Ninety-Six is accessible to tourists and is located in Greenwood County, South Carolina.

On a closing note, remember that when dealing with incomplete or incorrect information in pensions, it is best to utilize sources such as *The Virginia Continental Line* by John R. Sellers. Published by the Virginia Independence Bicentennial Commission, the 84 page book is still available.

The Roudabush Family of Page County, Part I
Article of 8/16/2001

Among the masses of emigrants from the Palatinate of Germany in the early 18th century was a man by the name of Hans Heinrich Raudenbusch. Born in Steinsfurt, Germany around 1712, he was the grandson of Hans Peter Raudenbusch.

The earliest professional miller to whom the Raudenbusch lines can be traced at present, Hans Peter (also the Courtier of Steinsfurt, Baden-Wurttemberg) had been born prior to 1600 and continued to operate a mill throughout the 30 Years War (1618 – 1648). For this amazing feat, the Kurphaz Government paid homage to him by giving him the flourmill. Hans Peter died October 17, 1657 in Reihen, Baden-Wurttemberg, Germany.

It is interesting to note that this family profession would carry on for over 300 years and well into the 20th century!

Alas, I digress, back to Hans Heinrich - he arrived (apparently with other family members) in Philadelphia on September 30, 1732 aboard the good ship *Dragon*. It is uncertain if he arrived with his wife or, that soon after arrival, he married Anne Maria Becker. Nevertheless, by 1743, he was warranted 150 acres along the Great Conawago Creek in York (now Adams) County. Seven years later, Heinrich/Henry was warranted yet another 200 acres nearby.

According to a very good descendant maintained website (http://www.habersack.com/geneology/hhr.htm), Henry's reasons for settlement in this area appeared to be "religious in nature." Specifically, "Henry was a member of the Church of the Brethren (German Baptist or Dunkard), and one of the first churches of that denomination in America was established around 1741, also near the Great Conawago Creek. Henry was one of the founding members. This congregation still exists and is known today as 'Mummert's Meeting House.'"

A constable in 1757, supervisor of highways in 1761, overseer of the poor in 1768, Henry was an active member in the community in Berwick Township, Pennsylvania. Though his sons may have served in a militia organization or even an regiment of the line, when the American Revolution came around, Henry remained firm in his religious beliefs as a Brethren and pacifist and refused to take the Oath of Loyalty. Henry died on February 5, 1784.

One of Henry's sons, Jacob, is the key tie to the line of Roudabush families that later came to the Shenandoah Valley. A brother of his – John – also came to Virginia but the last name was changed in his line, beginning with him, to RUEBUSH. Though John died while living near Hagerstown, his widow and children settled near Frieden's Reformed Church near Mt. Crawford in Rockingham County.

But back to Jacob - born in Adams County ca. 1752, he married by the 1770s to Anne Rickstacker and lived in Berwick Township through 1795. Moving to Rockingham County, Virginia, Jacob was listed in reference to a deposition being taken December 2, 1806 as living "at the sign of Cross Keys."

As a side note that may tie to this family, on his way home from the Ohio Valley at some point, George Washington stayed several days in Rockingham County at the home of a family known as "Rudiborts."

Jacob did not stay long in Virginia. By 1810 he had moved his family to Strabane Township in Pennsylvania. Another eleven years later, he moved yet again to Washington, Carroll County, Ohio. A member of the Whig Party and member of the Disciples of Christ Church, he died in 1837. He and his wife were buried near the farm that they built at Washington.

The Roudabush Family of Page County, Part II
Article of 8/30/2001

When last we were engaged in this topic, Jacob Roudabush, Sr. had moved on to Ohio. One son, (also named Jacob) after accompanying his father to Strabane, Pennsylvania, opted to go come back to Rockingham County in 1818. Jacob II's wife, whom he had married in 1808 in Rockingham County, was Mary Magdalene Whitzel. Her parents, Peter and Mary Tutwiler Whitzel, remained in the Valley and probably had something to do with the return of Jacob II's family.

Jacob – also a Roudabush miller like many others before him - died near Conrad's Store (Elkton) on July 4, 1848. His wife would follow before 1860. In all, Jacob and Mary saw the births of 11 children. Born August 10, 1826, the 8th child - Peter William Roudabush – also a miller by profession, would become known as the immediate progenitor of the Page County lines. Peter ran many mills including, but not limited to, one in Greene County, a mill near Honeyville, and a mill near the Peter Printz home in Ida.

In December 1853, Peter married Elizabeth Ann Koontz (the daughter of John J. and Mary Bingman Koontz – John J. Koontz was the grandson of the famous Elder John Koontz). From 1854 to 1872, Peter and Elizabeth had seven sons and three daughters.

During the Civil War, the Page County line of the Roudabush family did not serve. At the beginning of the war, Peter was exempt for 1) being a miller and 2) being "over age 35." Additionally, the oldest child was only 7. However, Peter's brother, John Hiram Roudabush (age 34) resided in Augusta County and joined Co. H, 14th Virginia Cavalry. Apparently, three of Peter's Rockingham County cousins served in Co. I, 7th Virginia Cavalry in the famous Laurel Brigade. It is unclear as to which family line these men were descended.

Clearly, at the very least, the names of two of Peter's children show allegiance to the Commonwealth's decision during the war. Major Ashby Roudabush and Virginia Jackson Roudabush revealed names prominent in the Valley in the war. In regard to M.A. Roudabush - there is an interesting story to note. It seems that, early in the war, then lieutenant colonel, Turner Ashby was riding with his regiment near one of the family mills. Ashby saw the new child (born Aug. 22, 1861) and asked if the boy had yet been named. When he learned that it had not – he pronounced that the boy be named "Major Ashby," for the boy could not outrank him.

However, there may be a tie to the naming of M. A. Roudabush and the July 3, 1861 death by brutal wounds of Turner's brother, Richard. Richard was a captain when mortally wounded and Turner, having himself been appointed to lieutenant colonel on July 17, 1861, and so terribly disturbed by his brother's death, when naming the young Roudabush, may have been wishing that they name the boy to honor his brother who might have also been promoted to major had he lived. How appropriate it would be that Major married a woman by the name Virginia Belle (McAllister)!

As an additional note, the first of Major Ashby Roudabush's sons was appropriately named for the family profession – "Miller."

Over the years, there have been many changes in spelling to the original name of Raudenbusch – Roudabush, Raudabush, Radabush, Roudebush, Ruebush and Rubush.

The Hessian and a Case of Good Fortune –
the Strole-Keyser Connection
Article of 1/14/1999

In 18th century Colonial America, immigrants were making it to North America by various means. Christian Strohl made his way to America, not as a colonist, but as a Hessian soldier sent to aid the British in putting down the upstart Continental Army. Born in Rumpenheim, Hesse, Germany in September 1758 to Peter (who was the son of Johan Conrad Strahl) and Margaretha Seybel Strahl, Christian was one of at least five siblings and was confirmed at his Lutheran Church in Rumpenheim in the spring of 1772.

Before recent information was uncovered and according to family history, Christian Strohl was believed to have settled in the Shenandoah Valley in 1776. Furthermore, he was also believed to have been one of the 8,000 Hessians that were captured at Saratoga, N.Y. while serving under General Baron Riedesel. These same captured Hessians were supposedly transported to Boston, Massachusetts to be sent back to their country. Upon arrival at Boston, many refused to leave. Thomas Jefferson, then governor of Virginia, suggested they be sent to Williamsburg instead and put in the stockade. After arrival at Williamsburg, they refused incarceration and consequently opened some sort of protest to remain in America. From Williamsburg, the men were divided into three detachments. One was sent to Charlottesville, Va., the other to Winchester, Va., and the last to Frederick, Md. A plan was then devised to indenture these men for some years to residents of the areas and then grant them freedom.

Recent information however, shows that in 1782, Michael Kiser purchased the indenture of a "recently captured Hessian soldier named Christian Strohl (Strole)." The difficult question to resolve is how recently Christian had been captured. Perhaps then his exact unit of origin and place of capture could be confirmed.

Nevertheless, Christian had come upon good fortune in being purchased by Michael Kiser. The Reformed Lutheran church records back in Rumpenheim show that the Kayser and Strohl families lived near each other, attended the same church, intermarried, and witnessed each other's baptisms. Therefore, it is very possible that Michael purchased Christian's indenture and was subsequently freed as a result of the family acquaintance.

A year after the purchase, Christian, along with the Kiser family left Berks County, Pennsylvania for Michael Kiser's new tract of 1,030 acres along the south fork of the Shenandoah River in what was then Rockingham County. Despite his obligation to Michael Kiser, Christian did have the opportunity to purchase a 300 acre tract from Martin Strickler on September 7, 1785. Today the same parcel of land, along with the house that Christian built, can be viewed along the Strole Farm Road in the bend of the river directly to the west of Grove Hill in the Shenandoah Iron Works District of southern Page County.

Michael released Christian from his indenture in 1788, which in turn, allowed his marriage to Michael's daughter Elizabeth in that same year. Christian found further good fortune in his efforts as a farmer, miller and father of four sons and eight daughters. The family attended Monger's Church (now St. Paul Lutheran Church) but were buried on their farm; Christian dying in 1841 and Elizabeth in 1854.

Further information on the Strole family can be found in the Page Public Library in the bound Christian Strole History. Information on the Strole-Kiser connection can be found on the internet at the URL: http://www.geocities.com/Heartland/Hills/6359/kiser/kiser.html.

"Surfing" Your Way to Page County Genealogical Research
Article of 1/8/1998

Ah yes, we're slowly becoming serious "netizens" on the "Web" these days. When it comes to the internet for some basic genealogy research there are boundless possibilities. For Page County there are currently three major sites that are beneficial to the new or experienced genealogy researcher.

The first reviewed Web Page is a part of the Virginia Genealogical Web Project or VaGenWeb for short. As a part of the VaGenWeb, this Page County site is maintained by Todd White. Like all sites listed in this review, this site is not commercial in nature and genealogy information found on these pages is freely available to the public; but like books, the sites are copyrighted. The VaGenWeb Page County site is a great reference point for checking various queries or the surname listing. Queries contained on the web page consist of other "netizens" who leave behind a particular surname or surnames with vital information in the hope that others might also be researching the same person. In the case that there might be information to share between one another, e-mail addresses are left behind so that a rapid exchange of information may take place. Likewise, various persons throughout the county and the country have been listed for voluntary look-ups of Page County ancestors. While at the site, be sure to click on the various links of Page County genealogy interests including, but not limited to, links to the "e-zine" entitled *Oh Shenandoah! Country Rag* and the Shenandoah Directory that lists various people in the Shenandoah Valley who are also on-line. Future growth and various upgrades are soon expected for the web page. The site can be found at: http://www.geocities.com/Heartland/2521/page.htm.

Once you've tapped into the first page, press on to the home page of the Genealogical Society of Page County. Maintained by Teresa Kelley and as a part of the "RootsWeb", this page is a definite contribution to Page County research on-line. This page gives a bountiful harvest when it comes to Page County genealogy research. While always being improved this page is a whopper including Bible records, cemetery information, local church history, mortality schedules, a Civil War diary of a Page County Confederate veteran, post office and towns and their name origins, etc.

Like the VaGenWeb Page County site, it too has a list of queries and a surname listing that gives member e-mail addresses and the surnames they are researching. In the future we can expect to see more Bible records, Voter Registrations for 1903 - 1908 and much more. Without a doubt, no Page County researcher should leave these pages unturned. This site can be found at: http://www.rootsweb.com/~vagspc/pcgs.htm.

Finally, we come to web page number three. In searching for my own Page County Confederate ancestors I struggled through many trips to Richmond to finally obtain all of the information necessary to quench the ever growing thirst for more knowledge. So that others would not have to go to such great lengths I created the Master Web Page of Confederate Units Formed in Page County. If your looking for a Confederate ancestor that served in a Page County unit or your ancestor served in another unit and resided in Page before or after the war, then this is your best cross-reference yet. While still under construction, the site will ultimately be provided with a multitude of links and other features that will benefit the Confederate ancestor researcher. The site can be accessed at:
http://www.geocities.com/Heartland/Hills/1850/pagecoconfeds.html

Researching Your Family History May be Just a Web Site Away
Article of 10/22/1998

Since fall is well underway and the winter months lie just around the corner, journeying to the library to do genealogical research may be a bit hindered due to poor weather. Some may remember that earlier this year I wrote an article regarding genealogical research on the internet. Since that article in January, several new things have either been modified or have recently blossomed anew on the web.

The Genealogical Society of Page County site and the Page County Confederate Veterans web sites have not moved from their URL's. However, the Virginia Genealogical Web Project page for Page County (currently under revision) has a new site that can be reached at http://www.geocities.com/Heartland/Hills/1850/PageCoVaGenWeb.html. Now, for what is new on the web horizon . . . .

The Mt. View Research site - designed and maintained by Judy Campbell - is an INCREDIBLE new web site. Located at www.geocities.com/Heartland/Valley/9793/, this site brings a veritable cornucopia of Page County genealogical items to your home. In addition to her personal genealogy profiles, Judy goes quite a few steps further and unleashes items that range from a biographical sketch of John Zirkle to marriage records and well beyond.

As a sneak peak, I will introduce a sampling of the Page County information sites she has placed on-line. The complete 1860 and 1870 census (arranged by House number); birth records from 1865-1885 (in alphabetical order by parents' surname); marriage records from 1831-1879 (in alpha order by groom as well as by bride); guardian bonds from 1850-1890; death records from records from 1864 - 1885; coroner's inquests; wills and list of heirs; divorce index from 1831-1923; and - my personal favorite for vital statistic finding - the cemetery index (which is listed in alphabetical order and makes research a snap).

In the event that your ancestor(s) might have crossed over from another county to Page or moved from Page to a bordering county,

Shenandoah, Rappahannock, Rockingham, and Warren County - as well as a few in West Virginia.

Overall, the Mt. View Research site in itself is all you need to kick-off your 1998-1999 research season. However, when combined with the other sites I have mentioned, all of the basic resources necessary for Page have been brought right to your home via computer monitor.

Other web sites worthy of mention for their detailed information include the Germanna Foundation site and the Broyles Family site. The reason that I mention these is due to the fact that several Page County families sprung forth from the Germanna "Colony." Both can be reached through:
http://homepages.rootsweb.com/~george/index.shtml.

Oh yes, and for your reading pleasure, in the event that you might have misplaced that issue of the *Page News & Courier* with the Heritage and Heraldry article that you meant to save - don't fret too much. In cooperation with the paper, I have placed an archive of the H & H articles on-line and will place future articles on-line approximately 30 days after their appearance in the paper. This web site can be found is available at:
http://www.geocities.com/Heartland/Hills/1850/heritageandheraldry.html.

Finally, as October draws nigh, I would be curious to hear from readers regarding ghost stories involving different historic characters from Page County history. While not normally my "haunt", it would be interesting to "dig-up" (pun intended in both) whatever I could in order to find information relating to the historic episodes that surround such stories.

America's Wars Have Left a Long Paper Trail for Genealogists
Article of 2/4/1999

While I haven't received any letters pointing it out yet, I figured I would bring up something that has probably surfaced on the minds of a few of my readers - "Why does he always write about war or war related items?" The answer is that wars have etched themselves, like some sort of indelible ink, on the minds of the participants and the families that either view the events first hand or read about them at home. The events of these times have become important facets of American history. From the French and Indian War to Desert Storm, the United States has averaged approximately 30 years between wars, not to mention all of the other smaller conflicts throughout. In turn, wars have required soldiers, sailors, marines, and in the most recent century, airman. These legions of men and women in the various armed forces have had their services documented in one form or another. While devastating in many ways these wars and the veterans that served within them have left "long paper trails" for contemporary genealogists.

As readers have seen in my columns over the past 16 months, I have mentioned several military related people and events when and how they have related to the history of Page County. I have written about military organizations, individual soldiers, pension records, wartime events and other things that have maintained Page County history in their themes. In fact, rare has it been where I have written about individual families and their histories without bringing up something to do with the military or military related events. The basis for all of these articles has come from various individual microfilmed military service records, pensions of these military members, books that contained information related to their military service, and books related to various events throughout history (books that might have no more than a sentence that mention Page County).

All of these records play an important part in genealogical research. The genealogist usually goes forth with a family story or name and in time, through birth, marriage, death, and cemetery records, form the stepping stone that leads into the creation of their basic "skeletal" family tree (not to be confused with the occasional skeleton in the family tree). Beyond that are the wills and deeds that provide a little light here and there into the lives of these people in the tree. But without turning over the "military stones," one might be missing even more enlightening tales of the family.

In summary, sure, I veer off once and a while (and will continue to do so) into other items that are viewpoints into history and how they relate to us and our family trees. I'll even continue to go off into a tangent here and there. However, with the vast stores of material relating to Page County and its people in war left yet untapped to historical transcription, I leave you with the reminder to hang on tight as I continue to be your tour guide to the past and maybe even give light to the path down your own family tree search. Likewise, I might even turn over a few stones and emerge with stories about characters in this century that have gone virtually unmentioned since Harry Strickler's *A Short History of Page County*. But before I leave you on this note, I will make the plea once again for copies (I don't need your originals) of diaries and letters of those same veterans (in particular in the 1800's) over the past.

Interpretation of History often Strays from Documented Fact
Article of 11/19/1998

"Just the facts please, just the facts." While I temporarily borrow a phrase from that favorite old show "Dragnet," it brings to mind thoughts of where American history has gone astray. Interpretation of history is a natural process for the genealogist, antiquarian, and chronicler - much like solving a mystery. However, just how many become strays from documented historical fact?

I'm personally a big fan of family legends and stories passed down by word of mouth through generations. There is in fact one story in regard to a great-great grandmother of mine that died - supposedly - as a result of a curse from a witch right here in Page County all because she had taken her tobacco pouch and used it as the object of her curse. Good ol' Appalachian folklore huh!? OK, OK, sounds wild I know - but an interesting story - that I have absolutely no way to prove.

So before we take the "word of mouth" for fact, try this simple test. In a classroom of a dozen or more people - take a story about a paragraph or more in length - and whisper it to one person, who will whisper it to another and so on (remember - say it only once) until the story has gone one-to-one throughout the room. Also remember not to allow any third parties in the class to listen in on the story as it is passed individually from person to person. Now, ask the last person who received the story to repeat aloud the story as he/she had received it. Has the story retained its meaning and how different is the story from when it was initially circulated? Odds are that several words have been altered if not the entire meaning of the story.

While we should continue to value and even document (A MUST that even I am occasionally guilty of in my genealogical research) these great family stories passed down from generation to generation, if possible we should also try to validate them through dependable historical resources. As my history professors used to say - "documentation, documentation, ..." Gee, odds are you have figured I was a history major. . . .

So where am I going with this? First, always take family stories with a grain of salt, and then work to prove these stories. Don't rely simply on other family stories. Though collaborating stories can help confirm, it is still not accurately documented. I'm cast from the mold of historians that originated from the pursuit of genealogy. Over the years I "evolved," in a sense, into a more objective and critical historian. I found it absolutely necessary to scrutinize an issue or subject before I proclaimed it as historical fact. If you stand by a conclusion that you simply cannot fully support with valid resources - the obvious need is to return to the grindstone.

There is an excellent book that delves into all of this that was written a few years ago. Joyce Appleby, Lynn Hunt and Margaret Jacob worked together and created the thorough book entitled *Telling the Truth About History*. Within one chapter entitled "Truth and Objectivity," the authors make several valuable points that sift through fact and fiction in history. They write:

"We have redefined historical objectivity as an interactive relationship between an inquiring subject and an external object. Validation in this definition comes from persuasion more than proof, but without proof there is no historical writing of any worth."

Pass Down those Nostalgic Tales to Future Generations
Article of 12/3/1998

My last column was about the necessity of keeping fact and fiction apart from one another when it comes to family stories. If you are dealing with an issue that needs positive back-up documentation in order for the story to be "certified" historic fact, then the rule still holds true. However, what of those good old nostalgic tales passed down over so many years? The stories that entertain and are told with a gleam in the eye and a warm spot in the heart. Just because you cannot document them, don't leave them by the wayside to disappear forever. They hold an important value of a different kind, and somewhere between the lines, there may be an iota of fact that leaves you to wonder.

Yes, there are the far fetched tales from old Appalachia that stir the blood of every warm blooded soul to hail from the hills. But there are also those tales that are of a day that is slowly fading from memory. How many are fortunate enough to recall (or still experience) the rain drops on a tin roof, the chill of the air during fall butchering, the warm gas stove in the kitchen that use to warm the kettle AND the house? These are all important stories to recollect and retain for your children and your children's children.

Defined in *The American Heritage Dictionary* (sorry - I don't have a *Webster's* handy), nostalgia is the "bittersweet longing for things, persons or situations of the past." Sound like I'm on a tangent again? Well, as the summer months come to a close and chill of the fall air sets in back there in the Shenandoah Valley, many remember several things of the past that have long since faded away. Oddly, it seemed like yesterday that my parents and grandparents reminisced on different things they had grown up experiencing. While a teenager, I stored these memories away, but still savored the nostalgia of their stories.

Now, in reflection, and several hundred miles from the Page Valley, I can still see the Blue Ridge or the Massanutten as it appeared in its fall brilliance to me in my youth. There are memories of bright colored leaves, the smell of burning leaves, family dinners on Sunday afternoons, that ever burning desire to draw pictures on a misty window. These are the things that memories are made of . . . .

and oddly they were no more than 25 years ago. It seems hard to imagine that a quarter of a century passes so quickly.

So now as the summer draws to a close and the autumn chimes in with all of its glory, families that didn't quite make it home during the spring and summer, take that journey to the Valley to spend a weekend or more of the various holiday dates before the winter snow sets in. With the weekend of the Heritage Festival on the horizon, the opportunity to conjure some of those old memories is at hand. To me, the season is best opened by taking that trek back to Page, walking around the buildings and exhibits and smelling the wood from the fires that heat those large cauldrons of apple butter. Maybe, just maybe, there will actually be a chill in the air to boot. By the way - if you have the chance, tell the kids one of those stories of growing up in the Valley again would ya?

Genealogical Research May Also Include World Wide Web
Article of 2/10/2000

It's about that time of year again when I place emphasis on genealogy research on the Internet. With shorter days and cold nights, now is the perfect time to become a "netizen" and explore genealogy resources on the Web. When it comes to the Internet for some basic genealogy research there are boundless possibilities.

In the era of web design frenzy, many people have taken their personal time to upload massive amounts of data that can be accessed for free. Whether it's the kind-hearted philosophy of sharing genealogy secrets or just that their respective genealogy sites were a test in their skills of web design, most of these independent sites are a wealth of knowledge. One such area is that of the USGenWeb Project (http://www.usgenweb.org/). Composed of a many, many web site designers interested in genealogy, this site leads to many other genealogy projects on the web that are non-commercial and "fully committed to free access for everyone." One such off-shoot of this site is found in the Projects state pages – the VaGenWeb being one of them (http://www.rootsweb.com/~vagenweb/).

However, for the genealogy "heavy-hitter" that enjoys the quick turn-around of our microwave society, there are some larger sites that offer a great deal up-front and are initially free, but may lead to a fee in order to find other information. Not that a web subscription is a bad thing, its just that these "big-boys" of the Internet are businesses and are using business tactics. Two of the largest sites on the web that fall in this category include Ancestry.com (http://www.ancestry.com/) and Genealogy.com (http://www.genealogy.com/). A free "heavy-hitter" site can be found through the Latter Day Saints and is titled Family Search (http://www.familysearch.org/).

The greatest advantage of going into these "heavy-hitter" sites is that they offer a researcher the chance to tie into the research of other people for free. Over the last two decades or more, several genealogists have contributed the work that they have done so that others may benefit from it. What a great gesture! However, even though the search is free – buyer beware! When it comes to family research, some amateur genealogists are less than thorough and might even follow a lead in the wrong direction. In other words, take all free net information with a grain of salt. If you're a truly discerning researcher, you will follow-up on the lead that you find on the web and back it up with your own research. Then again, you may tear down the myth that the other genealogists believed as gospel.

To launch the search effort on these site (lets take Family Search for example), all you need to do is place the first and last name of the ancestor your looking up and go for it! One word of advice however, the further back in your genealogy you are the better. If you input your father or mother, it is highly unlikely you'll crash into that proverbial potential treasure trove of data. However, if you input the name of a great-great grandparent or even further back, your odds are significantly improved in the search.

Ancestry.com gives a different angle for the search. Once at the leading page, type in the first name and surname of the person your trying to find more about. If your surname is really unusual, you can just insert that for a wide search – I wouldn't suggest it for common names however. For example, I wouldn't dare type in Moore (the 10th most common surname in the U.S.) for I know I would have various lines of Moores that had absolutely nothing to do with my own tree. Nevertheless, once you have typed in the data and have pressed search, just sit back and wait for a second and VIOLA! The resources that are listed before you are in detail as to whether you can access the information for free or for a fee. The Social Security Death Index is a nice free area that will usually give you, not only the Social Security number of an ancestor, but also – maybe – birth and death dates, the place of application, and last residence. Again, however, keep in mind that if the ancestor died before Social Security was established in the 1930's, this will be of no help. Still, for that NEW researcher, this database contains nearly 62 million records and might help to break into the 19th century.

About Me

So just who is this upstart columnist?
Article of 4/2/1998

Lets undo the tie (not that I often wear a tie) and allow the author some indulgences on the column for a moment. So here I am at my computer desk, my cats at my feet, books and files scattered all about me (as my wife often points out as an incredible mess) answering e-mail from people all over the place since I started writing this column. Ironically, the majority of the people that I respond to are those that either trace their ancestry to or have moved from Page County several years ago. I have received a handful of e-mail from people residing immediately in Page County as well as a handful of written correspondences. Oh and by the way, I'm not the Robert Moore that graduated from Page County High School in 1962, that's my dad, who now, after 30 years in the Marine Corps, resides once again in the county as the lone Moore of the "Blinky" Moore line of descendants remaining in Page.

Therefore, we have established that the circulation rate for the *Page News & Courier* is alive and well outside the county lines. However, I have to stop and think for a moment that maybe this upstart that writes the column and resides at a Georgia address doesn't appear to be from Page after all. Well, to answer this pressing curiosity, he is in fact of Page County origin.

First of all, the bulk of my ancestry carries common Page County surnames such as Roudabush, Koontz, Strole, Kibler, Shuler, Kite, Emerson, Bell Dorraugh (where did that surname actually originate anyway?), Ham, Nicholson, Richards, Cave, Knight, Hilliard, Offenbacker, Good, Stoneberger, Mayes, Painter, Purdham, Huffman, Nauman, Taylor, and Aleshire to name a few. It is the surname of "Moore" that alienates me in a sense from the mainstream of common Page County names. So to rectify this I will give a quick "background" check of myself.

Sometime between 1880 and 1884, John Howard "Blinky" Moore, a native of Clear Spring, Maryland, left home for Kentucky where he met Mollie Davison. To make a long story short, they married in Kansas, attempted, while Mollie was very pregnant, to go west, lost the baby along the way and, understandably disgruntled, returned east.

Around 1888, Howard was working on the Shenandoah Valley Railroad and saw the farm land that compelled them to eventually settle on Naked Creek in Page County. After moving to Shenandoah four children were born to Howard and Mollie including my great-grandfather, Hume. Howard was in a number of ventures in Shenandoah and worked for the Norfolk & Western R.R. and became a member of the Freemasons at Ashlar Lodge #125 in Shenandoah.

So that's the start of it all, but why am I in Georgia? Well, being a military brat and another "nomadic" adventurer of the Moore line, after some time in two colleges in North Carolina, I joined the Navy about nine years ago, and am now stationed at King's Bay Naval Submarine Base in Georgia. I've kept myself continually busy with Virginia history over the past eleven years with writing projects in the Virginia Regimental Histories Series, and freelancing for *Civil War Times, Illustrated* and *Blue and Gray* Magazine.

Oh and by the way, keep those e-mails and letters coming, it adds to my long list of ideas for articles for the column. Speaking of which, could that individual with information of Captain R.S. Parks write me again, I fell prone to the computer glitch and lost a few e-mail addresses.

Miscellaneous

Striving to Keep Tradition and History Alive
Article of 8/21/1997

Several years ago – about the same time Alex Haley's *Roots* became popular – a great interest began to grow in the examination of family trees. At about the same time, I too became interested and could hardly put the work to rest. Once bitten by the "genealogy bug," the project is hard to abandon.

Essentially, however, a family tree is just a stick with branches without understanding what all of those ancestors went through and experienced – not just the wars and political trials they endured, but the day-to-day lives of the farmers, millers, merchants, shoemakers, laborers, etc.

The history of Page County and the uniqueness of its community form of development was instrumental in the peoples' lives then as it is now. From the history of the county we have all emerged as the people we are today, each unique and different but tightly woven into the common bonds of a unique and special history.

Page County still abounds with researchers and people who strive to keep the history and traditions of the past alive.

This column will be dedicated to the interest in genealogy and the histories of the families, places and events that had an impact on Page County residents of yore. In addition to featuring articles about problems in genealogical research that are "Page" specific, the column will occasionally focus on a particular family and the resources available for further research into that family's genealogy. Events in Page County that played an important role in the lives of its people may also be highlighted.

In addition readers are encouraged to send in genealogical "queries" pertaining to family members they are having difficulty researching. Often two people may be researching the same family line, though different branches and they might cross at one common ancestor and possibly go back further than the other. In this case families might benefit from sharing common family tree information. Where one person may be having difficulties, another may help to provide the necessary boost to get the other back on the right track to further work.

Queries should be submitted with the last and first name of the persons about whom you wish to have more information and would be best responded to by making sure vital statistics information such as birth and death dates are included. If you are uncertain of the birth and death date, make a logical estimation.

For example, you know your great-grandmother was born in 1889 and her oldest child was born around 1900. So you could estimate that your great-great grandmother was born between 1859 – 1871 and died between 1901-1961. Your dates may be off a little, but it will give someone a good "ballpark" within which they can compare data.

Researching a Civil War Ancestor, and Where to Begin
Article of 9/4/1997

About four or five times a month I receive e-mail that asks how best to research a Civil War ancestor. The benefit of this research, whether personal or for membership in organizations such as the United Daughters of the Confederacy or the Sons of Confederate Veterans, can be thrilling to find.

Page County has several sources that can be accessed to aid in this venture and make it relatively uncomplicated and they can be found in the Page County Public Library to start.

Several books have been written as a part of the Virginia Regimental Histories Series and published by H.E. Howard, Inc. formerly of Lynchburg. All of the units formed in Page County have been covered in books written or are on the verge of publication. Page County men served in several units throughout the war, including Company D, 7th Virginia Cavalry; Company K, 10th Virginia Infantry; Company H, 33rd Virginia Infantry; Company E, 35th Battalion Virginia Cavalry; Captain William Henry Chapman's Dixie Artillery; the 97th Virginia Militia; the 8th Battalion Virginia Reserves; and Captain Peter J. Keyser's "Boy Company." The benefit of these books is that the rosters of the units have been nearly entirely transcribed, the only exception usually being the pay records.

Unlike the advertisements often seen for "capsule histories" that usually cost about $20 each, at an average cost of $19.95 each, the Howard's regimentals provide much more information for the buck. While the regimental series is a great source for information on your particular veteran's service with the unit, do not rely upon the book to give a full genealogical tree as this was not he focus of these books.

Another source for information is found in a book entitled *Page County Men in Gray*. This book lists the names of the men alphabetically, gives the unit in which they served and in some cases gives parental information, the names of the spouse and/or the names of some of the children.

Thomas Spratt, the author of the book, also took the opportunity to scan all cemetery books for Page County to give the birth and death dates of veterans. Usually, with the regimentals, this work was also completed for all units except the 35th Battalion Virginia Cavalry. *Page County Men in Gray* provides a handy cross-reference guide for further research into the regimentals.

Spratt's work covered all units organized solely in Page County. Disappointingly, his book shows he did not go through the Virginia pension records for Page County Confederate veterans. Upon examination of these records a number of years ago, I found that there were men who resided in the county at the outbreak of the war but served in other regiments such as the 7th Virginia Infantry (George E. Pickett's Division), the 23rd Virginia Cavalry, and the Stuart Horse Artillery, just to name a few.

I found an ancestor who served in Keyser's "Boy Company" and later enlisted with the 2nd Company, 62nd Virginia Infantry on May 4, 1864 and was fighting at New Market 11 days later. Upon close examination of Spratt's book I did not find his name, however, although he was descended from a family who had been in Page County since well before its formation, resided there before, during and after the war and even died there.

Nevertheless, in finding my own Confederate ancestors, I started with a family story, as I have heard others have done in Page County. First, I found out that a great-great grandfather had served in the war and the story behind his service. From there I figured out how he was exactly related to me and then I was off to the Virginia State Library (now known as the Library of Virginia) in Richmond. Other people start with Harry Strickler's *Short History of Page County* and go from the incomplete list of veterans published therein.

Within one or two years, and as the grand finale to the Virginia Regimental Histories Series, there will be a set of books (now estimated to be a two or three volume set) that will include all of the names of all of the veterans of all of the units from Virginia who served for the Confederacy. Therefore, by referencing this set of books one would be able to quickly reference the particular name and then find the unit-specific book(s) in which the ancestor's military record could be found.

Virginians Get to Your Posts for Gettysburg's 135th Anniversary Reenactment
Article of 6/25/1998

Civil War reenactors don't have to worry too much about minie balls, cannon balls, grape shot, canister, being captured, losing a limb or life or even typhoid and other camp related diseases. However, it is an experience to don a uniform similar to that worn by an ancestor and to endure at least a weekend remembering in a unique way, the "late war of unpleasantries." There are no barbeque grills, telephones, ovens, refrigerators, televisions or computers. It is just down to earth good clean living history.

That's what its all about this July for certain. At the release of this news clip, good citizens from throughout America (and in fact the world) are scrambling to muster with their local units to serve in what is anticipated to be the largest reenactment of a Civil War battle in the 20th century. In fact, the local Page County reenacting unit designated as Co. H, 58th Virginia Infantry will be heading for Gettysburg this coming fourth of July weekend. The 58th, with several members from Page, will be just a handful a people among the over 16,000 individuals already registered for the event. In the upcoming heated action, soldiers in Blue and Gray will reenact all three days of the famous battle that will include cavalry, artillery, and masses of infantry. Civilian activities will also occur throughout the large encampment. "We will be reenacting most of the key elements of the battle" say 58th Virginia members and Luray residents Charles Burner and Floyd Campbell. "From July 1st through July 5th, the scenarios covered will include First Contact, Little Round Top, Culp's Hill and The Wheatfield, as well as a proposed full-scale Pickett's Charge. For further information regarding the reenactment itself, call the 24 hr information line at 908-903-1064. However, if your one who enjoys surfing the "Net" to obtain information, try the 135th Gettysburg Anniversary web site at http://www.gettysburg.com/reenactment/index.htm.

While its a little late to obtain all of the uniform items necessary to participate and register as a reenactor, Campbell adds, "if your going to make this one as a spectator, you better make plans now. There may never be another event this large again in this century." For those who wish to find more information regarding joining the

58th Virginia for future events, both Floyd Campbell and Charles Burner may be reached at bluelight@rica.net and stonewall@rica.net respectfully. Otherwise, check-out the unit's web site at
http://www.geocities.com/Heartland/Hills/1850/patrickgrays.html.

Anniversary Date Targeted for Summers-Koontz Roadside Marker
Article of 8/20/1998

While a lonely graying monolith marks the site of the Summers-Koontz execution in Shenandoah County, there is nothing in Page, except the mention in books, regarding the incident that took the lives of the two young men. With that in mind, the Summers-Koontz Roadside marker fund has been established to erect a marker to be located along Route 340 in Page County, somewhere central to the respective grave sites of Summers and Koontz.

Contact has already been established with the Department of Historic Resources in Richmond, Virginia to obtain relevant information to erect the roadside marker. In accordance with guidelines established by the Historical Marker Program, the marker will be remain the property of the Commonwealth of Virginia. Beside the title and text, the marker will bear only the identification number assigned to it by the Department of Historic Resources, the seal of the Commonwealth, and the following signature line: "Department of Historic Resources, [date]." The name of the sponsoring individual or organization cannot be included. The marker will be silver-painted cast aluminum with black uppercase and lowercase letters.

Current objectives are to raise the funds necessary by January 1999 in order to raise the marker on the 134th anniversary of the incident on Sunday, June 27, 1999. Approximately $1,200 is needed to cast the marker. Raffle tickets will be sold to help in funding the effort beginning July 18, 1998 for a drawing to be held on the last day of the Page County Heritage Festival in October. Prizes include: 1st Prize – The Joe Umble Civil War art print entitled An Affectionate Farewell. 2nd Prize –Five books of the Virginia Regimental Histories Series that include Page County units - these books include Robert Moore's Danville, Eighth Star New Market and Dixie Artillery, Rick Armstrong's 7th Virginia Cavalry, John Divine's 35th Battalion Virginia Cavalry, Terrence Lowry's 10th Virginia Infantry and Lowell Reidenbaugh's 33rd Virginia Infantry. 3rd Prize – A one-year subscription to Blue and Gray Magazine.

History, a researcher, and one of many spooky ironies
Article of 11/5/1998

In 1995 I wandered upon a military record for cousin James Draper Moore. A native of Washington County, Maryland, James had served in Co. B of Cole's 1st Potomac Home Guard Cavalry. After combing the record for extensive details, I found that the redheaded twenty-three year old had died at Andersonville. It wasn't until April 1997 however, that I finally had the opportunity to visit him at grave #7273. What awaited me was a genealogist's nightmare, but a personal challenge to a historian. Imagine my surprise when I realized that the stone bore the name of another soldier.

Now for someone with five direct Page County Confederate ancestors, this lone Maryland Yankee was quite impressive. So far he had been captured in a fight with Mosby's men, ended up in one of the war's infamous POW camps, and offered this historian a mystery to solve. But from one mystery springs another. While I have been concentrating on efforts to convince Andersonville that the grave had been mis-marked and that my half 1st cousin 4 times removed actually lies quietly in grave #7273 (which I have finally succeeded in doing and am awaiting a new tombstone to reflect the same), a native of Page County COULD have had the responsibility in saving young James Moore's life. But more on this in a little while. . . .

The events that led to young Moore's unwanted trip to Andersonville began on January 10, 1864. Just before dawn on that freezing morning, Mosby and his raiders struck Cole's Battalion on Loudoun Heights. Moore was in fact stationed with the ill-fated picket along the Hillsboro road, where Piney Run crossed. Mosby had to make certain that this picket was taken out in order to free a path for his escape from the night assault.

By the time that Mosby had decided to withdraw, he had suffered severe losses, including the wounding of his younger brother "Willie". In addition to the six captured Federal troopers, Cole's battalion had lost six killed and fourteen wounded. However, the men lost from Mosby's command were deemed by one ranger as "worth more than all Cole's Battalion." Considering all of this, a truce was made later that morning and Captain William Henry

Chapman, a native of Page County and one-time captain of the county's own Dixie Artillery, dispatched a messenger into the Federal camp with an offer for an exchange. For the recovery of his men, Mosby would return the six captured Federal troopers. Cole refused to receive the offer, sealing Moore's fateful journey to Andersonville.

Had Chapman succeeded in his attempt to negotiate an exchange, Moore might have survived the war. However, this author has to sit back for a minute to appreciate a personal irony in all of this. True, it might have been purely coincidental that Chapman, a Page County man, had nearly been responsible for sparing a distant Maryland relative. However, little did I know that two totally separate personal "crusades" would ever meet at a crossroad. For you see, years before the "discovery" of my Yankee cousin, in my research to publish a book about the Dixie Artillery, Chapman was a main focal point of research. I contacted several of his descendants, sought out his personal papers with a very insatiable hunger, and emerged from it all with a never before published photo of this right-hand man to Mosby. Was it all purely coincidental, or did I unknowingly attempt to return a good gesture extended a distant relative over 133 years ago? Goose bumps are in order here, but it isn't the most haunting aspect of my research nor the first instance, and I feel certain that it won't be the last . . . . I hope.

The Need of Keeping Page County's Documented History in Page County – Part 1
Article of 8/5/1999

For openers, don't read the title the wrong way here. I'm not saying to "hoard" Page County's historical documents so those living outside the county don't have access to things like letters, diaries, memoirs, etc. (some of these same people, like myself, are natives of Page and reside out of the county and have a genuine interest in the contents of these same documents). My plea is actually for the overall preservation of documents relating to Page's rich history. While it would be fantastic to have as many of the county's historic documents as possible in a safe repository right here in Page; realistically, there is no true repository in Page that can offer climate control and the best situation to preserve our ancient pieces of paper from deterioration, theft or anything else. Additionally, why would a descendant want to part with his or her ancestor's priceless documents? Rather, what is first and foremost important at this time? Before anything else happens to those priceless documents, as a minimum we should make photocopies to maintain in one or more public master file (preferably at county or local university libraries). Who really knows just how many original documents have already been lost to time? But for those that we know are in existence today - how can you best preserve them and prevent their loss forever more? Sadly, at one point in time, for whatever reason, many of our priceless documents are sold outside of the county, OR, Heaven forbid, they are lost tragically and FOREVER in a house fire, flood, hurricane or other natural disaster.

On a tangent of my own again? Perhaps, but, at the writing of this article I'm also working with a renewed awareness after a recent personal episode. Specifically, I recently was on the famous e-bay auction site and found a most fascinating document relating to Page's history. To most it wouldn't appear to be anything spectacular or earth-shattering, but to me it was absolutely wonderful just by virtue of the person who signed the document up for bid. Someone in Shenandoah County had found a document signed by William Townsend Young and placed it for bid on e-bay. Now in itself, the name probably means little to anyone. However, if one takes the time to look, they would find that Young was the first captain of the "Page Volunteers," also known as Company K,

10th Virginia Infantry. Though it was advertised with these facts of Young's Civil War service, this document wasn't anything of great significance. It wasn't endorsed by Robert E. Lee nor were the contents of great value. Additionally, it wasn't even signed by Young during the war, but rather while he was a merchant in Luray in the 1850's. Well, I saw an ideal opportunity to save another piece of Page's past and placed my bid amounting to no more than about $12.00 in all. The auction had days to go before ending and I was safe until the absolute last minute. Now I've played the auction game on e-bay before and I know to look out after my bid - but this unknown person that wasn't residing in or even -in all likelihood- from Page County (his e-mail handle was "warmonger" I believe) outbid me by 50 cents. Now I know its a "shame on me" thing for not keeping a better eye out, but the moral is much greater here in the long run - how can we preserve those documents rich with important information for all posterity TODAY? More on this in a following article.

The Need of Keeping Page County's Documented History in Page County – Part 2
Article of 8/19/1999

Since I've already laid the groundwork with the Civil War in Part 1 of this article, I might as well continue the path on which I'm running (a sigh goes up from the readership no doubt - ha ha!). Anyway, in a previous article I stated that Page had WELL OVER 1,200 veterans to wear the gray. Remarkably, less than twenty of those soldiers' personal reminiscences, letters, diaries or otherwise have been found in some form or fashion and are available to the public through various libraries (from Chicago to North Carolina), published works, or on-line. Up front - the preservation of written documents by twenty soldiers seems like a great deal, but when you break into the averages, we aren't really doing very well. As for myself - for having direct lineage to five Confederate veterans, I don't have one letter, diary or memoir written by them of their service, nor do I have a photo of one of them in a uniform.

So what is the specific problem? Why aren't there more of these things available for exhibition or research to the general interested population? From experience over the past decade I have found that there is a general reluctance to let anyone know that they had such things as they would be bothered to death by someone trying to buy the items. I can cite at least one instance that documents - that had been maintained within their "home" county for years - have been bought by someone outside of the county and that had no family ties with the author or family of the same documents. Furthermore, they intended to keep them as a part of their private collection and would deny the allowance of photocopies to anyone for public depository. A sad ending.

There are even those who are concerned that they would be worried to death by a family member for copies. Additionally, there is also a great concern that those that have these items might be in a compromised position with other family members in the instance that those other family members found out that they had these documents rather than someone else in the family. The solution to this would be simple. Make photocopies - deposit them anonymously in the public library - and if asked about them, just state that you had seen copies once at the library and were certain that they could get copies there. Of course, for those wishing to seek copies, when going to the library, don't become a part of the overall problem and take the photocopies for your personal copies, leaving us back at the starting gate.

Finally, the point here is that we need to take a deep concern over what is happening to our heritage. If you wish to sell your families letters, diaries, photos, etc., that is of course your prerogative. Just please, before doing so, make copies to preserve for generations to come, as there are no guarantees that they will be safe in their next home.

When it comes to descriptive wartime letters, diaries, memoirs, or even photos in uniform, if all of what I have said still isn't enough to insure you - please send photocopies (no originals please as there are no absolute guarantees with delivery services without a steep price) to me anonymously. I will make certain that copies are deposited in the Page Public Library - both the Luray and Shenandoah branches AND the Heritage Association's Calendine- to help to insure preservation for all generations to come.

Page's Part in the Early History of the Baptist Church in Virginia
Article of 1/20/2000

Founded by members of the Church of England, the Virginia colony established in its charter that no other churches were to be tolerated. With the notorious bloody code of 1611, the first published for the government of the Colony, every man and woman in the Colony,

"or who should afterwards arrive, should give an account of faith and religion to the parish minister, and if not satisfactory to him, they should repair often to him for instruction; and if they refuse to go, the Governor should whip the offender for the first offense, for the second refusal to be whipped twice and to acknowledge his fault on the Sabbath day in congregation; for the third offense to be whipped every day till he complied."

Over forty years into the establishment of homesteads on the Shenandoah frontier, the Baptists began to find hope in escaping the long-experienced persecution in Virginia. By 1756 several Baptist congregations were organized in what is now Rockingham, Shenandoah Page Counties. By the 1770s, on the east side of the Massanutten Mountain, in what is now Page County, a congregation was being built up by Baptists, partly, as it appears, from the Mennonite community and centered around the famous White House.

Elder John Koontz and others began teaching the gospel according to the Baptist faith in the area of Mill Creek. Preaching in both German and English, Koontz's sermons were moving and eloquent enough to convert many, including Martin Kauffman and many of his Mennonite flock. Reportedly, his efforts to convert so many subjected Koontz on more than one occasion to beatings by "ruffians" of the Massanutten neighborhood.

As a result of the great deal of concern over the preachings of Koontz and the influence that it bore upon the local Mennonite congregation, local Mennonites sent for preachers from Pennsylvania. As a result, Peter Blosser arrived on the eve of the Revolutionary War and began preaching non-resistance among many of the area's residents.

Interestingly, Martin Kauffman, the aforementioned Baptist preacher convert from the Mennonites, supported Blosser's anti-war sentiment, and supported that ideology in this area of the Valley — ultimately resulting in a division in the White House congregation.

Nevertheless, by 1775, according to church historian Robert Semple, the Baptists were facing a "Very favorable season." The concept of revolution against the noted "Establishment" was favorable to many. As a result of the regular session in their General Association, the Baptists of Virginia submitted petitions throughout the state, to be forwarded to the Virginia Convention or General Assembly to in fact abolish the current established church of the colony, "and religion left to stand upon its own merits; and, that all religions societies should be protected in the peaceable enjoyment of their own religious principles."

By 1776 this bill had been passed. Unremarkably, there is said that there were no Tories among the Baptists during the War for Independence. By 1784, Baptists were finally being recognized and supported by individuals from all denominations.

Thomas Jefferson, in preparing his "Act for Religious Freedom" which passed the Virginia General Assembly in 1786, made clear the right for religious freedom when he wrote that:

"no man shall be compelled to frequent or support any religious worship, place or ministry whatsoever, nor shall be enforced, restrained, molested, or burthened in his body or goods, nor shall otherwise suffer on account of his religious opinions or belief; and by argument to maintain, their opinions in matters of religion, and that the same shall in nowise diminish, enlarge, or affect their civil capabilities."

That Which is Important to Preserve and Why
Article of 6/29/2000

Recently, I drove by the site of Page's own White House and my heart literally dropped. To have served as such an historic icon for so many generations, the once proud little meetinghouse shows significant wear and undoubtedly could be listed in the highest of risk categories. Having been built in the earliest days of the settlement of the Shenandoah Valley, this building has seen an amazing transformation in both the culture and technology that has developed as well as that which has passed through the Valley. Yet, in its quiet and serene location, it remains as a tranquil reminder of a more simple time. Not that life wasn't difficult to Valley settlers in the earliest existence of the White House; rather, the complexity of problems faced on a daily basis has changed dramatically.

Certainly, I applaud the efforts made to restore the train station in downtown Luray, but regretfully, our oldest structures in the Page Valley remain in harms' way. Some have just recently been lost in the past 10 years. When I say structures, I not only mean physical buildings, but documents, artifacts, and even cemeteries. Lets take Green Hill Cemetery for example – please take the opportunity to finger through Harry M. Strickler's *A Short History of Page County* (even more, take s stroll through the index of names) and then take a walk through Green Hill. First, please brace yourself for the site that will lie before you. While Luray is not the only town in Page County nor does it have hold on being the absolute final resting place of all of its historic characters throughout history, with its government seated in that town, one can literally say when walking through the cemetery "here lies Page County."

What I am trying to get across is the point that strides must be taken now to preserve critical places that relate to the unique history of Page County. Surely, we neither have the time or money to secure everything for posterity. At the very least, why not start with those structures that are crucial to the understanding of the history of the Valley and then to those in the worst of conditions, yet showing great potential for preservation?

Without action, what remains for us to pass on to our children? If we take no action now, what remains for them tomorrow? Then too, there are some that may say the new and next generations don't and won't care. I can think of several people who did not care a bit for history and then something changed in their philosophies later in life.

Sometime this week or very soon (please don't wait too long), take a drive to the marker looking toward the White House, gaze upon it and try to think of its earliest days. You may choose another structure of your choice (but remember not all of those in Page's *Old Homes* book remain today). Just make sure that the image before you remains emblazoned on your memory, for the true question remains – "will it be there for your children or grandchildren to see in 15, 10, or even 5 years or will it be reduced to that memory?" What can we do as those that watch OUR history deteriorate? What can you do as the owners? The answer may not be as difficult as you think.

Page County Civil War Commission Update
Article of 9/07/2000

With the exception of the Civil War Trails marker dedication at Verbena (Shenandoah) on Memorial Day weekend, the summer has been relatively quiet. However, with the opening of September, at least four more Civil War Trails dedications in Page County loom on the horizon.

By the end of November, Page County (with the help of demonstration grants from the Shenandoah Valley Battlefields National Historic District and aid from Page County Economic Development) will have more Virginia Civil War Trails markers than any other county in the state (and some folks say that nothing happened in Page County during the Civil War!).

It is the intent of the Page County Civil War Commission to remain focused on historically accurate and educational interpretive resources in Page County for increased Civil War tourism over the next 15 years, especially with the Sesquicentennial of the Civil War just 11 years from this past April (2011) and ending in 2015.

The Civil War Trails markers are a critical element of Virginia's Civil War tourism, as they do not really take away from the character of the county. Even today there are many areas within the county where tourist can visualize an event without too much interference from the modern world. This is extremely important to those who want to gain an educational perspective while touring the hallowed fields. With over $8,500 in demonstration grant money and supplemental monies to cover the difference, the upcoming schedule for marker dedications is as follows:

1) Willow Grove Mill (Luray) indicating that Page County was the northern-most portion of Union Gen. Philip Sheridan's "burnings" east of the Massanutten. Willow Grove Mill was one of several mills destroyed in October 1864. Though the mill is not now original to the war, the foundation remains original and the site is one of the few that were rebuilt and remain today. This marker is to be dedicated the first weekend in October at the same time as the Page County Heritage Festival.

2) Graves Chapel (Stanley) for the passage of "Stonewall" Jackson's troops (then the 2nd Corps of the Army of Northern Virginia) out of the Valley in November 1862. This marker concentrates on Jackson's "last glimpse" of the Valley as a glimpse upon the Page Valley from the area of Franklin Cliffs near Fishers Gap. This marker is to be dedicated in November.

3) Luray/New Market Gap (Rt. 211) also to mark Jackson's last march out of the Valley toward Fisher's Gap. It was after a night's rest in the gap on the Page County side, that Jackson emerged from a tent and surprised his staff by having donned a completely new uniform and announced that his troops were now to be known as the 2nd Corps of the Army of Northern Virginia. This marker is to be placed in conjunction with the Graves Chapel marker in November.

4) Red Bridge (Grove Hill) to mark the site of the burning of one of three bridges in Page County to slow Union Gen. Shields' advance up the Page Valley in June 1862. This episode also played a major role in the relationship between Jackson and Turner Ashby and nearly caused a major rift in Jackson's Valley army. This marker is to be dedicated this fall.

Though this will wrap-up dedications in 2000, more possibilities await next year with yet another round of demonstration grants made available by the Battlefields Commission.

Milam's Gap and the Legendary Milam Apple
Article of 9/21/2000

Now this may be a bit off the normal beaten path that I take as the author for this column, but this article does remain heritage/family focused. As some readers know, I get a bit nostalgic from time to time and recently, upon remembering Page County tales of the tasty Milam apple (which I have yet had the opportunity to try) it occurred to me that one of the many gaps that cross into Page County bears the Milam name. Was there a correlation and did the apple generate in Page County or nearby? A quick search of the Internet gave me a bit of insight. There isn't a great deal of data, but it is interesting. By the way, if somebody knows of a few good TRUE Milam saplings that they are looking to "liberate", let me know!

From a Milam family web site I discovered a story that was uncovered in a book written by Vera Milam Ryker. While disappointing that the Milam apple did not originate in Page, it still remains worthwhile to note that it did take root (no pun intended – well, maybe a little) in Madison County. The first mention of the elusive apple came from a letter written by Judge W. E. Bohannon of Criglersville, VA, dated October 16, 1927. "Judge Bohannon was a descendant of Thomas Milum through a daughter, and in 1927 he was past 80 years of age. According to Judge Bohannon:

Thomas received a grant of 203 acres from Lord Fairfax on January 31, 1749. It was here that Thomas lived and died in 1785. This grant of land is located in Madison County, Virginia at the eastern foot of the Blue Ridge range and is situated 10 miles northwest of Madison, the county seat. The "Milam Apple" known all over the country originated on this farm, and got its name from Thomas Milum. Also the first pass over the Blue Ridge Mountains from this county to the valley was opened by Thomas Milum and bears his name to this day, "Milam Gap."

Yet another version confirms Madison County origin but gives credit to a different family member. In the *History of Madison County, Virginia* (1926), Claude Yowell claimed that "the Milum Apple, a native of Madison County and very highly prized by the citizens of this county, had its origin near Milum's Gap. It originated from a seedling that came up in the yard of one Joseph Milum. The apple proved to be so good that people came from far and near to graft trees from this one. The apples were named for the man who owned the seedling, Joseph Milum and afterwards the gap in the Blue Ridge near his home was also named for him."

So, in summary, that's the story. Oh yes, take a look in Chapter 18 of Mark Twain's Tom Sawyer and you will see a passage mentioning the Milam apple. Additionally, the famous apple also appeared in S.A. Beach's *The Apples of New York* in 1905.

As for the Milam/Milum family, by the time of Beach's book, most had long-since removed from Madison County. As a matter of fact, there are none listed in the 1850 census of Madison County; the name being much more predominant in Southwest Virginia and in the Kanawha Valley of what would become West Virginia in just over a decade.

Page was Once Known for Orchards and New Apple Varieties
Article of 4/19/2001

Some may recall my story on the Milam apple and its ties to Page County. However, some may not realize just how active the county was in apple production since before the Civil War.

Page County ranked last in acres of improved land in farms in 1860 in the ten-county area of the Shenandoah Valley (Augusta, Berkeley, Clarke, Jefferson, Frederick, Page, Rockbridge, Rockingham, Shenandoah, Warren), but it also ranked 4th in value of orchard products (standing only behind Rockingham, Augusta, and Rockbridge).

Seemingly, the greatest amount of orchard activity changed little over the years with dominance being in the northern areas of the county – Beahm's Gap, Thornton's Gap, Kimball and Luray holding the greatest prominence.

It appears that the cash crop grew over the years, and with growth came creativity in finding new varieties. While the exact numbers of apple varieties introduced from Page County is unknown, there were no less than six recorded and mentioned in *Old Southern Apples* by Creighton Lee Calhoun, Jr.

As early as 1860, Page County introduced two varieties– "Kimball" and "Shenk." While "Kimball" (also known as Dr. Dunn's Sweeting or Dunn's Sweeting) was said to have had origins east side of the Blue Ridge near Beahm's Gap (incorrectly identified in the above mentioned book as "Brahm's Gap"), Kimball was being grown and sold in Kimball in 1899.

"Shenk" originated "on the west side of Thornton's Gap." "Honest John" followed "Shenk" as being from Beahm's Gap in 1865. "Harrah" or "Billie's Favorite" was another Thornton's Gap introduction brought to light in 1882.

Perhaps the most notable person to bring Page County apple varieties to the attention of the industry, Albert Bolen introduced the "Armintrout" in 1873.

Born in 1868, Bolen, a descendant of a Rappahannock County family, made Page his home and was advertising his "Page Valley Nurseries" in Kimball in the 1894 *Page News* – "250,000 fruit trees and ornamental trees of all kinds for sale."

In 1899, Bolen sent yet another variety, known as the "Beahm" apple, to the USDA. This may be the last recorded of those to originate from Page County.

Regretfully, all six varieties are considered extinct southern apples and cannot be found in the market or nurseries today. "Milam," (also known as Harrigan, Blair, Thomas, Red Milam, Red Winter Pearmain, or Haragan) is the only variety known to be available today with slight historic ties to Page County.

Though a sidebar business to his larger enterprises, Miller Elbea Roudabush of Luray, is perhaps one of the best known for apple propagation and sales in Page during the mid-20th century. Apples faded from prominence as a major cash crop for the county by the latter third of the century. A relic of sorts from the end of the "heyday" - labels from bushel baskets of "Red Fox" brand apples, one of Roudabush's many business activities, can still be found for sale on Internet auctions today.

Born in 1886 and the oldest of five children, Roudabush was the son of Major Ashby and Virginia Belle McAllister Roudabush. True to his given name, Miller Roudabush was also highly known for his efforts in continuing the family milling tradition.

Roudabush was not only president of the Page Milling Company but was also instrumental in converting the famous Stanley Flour Mill to electricity after 1921. The electric power for the mill originated from yet another project of Roudabush's - the hydroelectric plant at Newport that became known as the Page Power Company.

Honoring our Veterans with a Headstone is an Easy Process
Article of 11/30/2000

It is interesting to know that not all of our ancestors have headstones to honor their lives or their military service. Equally interesting is the fact that several living veterans do not realize their entitlement to the same.

A few months back, I was walking through the National Cemetery in Staunton recording the names of those buried there. During that time, a veteran from World War II walked up to me and asked if I knew how much the Department of Veterans' Affairs charged for the headstones and what the process was in obtaining one.

He was absolutely floored when I pronounced that, to eligible veterans, the markers are free and the stones are shipped free of charge!

Ultimately, the Department of Veterans Affairs "(VA) furnishes upon request, at no charge to the applicant, a headstone or marker for the unmarked grave of any deceased veteran discharged from the U.S. Armed Forces under conditions other than dishonorable."

More information about obtaining a headstone can be found either on the web (http://www.cem.va.gov/hm.htm), or by contacting the National Cemetery Administration (a part of the VA) directly.

Perhaps the most intriguing aspect of obtaining veterans headstones has surfaced in the past few years. Many people, including myself, have persons in their family tree that served in the military over the course of the history of the United States but were not wealthy enough to have a headstone purchased to mark their grave. Just last year I marked two graves * one of an ancestor who served in the War of 1812 and the other * a Confederate veteran (yes you read that right).

But remember, when ordering headstones for veterans of wars prior to World War I you are required to have detailed documentation to prove eligibility such as, muster rolls, extracts from State files, military or State organization where served, pension or land warrants, etc.

A trip to the National Archives or a mail request to that organization isn't so difficult. Perhaps the biggest mystery is establishing exactly where that veteran is buried.

In the case of the Confederate veteran, I knew where the family graveyard was located. I went there, cleared the plot, was able to identify which graves were for the children and which ones were for the adults (there were larger stones to mark the head and smaller stones to mark the footstone), and, by process of elimination identified only two adult graves located prominently in the graveyard.

This is where a little speculative work had to be conducted, who was buried on the right or left. Based upon typical graveyard scenarios, I established that the husband was buried on the (as your facing the graves) left (or was that the right - its been a year so pardon my memory).

Now, as far as the VA guidelines for marking the grave of a Civil War ancestor, remember what I stated above. Also, you can order either upright headstones or flat markers to mark the graves of Union and Confederate Civil War dead.

Also remember that it takes about three (3) months (depending on how busy they are) to get the stone delivered.

AND, when it comes in, be prepared if you ordered an upright stone * they aren't light of weight! Especially keep this in mind when, as in one of my situations, you have to figure how to get the stone to the site of the grave. Then too, remember that you have to set the stone and hope that the ground is soft!

What's in a Name: Luray and Shenandoah
Article of 6/21/2001

Writer's block can be a terrible thing (especially when attributed to sleep deprivation) and to move things along, I find the Internet to be a valuable source for ideas. Which brings me to the topic this week. In the wake of the arrival of a new baby (ah yes, the reason for sleep deprivation and for my delays in getting back to some who have recently written to me), I thought about the originality in names. With that in mind, I thought of Luray and Shenandoah (nope, the new daughter was not named for either).

Most local folks know the story about the possible origins of the name of our very own Luray, Virginia. Some subscribe to the tale of Mr. Louis (Lou) Ramey and then there are some that believe that Lorraine, France may have been a source. But, what about those towns named after? Were they named for our Page County town? Hard to say for certain with only the Internet as a source.

The answer to that may be more readily available in the respective county histories, if written. I do know that by typing "Luray" in a search engine, you'll probably find that about 98% of the entries that come up have something to do with Luray, Virginia. The other 2% deal typically with the Lurays of other states. One that was interesting showed that Russell County, Kansas' very own Luray claims the fame to being "Halfway between Paradise and the Garden of Eden" . . . and it is . . . geographically between towns with those names.

Other finds on the web relate to Luray, Henderson County, Tennessee; Luray, Clark County, Missouri; and Luray, Hampton County, South Carolina. Then I stumbled upon a site called "placesnamed.com" and discovered Luray, Henry County, Indiana; Luray, Marshall County, Iowa; Luray, Fayette County, Ohio; and Luray, Licking County, Ohio.

Of all of those found, I feel relatively confident in saying that Luray, Virginia has 1) the highest population of them all, and 2) has the highest elevation.

Apart from town names, you may also find something to do with china patterns. Made of soft pastels of pink, pale yellow, pale green and baby blue, LuRay china was popular during the 1940s and was a "reaction against the very intense colors of Fiesta (another pattern) and provided a solid glazed dinnerware alternative to housewives who preferred a quieter palette."

So, what about the name "Shenandoah?" Certainly, you may think, as I did at one time, that the "daughter of the stars" name must be held to sacred form here in our very own Valley. But alas, I found in once traveling that there is a Shenandoah, Georgia and I also know of a Shenandoah, Iowa.

Going back to "placesnamed.com" I also found that the name Shenandoah graces towns in Florida, Louisiana, New York, Ohio, Pennsylvania, and Texas! Additionally, there are places (legitimately speaking since the "river runs through it") in West Virginia. But be careful, don't try to pull out an atlas and try to find all of these places. Some still have not quite made it to the big maps.

Virginia Civil War Trails and Marking Page County History
Article of 7/4/2001

One-hundred-forty years ago this year, the American Civil War was well into its second month. In the nearly four years that remained, the landscape of Virginia and other states would show the stress of a devastating war.

While Page County had no large-scale battles, it was very much a part of the war as an avenue for armies. By 1863, one topographical engineer for the Confederate army mentioned the deplorable state of the roads in the county – roads that, only twelve years before, had been the pride of the county in the midst of a major development of turnpikes.

Fortunately, Page County is a part of the Shenandoah Valley Battlefields National Historic District and has benefited from grants from the Shenandoah Valley Battlefields Foundation. With the financial help from these grants (covering 80% of the overall costs of markers), there are presently six markers in Page that point out the relevance of individual sites to historic activities.

You can find these markers at the sites of Red Bridge, White House Bridge, Price's Mill or Verbena, Luray/New Market Gap, Graves' Chapel and Willow Grove Mill.

As indicated in the accompanying story, the latest round of grants allow us to continue to tell the story of the county's role in the war through the addition of three more markers and preservation/restoration of Graves' Chapel as an historic site.

The first of the three new markers will deliver the story of the May 7, 1862 clash between elements of Gen. Richard S. Ewell's men and Federal forces under Gen. Jeremiah C. Sullivan. The second marker, to be located in the vicinity of Pass Run, will identify with the Confederate retreat from Gettysburg and the engagement at Wapping Heights/Manassas Gap near Front Royal in July 1863. The third marker will tell of the engagement of Yager's Mill (near the old Redwell Furnace) and the significance of that action and the fight at Milford (on the Page/Warren County line) that saved Gen. Jubal Early's Confederates total destruction in the wake of the

Battle of Fisher's Hill.

So what does this mean for Page County? A few years back the Virginia Tourism Corporation reported that of the tourist that come through the Commonwealth, nearly five million people annually are drawn to Civil War attractions. Certainly this does not mean that Page would receive that many visitors. However, it will tap into this number and will ultimately benefit economically as visitors add the county to their tourism itinerary - either making their way through Page on the way to other major battlefields or making Page a "base of operations" for outreaching tours. In addition to this, the Shenandoah Valley was recently rated in *Money Magazine* as 12th best tourist destination in the United States, specifically mentioning the Valley's Civil War sites.

Along with economic benefit, by purchasing Virginia Civil War Trails (actually a non-profit organization)signs, historic preservation conscious organizations in the county tap into a program that offers a premier, self-paced, free mobile history experience.

Through colorful images, maps and sidebar information, signs introduce travelers to personalities, historic structures, troop movements and battles at nearly 300 sites statewide. By heightening awareness to the particular significance of historic activities, the signs also focus tourists on the importance of preserving historic structures that may stand before them.

The Virginia Civil War Trails logo is seen on highways and interstates throughout the Commonwealth is one of the most highly recognized signs in Virginia tourism. The distinctive bugle-logo was recently added to the VDOT's official state map.

Most recently, the National Trust for Historic Preservation has heralded Civil War Trails as one of the most sustainable heritage programs in the nation.

The program has also recently expanded into Maryland and will receive funding in that state to continue to expand the story of the war. Future expansion into West Virginia and Pennsylvania is also anticipated.

Belsnickling – When Dressing in Costumes Wasn't Just for Halloween
Article of 9/13/2001

Halloween isn't even upon us yet and the latter 20th century tradition of Halloween AND Christmas decorations in the store is before us already. So, in the same spirit, I say, "why not?" – time for a story that does justice to both seasons that the retailers bring to us so early-on this time of the year. And yes "Virginia," this story does pertain to Page County and the Shenandoah Valley . . .

Sometime during the third quarter of the 20th century, an old custom seemed to fade away. Perhaps only few recall the name "Belsnickle," but there are some – even here in Page – that might recall a time when, on Christmas Eve (not Halloween as some may think), some folks would dress in hideous disguises and distribute nuts and cakes to naughty boys and girls. These "gifts" were thrown upon the floor, but if a child were to try to recover them in the presence of the Belsnickler, the child would quickly receive a "whack" on the backside with a whip. In "Pennsylvania Germans of the Shenandoah Valley," it was noted that this practice might even go well beyond just one evening, running for nearly two weeks, starting a week before Christmas and continuing until New Year.

Seemingly a strange old custom, Belsnickling had roots in German ancestry. Belsnicklers usually traveled in groups – much like trick-or-treaters of contemporary times – from farm to farm, "making merriment as they went, a boisterous, noisy, and happy group." Starting shortly after dark, the practice would end long before midnight. While not welcome in all homes, in some instances, Belsnicklers were invited in, and after unmasking and identifying themselves, were rewarded with refreshments of doughnuts, molasses cakes, coffee, lemonade, or cider.

Early on, costumes were typically made from stockings and burlap or paper bags. In many cases, people used charcoal to blacken their faces – the ultimate goal being to disguise yourself enough as to prevent identification. In time, the art of creativity in costumes, much like the changes in Halloween today, seemed to fade away and was replaced by costumes and masks manufactured and sold at various retail stores.

Another practice similar to Belsnickling was "Kris Kringling."

The roots of "Kris-Kringling" can be found in the original "St. Nicholas the gift-giver" who was superseded by a representation of the infant Jesus (the Christ child, or "Christkindlein"). Ultimately, both Belsnickling and Kris-Kringling have common ties in the "Christkindlein" that accompanied Nicholas-like figures. In time, this person changed into a dwarf-like helper who wore furs (known as "Belsnickle" or "Pelznickel"). While the Belsnickle greeted awake children on Christmas Eve, the Christkindlein was credited with bringing gifts to children that slept – the same gifts that would be found on Christmas morning. In time, the word Christkindlein seemed to mutate into "Kris Kringle" and ultimately became the more recognized Santa Claus that we know today.

While Santa began to come into a more recognizable form around the 1840s with Clement Moore's famous story and in the 1860s with caricatures by Thomas Nast, Belsnickling still existed – as I've mentioned – into the 20th century. However, the fur-wearing Belsnickler also contributed one other thing to Santa before all was said and done – ah yes, Santa does were a fur-trimmed red coat doesn't he?! Who would have ever thought that a custom practiced right here in Page and the Valley contributed something to that jolly old fellow?

Fall Celebrations of Heritage and the Spirit of America
Article of 9/27/2001

Before I open this article, it is difficult not to pause for a brief moment without paying respect to the over 6,000 people that are listed as missing as a result of the events of September 11. Likewise, enough praise cannot be directed toward the rescue workers that work day and night in the recovery operations as well as the large number of American servicemen and women that are mobilizing around the globe to defend the very day-to-day liberties that we so often take for granted.

That being said, and in tune with American spirit of moving forward, I also write this week of a celebration of Americana - the Page County Heritage Festival.

The festival truly does bring to mind the "old-times" with music, clogging, wagon rides, apple cider, home-cooked food, a steam and gas engine and numerous crafts on display. As a fine time to celebrate the unique and special culture of the Page Valley, I hope that everyone will take the time to come out and reflect on our culture as it fits within the great "American quilt."

Of course, one of my personal favorites is seeing the apple butter boil. But, the boil isn't quite the same festive event that it was even well into the 19th century.

In an October 1862 letter, a Confederate officer summed-up a Shenandoah Valley "boil" – perhaps the best account found to date. Though finding the event "disgusting," he rather enjoyed the delicious apple-butter in the end. The brief story reveals a slice of charm that forms the foundation of Valley folk life. Furthermore, even in the face of war on the home front, Valley civilians knew how to move on with life - even with entertaining customs.

The Richmond native recollected: "They put a large cauldron on the fire and fill it with cider and as the cider boils all the young girls from the neighborhood are there to cut apples. We were invited to one the other night and I tell you twas a sight to see. The girls form a ring around the pot . . . The first one is placed and she says, 'I form a wreath' – 'what kind of flower?' – 'a rose' – 'who shall the next flower be?' – 'Capt. M[acon]' and he walks up, and kisses the young lady, or as they classically express it, 'puts on the trimmings' and there he is questioned as above and the young lady chosen comes up 'puts the trimmings on' takes her place in the ring and so on until all the party are circling around the fire, dancing and singing and kissing – it is altogether very disgusting. They go thro' a great many games too numerous to mention; but in all of them the chief aim and object is to accomplish as much kissing and hugging as possible. The closing of the ceremony is the forming of a bridge for the apple butter to pass over – this is formed in a manner very similar to the ring. I proposed a regular dance and a fiddler but they were all horror-stricken and said they could not as they belonged to the church – What a parody this is on religion and virtue! A good many of the boys seemed to think however it was fine fun. I can't say I did not enjoy the 'boil' for the apple-butter was delicious. This beats a So. Ga. shinding all to pieces . . .

Index

Abell, Captain, 49, 73
Adams, Thomas Jackson, 126, 127
Adams County, Pa., 76, 170, 171
Adams County Militia, 76
Aerie Insurance Company, 113
Albany, New York, 48
Aleshire, Henry P., Jr., 145
Aleshire, John Conrad, 144
Alexandria, Va., 153
Alleghany Co., Va., 152
Alma, Page County, Virginia, 23, 33, 38, 41, 77, 107, 110, 157, 165
Alma Bridge, 133
Almond, Isabella C., 48
Almond, Mann, 48, 113
Alves, Mrs. L. Wallis, 139
American Revolution, 19, 45, 46, 119, 171, 204, 205
Amiss, Frederick T., 82, 141
Amiss, Thomas Benjamin, 140
Anderson, Richard H. (Gen.), 85
Andersonville POW Camp (SEE Camp Sumter)
Anglican Church, 26, 27
Anne, Queen, 12, 146
Annweiler, Bavaria, 22
Apache Indians, 113
Appalachian Mountains, 16
Apple boil, 222, 223
Appomattox, Va., 76, 106, 153
Archer, James J. (Gen.), 105
Arlington National Cemetery, 132
Armintrout apple, 212
Army of the Mississippi (Confederate), 51
Army of Northern Virginia (Confederate), 58, 75
Army of the Potomac (Confederate), 51
Army of the Potomac (Union), 85, 121
Army of the Valley (Confederate), 77
Army of Virginia (Federal), 71
Arslan, Mark B., 163
Ashby, Richard, 173
Ashby, Turner, 69, 143, 173
Ashlar Lodge #125, 189

Atlanta, Ga., 121, 131, 153
Atlantic Monthly, 132
Atlantic Ocean, 22
Augusta County, Virginia, 34, 105, 172
"Aventine," 48
Averell, W.W. (Gen.), 87

Baker, Isaac N., Dr., 127
Baker, John T., 123
Baltimore, Md., 142, 143
Banckard, Anna Ursula, 162
Bantz, M., 127
Barbee, Mrs. Herbert, 138
Baptists, 23
Barber, Captain, 73
Barbour Co., Va. 158
Battles and Leaders of the Civil War, 52
Bauserman, Mrs. Raymond, 139
Bavarian Wittelsbachs, 10
Baybutt, Philip, 96, 97
Beahm's Gap, 212
Bealeton Station, Va., 87
Beasley, Mark, 34
Beauregard, Pierre Gustave Toutant, 51, 112
Becker, Anne Maria, 170
Beefsteak Raid, 76
Beidler, Charles Edward, 140
Belgium, 144
Bell, Erasmus Lee, 140
Bell, John Wesley, 35, 36, 123
Bell, Mitkalf A., 112
Belsnickling, 220, 221
Benet, Stephen Vincent, 117
Bentonville, Va., 159
Berkeley, William (Governor), 16
Berkeley Co., Va., 158
Berk's Co., Pa., 162, 175
Berry family, 45
Berry's Ferry, Va., 87
Berwick Township, Pennsylvania, 170, 171
Beverly, Virginia, 59
Big Meadows, 16
Bird, Judge, 50
Bixler Ferry Road, 36

Black Confederates, 116-117
Black, Mrs. Lynn, 139
Blosser, Daniel (Sheriff), 36
Blue Hole (in Naked Creek), 133
Blue Ridge, 16, 17, 18, 26, 32, 33, 43, 48, 100, 120, 166, 184
Bohannon, W.E., 210
Bohemia, 11
Bohme, Anton Wilhelm, 27
Bolen, Albert, 212, 213
Booth, Bessie, 143
Booton, John Kaylor, 57, 151
Borst, Addison D., 49
Borst, Charles, 48
Borst, Cornelia, 48
Borst, Elizabeth, 48
Borst, John B., 49
Borst, Peter Bock, 48, 49, 50, 73, 118, 119
Borst, William, 48
Borst's Tannery, 49, 88
Bostick, Mrs. Lena Stover, 139
Boston, Massachusetts, 174
Boteler's Ford, Maryland, 58
Bowers, Albert, 76
Bragonier, Robert C., 140
Brandy Station, Va. 75
Brantley Baptist Church, Baltimore, Md., 143
Breathed, James (Major), 95
Breckinridge, John C. (Gen.), 89
Breyhel, Conrad, 146
Breyhel, Hans Jacob, 146, 147
Breyhel, Margaretha Schelling, 146
Breyhel, Johannes, 146
Brick Church, 86
Bristoe Campaign, 86
British/English colonies, 13, 14, 24, 25
Britton's shops, 49, 88
Broadus, Andrew, 124
Brown, John, 91, 116
Brownsville, Pa., 144
Broy, W. Peter, 141
Broyles, Zacharias, 147
Bruner, William F., 83, 84
Bruton Heights School, 31
Bundy family, 45
Burke Stage Line, 53
Burner, Charles, 143

Burner, Charles A., 195
Burner, Hamilton Vincent, 143
"Burning, The," 70, 98
Butterfield, Francis W. (Colonel), 107, 108, 109

"Calendine", 53
California, 89, 104, 105
"California 100," 96
Calvinists, 15
Camden, S.C., 168
Camp Chase, Ohio, 63, 92, 138
Camp Sumter/Andersonville POW Camp, 115, 198, 199
Camp Winder, Va., 80
Campbell family, 44, 45
Campbell, Andrew Jackson, 80
Campbell, Floyd, 195
Campbell, Samuel, 41
Canada, 12, 24
"Captain" (slave), 35, 36, 37
Captain Colwell Post No. 201, G.A.R., 124
Carlisle, Pa., 124
Carlisle Herald & Mirror, 125
Carman, Charles H., 123
Carroll, Samuel S. (Col.), 69
Carter, Colonel John, 30
Carter, Judith, 30
Catherine Furnace, 41
Catholics/Catholicism, 11, 14
Cave, Francis P., 122
Cave, Lucy Virginia, 123
Cave, Reuben, 45, 148, 149, 168
Cave Hill, 67
Cedar Creek, 144
Cedar Grove Cemetery (Covington), 152
Cedar Mountain, Battle of, 53
Cedar Point, Page County, Virginia, 34
Champaign Co., Ohio, 120
Champion's Hill, Mississippi, Battle of, 113
Chancellorsville, Battle of, 53, 98
Chapman, Edmund Gaines, 150, 151
Chapman, Samuel Forrer, 57, 58, 150, 151, 152, 153
Chapman, William Allen, 150

Chapman, William Henry, 57, 58, 150, 151, 152, 153, 192, 198, 199
Chappell, Edward, 20, 21
Charles Town, Va., 91
Charleston, S.C., 169
Charlottesville, Va., 174
Chesapeake Bay, 168
Chicago, Illinois, 130
Christmas, 88, 138
Church of England, 28
City Point, Va., 98
Clarke County, Virginia, 34, 39
Clear Creek Monthly Meeting (Ohio), 112
Clear Spring, Md., 188
Clem, Franklin, 75
Clem, Isaac, 75
Clinedinst, John W., 127
Clore, Delilah, 147
Clore, Peter, 147
Clummer, George (Captain), 149
Coffman, J.H., 82, 83, 84
Coleman, Frank, 148
College of William and Mary, 30
Colonial Williamsburg Foundation, 166, 167
Colonial Williamsburg Foundation Center, 31
Colston, John T., 127
Columbia Bridge, 32, 33, 64, 65, 69, 73, 77, 78
Columbia Ford, 108
Columbia University, 150, 152
Columbus, Mississippi, 143
Columbus, Ohio, 113
Confederate Reunion and Memorial Day, 138
Confederate Units:
    Dixie Artillery, 45, 55, 57, 58, 63, 91, 134, 150, 151, 192, 199
    Captain Peter J. Keyser's Boy Company, 59, 60, 134, 135, 192
    Eighth Star New Market Artillery, 127
    Purcell Artillery (Cayce's Battery), 58, 151
    Wheat's Tigers, 65
    Washington Artillery Battalion (New Orleans, La.), 58

    3rd Georgia Infantry, 85
    7th Louisiana Infantry, 65, 66
    9th Louisiana Infantry, 65
    1st Maryland Cavalry, Co. C., 102, 104
    1st Cherokee Regiment (N.C.), 83
    2nd South Carolina Cavalry, Co. D (Wassamassaw Cavalry), 84
    1st Tennessee Infantry, 92
    1st Texas Cavalry, 90
    1st Battalion Valley (Va.) Reserves, 60
    1st Virginia Cavalry, 127
    2nd Virginia Cavalry, 95
    3rd Battalion (Chrisman's) Virginia Reserves, 60
    4th Regiment Virginia Volunteers, 91
    4th Virginia Cavalry, 95
    6th Virginia Cavalry, 65, 97
    7th Brigade Virginia Militia, 59, 60, 61
    7th Virginia Cavalry, 127
    7th Virginia Cavalry, Co. D ("Massanutten Rangers"), 63, 64, 87, 91, 92, 101, 106, 110, 124, 129, 134, 143, 154, 192
    7th Virginia Cavalry, Co. I, 172
    7th Virginia Infantry, 193
    8th Battalion Virginia Reserves, 60
    10th Virginia Infantry, 78, 91, 92, 127, 140
    10th Virginia Infantry, Co. F (Muhlenberg Rifles), 130
    10th Virginia Infantry, Co. I (Riverton Invincibles), 132
    10th Virginia Infantry, Co. K ("Page Volunteers"), 49, 53, 54, 57, 59, 98, 100, 102, 130, 134, 151, 192, 200, 201
    12th Virginia Cavalry, 127
    13th Virginia Militia, 59

13th Virginia Infantry, Co. G., 104
14th Virginia Cavalry, Co. H, 172
17th Virginia Infantry, Co. B, 150
18th Virginia Cavalry, 127
23rd Virginia Cavalry, 126, 127, 193
33rd Virginia Infantry, Co. H ("Page Grays"), 44, 55, 56, 59, 79, 115, 134, 151, 192
35th Battalion Virginia Cavalry, Co. E, 75, 76, 98, 102, 134, 192, 193
39th Battalion Virginia Cavalry, Co. C., 92, 124
43rd Battalion Virginia Cavalry (Mosby's Rangers), 55, 151, 152
43rd Battalion Virginia Cavalry, Co. C, 151, 153
48th Virginia Infantry, 80
58th Virginia Militia, 59
62nd Virginia Infantry, 60
62nd Virginia Infantry, 2nd Co. M, 135, 193
97th Virginia Militia, 59, 128, 134
116th Virginia Militia, 59
136th Virginia Militia, 59
145th Virginia Militia, 59
146th Virginia Militia, 59
149th Virginia Militia, 59
Confederate Veteran Magazine, 82, 140, 142
Conger, Captain, 65
Congressional Medal of Honor, 96, 97
Connel, John H., 127
Conrad's Store (Elkton), Va., 87, 172
Continental Army, 28, 29
Continental Can Company, 132
Continental Regiments:
1st Virginia Infantry, 28, 168
2nd Virginia Infantry, 148, 168
4th Virginia Infantry, 145
5th Virginia Infantry, 28
9th Virginia Infantry, 28
13th Virginia Infantry, 28
Corbin Hollow, 167
Corinth, Mississippi, 113
Cornwallis, Lord, 149
Count Palatine, 10
Covington, Va., 152
Cox, Walter M., 127
Cowes, England, 164
Cowpens, S.C., 169
Coyner, Samuel Brown, 64
Crawford, Malcolm F., 33
Criglersville, Va., 210
Crippen, William C., 67, 68
Crisp, Charles Frederick, 130, 131
Crisp, Harry, 130
Crisp, William H., 57, 130
Crittenden, Alexander Parker, 105
Crittenden, Churchill, 102, 103, 104, 105
Crittenden, John, 105
Crittenden, Thomas Turpin, 105
Croghan, George, 25
Cross Keys, Rockingham Co., Va., 69, 171
Culpeper, Virginia, 49, 168
Culpeper County, Virginia, 26, 86, 116, 147
Culp's Hill, Gettysburg, Pa., 44, 56, 120
Cumru Township, Pa., 162
Cuntz, Elizabeth Catherine Stoever, 22
Cuntz, John, 22
Custer, George Armstrong (Gen.), 94, 96

"Dan" (slave), 34, 35
Danzig, 26
Daughters of the American Revolution, 148
Davis, Miss A.A., 138
Davis, Miss A.J., 138
Davis, Jefferson, 52, 61, 62, 74, 79, 142
Davis, Mary Ann Dorraugh, 154
Davis, Samuel B., 154
Davis, T. Sturgis (Major), 102
Davis, Varina Howell, 142

Davison, Mary Rosanna "Mollie", 188
Dayton, Virginia, 21
De Villiers, Commandant Neyon, 25
Dearing, James G. (Gen.), 75
Deep Hole (in Naked Creek), 133
Delaplane, Va., 152
Delaware River, 145
Department of Veterans Affairs, 214
Dickson, Louise Catherine, 138
Disciples of Christ Church, 171
Dixie Artillery, 45, 55, 57, 58, 63, 91, 92, 130
Dixon, John, 41
Dogans, John, 128
Dogtown, Page Co., Va., 65
Dorraugh, Elijah Russell, 154
Dorraugh, James Hiram, 154
Dorraugh, Mary Ann, 154
Dorraugh, Rachel, 154
Dorraugh, Sarah, 154
Dorraugh, William M., 154
Douglas, Henry Kyd, 79
Dovel family, 38, 39
Dovel, Adam Beauregard, 38
Dovel, Cecilia, 39
Dovel, Charles C., 38, 39, 133
Dovel, David, 39, 157
Dovel, Drucilla, 39
Dovel, Priscilla, 39
Dovel, Russell, 39
Dovel, William, 157
"Drucilla" or "Old Sill" (slave), 38
Dugans, John A., 128
Duke of Abercorn, 15
Dulaney, Richard H. (Col.), 127
Duncan, George, 75
Dusslingen, Wuerttemberg, 146

Early, Jubal (Gen.), 86, 87, 94, 95, 96, 218
Eaton, Amanda Shifflett, 161
Eaton, Nancy, 161
Eaton, Thomas, 161
Eaton, William, 161
Edict of Nantes, 156
Edom, Rockingham County, Virginia, 46
Ehlscheid, Germany, 144
Elgin, Catherine Lewis Smith, 152

Elgin, Eliza Rebecca, 152
Elgin, S. Gustavius, 152
Elizabeth II, Queen, 15
Ellaville, Ga., 130
Ellis, Martin, 128
Elliot, Phoebe, 159
Elmira, New York, 49, 114, 115, 132
Elscheit, Conrad, 144
England, 12, 13, 19, 28
English, 13, 14, 28
English Protestants, 14
Essex Co., Va., 146
Ewell, Richard S., 51, 85, 218

Fairfax Court House, Va., 97
Fairfax, Lord, 210
Fall Creek, Massachusetts, 96
Fauquier County, Virginia, 23, 151, 152
Federal troops, 39
Financial and Mining Record of New York, 52
Finch, Surgeon, 49, 73
First Congress, 29
Fishers Gap, 33, 77, 78, 86, 209
Fisher's Hill, Va., 94, 95, 96, 219
Fitch, George K., 140
Fleischmann, Maria Catherine, 147
Fleischmann, Zacharias, 147
Fletcher, James, 42, 43
Fletcher, Lucy, 42
Fletcher, Nasenath, 43
Flinn, George (Sheriff), 37
Flinn, John H., 76
Florida Territory, 51
Forrer, Catherine F. Ebersole, 150
Forrer, Elizabeth, 150
Forrer, Judah, 63
Forrer, Samuel, 150
"Fort" Homes, 20
Fort de Chartes, 25
Fort Delaware, Delaware, 54
Fort Detroit, 25
Fort Harrison, 21
Fort Mifflin, 149
Fort Ninety-Six, 169
Fort Philip Long, 20
Fort Pulaski, Georgia, 54
Fort Redstone, Pa., 144

Fort Quiatenon, 25
Fort Stover, 20
Fort Sumter, 119
Foster, Robert S. (Col.), 65, 66
Frankenburg, Hesse, Germany, 22
"Frankey" (slave), 34
Franklin Cliffs, 77, 209
Frazier's Farm, Virginia, Battle of, 58
Frederick V, 11
Frederick, Md., 174
Frederick County, Virginia, 42, 126, 144, 158, 159, 178
Fredericksburg, Va., 77, 87
Free Blacks, 40, 41, 44
Free State Hollow, 166, 167
Fremont, John C. (General), 64, 69
French, William H. (Gen.), 85
French, 13, 24
French army, 11
French Protestants, 14
French & Indian War, 24, 28, 30, 181
Frieden's Reformed Church, 171
Friermood, Mathias, 165
Fristoe, Charles B., 75
Front Royal, Virginia, 23, 32, 69, 70, 85, 86, 87, 94, 95, 96, 218

Gaelic Lords, 14
Gaines, Edmond Pendleton, 150
Gander, Martin Van Buren, 140
Gates, Horatio, 168
Gatewood, Wright, 62
Genealogical Society of Page County, 176, 178
General Order #5, 71
General Order #11, 71
George III, King, 119
"Georgia" (proposed colony west of the Blue Ridge), 19
German element, 26
German immigrants, 18, 19
Germanna Colony, 18, 22, 146
Germanna Foundation, 179
Germany, 10, 11, 12, 22, 28
Gettysburg, Pennsylvania, 44, 56, 85, 86, 99, 120, 132, 218
Gibbons, Christina Miller, 90
Gibbons, Samuel, 90

Gibbons, Simeon Beauford, 89, 90, 91, 92, 140
Gibbons, William Stephens, 91, 92
Giddings, Charles, 75
Gilmor, Harry (Major), 49, 87
Glaize, Henry W., 127
Glaize, Sallie, 127
Gloucester County, Virginia, 30
Gloucester Historical Society, 31
Goessel, Christopher, 144
Goessel, Maria Catherina, 144
Goldsborough, W.W., 102, 104
Gooney Run, 94
Gordon, John B. (Gen.), 75, 76, 131, 142
Grabill, John Henry, 75
Grandstaff, Alonzo F., 127
Grant, Ulysses S., 52, 95, 153
Graves' Chapel, 77, 78, 81, 82, 84, 209, 218
"Gray Ghost" (John S. Mosby), 150
Grayson, Benjamin Franklin, 53
Grayson, David Coffman, 53, 54, 98, 99, 141
Grayson, William E., 140
Great Britain, 149
Great Conawago Creek, Pa., 170
Green, John, 168
Green Hill Cemetery (Luray), 50, 54, 123, 206
Green Meadows (Adam Miller House), 21
Greene, Gen. Nathanael, 28, 168, 169
Greene Co., Va. 172
Greensboro, North Carolina, 52, 153
Greenwood Co., S.C., 169
Grove Hill, Page County, Virginia, 55, 107, 108, 110, 128, 175
Grove, Anita, 139
Grove, Arthur Ashby, 141
Grove, Benjamin Franklin, 55
Grove, John Pendleton, 141
Grove, John W., 76
Grove, Mrs. J. Gill, 139
Groves, Joseph, 140
Guadalupe County, Texas, 90
Guadalupe Male Academy, 90
Guiamiro, Cuba, 52
Guice, Benjamin D., 127

Guilford Court House, N.C., 149, 169

Hagerstown, Md., 171
Haley, Alex, 190
Ham, Sarah, 154
Hamburg, Germany, 16
Hamburg Academic Gymnasium, 16
Hamburg, Page County, Virginia, 63
Hancock Creek, Illinois, 99
Hancock, Winfield Scott, 153
Handright, Thomas J., 75
Hanover, Germany, 164
Hardert, Germany, 144
Hardin County, Kentucky, 46
Hardt Mountains (Bavaria), 22
Hargest, Judge, 50
Hargrove, Mary Ida, 138
Harold E. Howard, Inc., 134, 137
Harpers Ferry, Virginia, 32, 58, 91
Harper's Magazine, 52
Harrison, Josiah, 158
Hartigan, John James, 102, 103, 104, 105
Harrisonburg, Va., 69, 74, 91
Hawksbill Creek, 32
Hayes, Rutherford B., 153
Hebron Evangelical Church, 26
Hebron Lutheran Church, 22, 146
Hedgesville, Virginia, 92
Heidelberg, Pa., 162
Helmsted, Germany, 26
Henderson, Judge R.M., 125
Henkel & Co. Publishers, 127
Henkel, Socrates, 109
Henry, Thomas, 167
Henry Hill, Manassas, Va., 56
Henry, Patrick, 30
Hermann I, 10
Hershberger, Elizabeth, 100, 101, 102
Hershberger, Henry Pendleton, 100
Hershberger, John S., 100, 140, 141
Hessian Soldiers, 149, 174
Heth, Henry (General), 51
High Bridge, Va., 76
Highland Co., Ohio, 112
Hill, Ambrose Powell (Gen.), 85, 86
Hilliard, Bessie Comer, 161
Hilliard, Charles Robert, 159, 160

Hilliard, Ella Nauman, 161
Hilliard, Grafton, 158
Hilliard, Jacob, 158, 159
Hilliard, Jacob Taylor, 158
Hilliard, Jacob Theodore, 159
Hilliard, John T., 158
Hilliard, Margaret Elizabeth Eaton, 160, 161
Hilliard, Martha Susan Monger, 160, 161
Hilliard, Mathias, 158, 159
Hilliard, Nancy Ann, 158
Hilliard, Sarah Elizabeth Breeden, 161
Hilliard, William Christopher, 159
Hillyard Cemetery, Weaver, W.V., 158
Hilton Head, South Carolina, 54
Hilyard, Amos, 158
Hilyard, Amos, Jr., 158
Hilyard/Hilliard, Jacob, 158
Hilyard, John, 158
Hilyard, Mathias, 158
Historical Register of Virginians in the Revolution, 29
History of Rockingham County, 16
Hite family, 55
Hite, Daniel, 55
Hite, David C., 56
Hite, John P., 56
Hite, Rebecca, 55
Hite, William F., 55, 56
Hoak, Mrs. Lester, 139
Hobart College, 105
Hobkirk's Hill, S.C., 169
Hochman, Jacob, 34
Hodson, Rebecca, 112
Holland, 11
Holy Roman Empire, 10
Honer, T., 75
"Honest John" apple, 212
Honeyville, Page County, Va., 57, 65, 66, 78, 151, 172
Hopkins, John E., 127
Hotchkiss, Jedediah, 77, 86
House of Burgesses, 28
House, Benjamin, 123
Huffman, Ambrose, 133
Huffman, Ambrose C., 140
Huffman, James, 132, 133

Huffman, Oscar C., 132
Huffman, Mrs. R.R., 139
Hughes family, 45
Hughes, Jake, 45
Hughes River, 166
Huguenots, 14, 18, 156
Huntsville, Al., 153
Hussey, Cyrus, 108, 110, 112, 113
Hussey, Joshua, 113
Hussey, Stephen, 112
Hussey, William, 113
Hutchinson, William, 148

Ida, Page Co., Va., 172
"Immortal Six Hundred," 54, 115, 130
Indiana, 122, 123
Ingham, 154
Interstate Commerce Act of 1887, 131
Ireland, 14, 15
Isaac, Washington, 123

Jackson, Thomas Jonathan "Stonewall", 55, 59, 63, 64, 65, 69, 77, 78, 79, 86, 89, 90, 143, 209
James I, King, 14
James River, 168
JEB Stuart Monument Fund, 139
Jefferson, Thomas, 30, 33, 174, 205
Jeffries, Esther Foote, 152
Jeffries, James Eustace, 152
Jeffries, Josephine H., 152
Jennings, Mrs. Jean, 139
Jennings, Mrs. Thomas C., 139
"Jerry" (slave), 43
"Joe" (slave), 34
Johnson, Albert Sidney (General), 52
Johnson, Edward "Allegheny" (Gen.), 86
Johnson, Sir William, 25
Johnston, Joseph E. (General), 57, 61, 91
Jones, Harriett, 97
Jones, Hugh, Rev., 146
Jones, J. William, Dr., 142, 143
Jones, William E. "Grumble," 75
Jordan, Elizabeth Ann Sibert, 51
Jordan, Francis Hubert, 51

Jordan, Francis Hubert, Jr., 124
Jordan, Gabriel, 51, 89
Jordan, Gabriel, Jr., 89
Jordan, Irvin L., Jr., 116, 117
Jordan, Macon, 51
Jordan, Mary Betsy Seibert, 89
Jordan, Thomas (General), 51, 52, 112, 124
Joyce (ship), 22
Judd, Mrs. Dorothy H., 139
Judd, Samuel N., 140

Kaufman, Anna, 46
Kaufman, Benjamin, 46
Kaufman, George W., 46, 47
Kauffman, Barney, 98
Kauffman, Enoch Van Buren "Mac," 98, 99, 102, 105, 140, 141
Kauffman, Joseph Franklin, 98
Kauffman, Martin, 23, 204, 205
Kauffman, Philip Monroe, 63, 64, 98, 99, 102, 105
Kauffman, Rebecca Mauck, 98
Keiser, Agnes. 162
Keiser, Valentine, 162
Kelly/Celly family, 29
Kendrick Farm, 100
Kernstown, Virginia, Battle of, 55, 120
Keyser, John W., 81, 82
Keyser, Peter J., 134, 192
Keyser, Thomas, 59, 60
Kibler, David, 43
Kibler, Dorothy "Polly", 43
Kibler, Helen, 139
Kibler, Isaac Newton, 75, 140
Kibler, Martin, 43
Kiblinger/Kepliner family, 29
Kimball, General, 67
Kimball, Va., 212
Kimball apple, 212
King of Bohemia, 11
King George County, Virginia, 49
Kingree, David, 127
Kip, Lawrence (Col.), 104
Kiser, Elizabeth, 175
Kiser, Michael, 162, 163, 174, 175
Kiser, Valentine, 163
Kite, Andrew Jackson, 106, 108, 110

Kite, Mrs. Frank, 139
Kite, Reuben, 128
Kite's Mill, 108
Klug, Rev. George Samuel, 26, 27
Knight, Andrew J., 79
Knights of the Golden Horseshoe, 18
Koiner, Gideon, 127
Koontz family, 29, 38
Koontz, Anna Keyser, 106
Koontz, Elder John, 22, 23, 172, 204, 205
Koontz, Elizabeth, 38
Koontz, Elizabeth Ann, 172
Koontz, Daniel, 39, 108, 109
Koontz, George William, 127
Koontz, Isaac Sr., 38, 106
Koontz, Isaac Newton (Sergeant), 106, 108, 109, 110, 111, 126, 107, 109, 110, 111
Koontz, Jacob D., 106, 108, 110, 111
Koontz, John J., 172
Koontz, Mary Bingman, 172
Koontz, Susannah Kiblinger, 38
Krick, Philip, 162
Kris Kringling, 220
Kurphaz Government, 170

Laconia, James Wade, 123, 140
Lacy, Beverly Tucker (Rev.), 86
Lafayette, Indiana, 25
Lantz, R.M., 127
Larkins, Samuel M., 83
Lauck, Theodore H., 140
Lauck, William C. (Elder), 37
Laurel Brigade, 75, 140, 172
Leaksville, Va., 79, 128
Leavill, Mary Ann, 43
Lederer, John, 16, 17, 18
Lee Chapel & Mausoleum, 139
Lee, Fitzhugh (Gen.), 94
Lee, Robert Edward, 54, 76, 77, 79, 85, 97, 106, 143, 153
Lehigh Co., Pa. 162
Leicester, England, 97
Letcher, John (Governor), 61, 62, 107
Libby Prison, 114
Library of Virginia, 136

Lincoln, Abraham, 46, 47, 49, 119
Lincoln, Abraham L., 46
Lincoln, Jacob, 46
Lincoln, John, 46
Lincoln, Nancy Hanks, 46
Lincoln, Nancy Todd, 47
Lincoln, Thomas, 46
Lincoln, Illinois, 46
Lingel, Jacob, 162
Lingel, Mary, 163
Linville Creek, Rockingham Co., Va., 46
Lionberger, John, 91
Lionberger, John Henry, 91, 92
Lionberger, Lavinia Seibert, 91
London, England, 12, 17
Long, Isaac, 133
Long, Mrs. R.B., 139
Longstreet, James (General), 58, 77, 86
Lorraine, France, 216
Lowry, Eliza Wharton, 138
Lookout Mountain, Tennessee, 120
Louderback, John P., 78
Loudoun Co., Va., 120
Louis XIV, King 12
Lloyd, William R. (Colonel), 49, 73, 74
Long, Caroline, 138
Long, Frank, 100, 101
Lowell, Charles Russell, Jr., 96
Lubeck, Germany, 28
Luray, Indiana, 216
Luray, Iowa, 216
Luray, Kansas, 216
Luray, Missouri, 216
Luray, Ohio, 216
Luray, S.C., 216
Luray, Virginia, 32, 33, 36, 42, 43, 48, 49, 53, 54, 55, 60, 67, 70, 72, 73, 74, 80, 86, 87, 88, 95, 96, 97, 98, 120, 124, 125, 128, 130, 140, 212, 216, 217
Luray Cave, 124
Luray Cave & Hotel Company, 125
Luray Caverns, 80
Luray Chapter #436, United Daughters of the Confederacy, 138, 139, 140
Luray College, 48

Luray Depot, 124
Luray-Front Royal Turnpike, 32
Luray Gap, 33
Luray Manufacturing Company, 90
Luray Orphanage, 142
Luray Valley, 108
LuRay China, 217
Lusk, Lycurgus, D., 108, 109
Luther, Martin, 11
Luther's 95 Theses, 10
Lutherans, 11, 22, 23, 27, 28
Lutheran Reformed Church (New Market), 104

Madison Co., Va., 78, 87, 146, 147, 150, 166, 210, 211
Magruder, Philip W., 127
Maguire, Laura, 92
Main Street, Luray, Va., 36
Manakin Town, 18
Manassas Gap, Va., 85
Manassas Gap Railroad, 120
Manassas Junction, Virginia, 51
Manassas Monument, 138
Manassas, First Battle of, 52, 56, 77, 91, 124
Manassas, Virginia, Second Battle of, 56, 58, 98
Manchester, England, 96
Manning, Joseph M., 123
Manson, Andrew, 148
March to the Sea, 122
Marksville, Page County, Virginia, 33, 41, 78, 81
Marsh Creek (Pa.), 76
Marshall family, 45
Marshall, Va., 152
"Martin" (slave), 35, 36, 37
Martin, Virginia, 139
Marye, Elizabeth Ruffner, 89
Marye, William Staige, 89
Marye, Willis Young, 89
Massanutten District, 44
Massanutten Gap, 33
Massanutten Mountain, 18, 19, 29, 32, 33, 63, 67, 77, 89, 94, 95, 107, 109, 184
"Massanutten Rangers", Co. D, 7th Virginia Cavalry, 63, 64, 87, 91, 92, 100

Massanutten Settlement/Tract, 18, 19, 20, 21, 23, 204
"Matilda" (slave and sister to Bethany Veney), 42
Matthews, James A., 140
Mauck, John P., 76
Mayari, Cuba, 52
McAllister, Virginia Belle, 173
McClellan, George B. (Gen.), 72
McCormick, Patrick, 158
McCoy, James W., 140
McCullough, Benjamin M., 123
McDaniel, Mary, 34
McDowell, Virginia, Battle of, 53, 65, 91, 140
McInturff, Marcus, 75
McKay, David, 42
McKay, Enos, 34, 35
McFarland, Susan, 158
McLean, Wilmer, 52
Meade, George G. (Gen.), 85
Mechanicsville, Virginia, Battle of, 58
Meem, Gilbert Simrall (General), 59
Melton, James A., 140
Memorial Foundation of the Germanna Colonies of Va., 147
Memphis Appeal, 52
Menefee, Jonas (Mannyfield), 43
Mennonites, 23
Merritt, Wesley, 94
Methodist Episcopal Church, 112
Mexican War, 51
Michel, Franz Louis, 18
Middlesex, England, 30
Milam apple, 210, 211, 212
Milam Gap, 33, 83, 86, 210
Milford, (Overall) Virginia, 41, 86, 94, 95, 96, 218
Mill Creek (Page Co.), 23, 55, 62
Miller, Adam, 21
Miller, Paul, 140
Miller, W.A.J. (Major), 60
Miller, W.E., 125
Miller, William H., Dr., 63
Milroy, Robert (Gen.), 72
Milton, N.C., 153
Milum, Joseph, 211
Milum, Thomas, 210
Mimslyn, 48

Miskel's Farm, Va. (Battle of), 151
Mississippi, 105
Missouri, 122
Modesitt, Mrs. A.S., 139
Modesitt, Elizabeth Kaufman, 46
Modesitt, James Robert, 46
Modesitt, James William, 55, 60
Monger's Church, 108, 175
Monongahela River, 144
Montgomery Co., Pa., 162
Moore, Clement, 221
Moore, James Draper, 198
Moore, John Howard "Blinkey", 188, 189
Moore, Robert Hume (1896), 189
Moore, Mag, 127
Moravians, 26
Morris, Haley, 44
Morris Island, South Carolina, 54, 130
Mosby, John S., 55, 58, 63, 96, 151, 152, 153, 198, 199
Mosby, Willie, 198
Mount Hope Cemetery, Hastings-on-the-Hudson, N.Y., 52
Moyers, David & Cass, 127
Mt. Crawford, Va., 171
Mt. Jackson, Va., 86, 87, 106
Mud Point, 149
Muhleck, Lieutenant Col., 73, 74
Muhlenberg, Rev./Gen. John Peter Gabriel, 28, 29
Muhlenberg, Rev. Heinrich Melchior, 27, 28
Munford, Thomas T. (Col.), 94
Munson's Hill, Va., 104
Myers, John H., 127

Naked Creek, 69, 132, 133, 189
Nassau-Siegen District, Germany, 18
Nast, Thomas, 221
National Archives, 129, 136, 148, 168
National Cemetery Administration, 214
Native Americans, 13, 24
Nauman, Barbara, 165
Nauman, Benjamin Harrison, 165
Nauman, Catherine, 165

Nauman, Christian, 164
Nauman, Christina, 165
Nauman, David, 165
Nauman, Elizabeth, 165
Nauman, Emil, 164
Nauman, Eva, 165
Nauman, Hannah, 165
Nauman, Johannes Gottlieb, 164
Nauman, John Christian, 164, 165
Nauman, John Christian, Jr., 164
Nauman, John Gottlieb, 164
Nauman, Mary, 165
Nauman, Thomas, 164
Nazer, Lieutenant Col., 73, 74
New Bern, North Carolina, 18
New England, 43
New Kent Co., Va., 105
New Market, Virginia, 28, 46, 67, 74, 84, 89, 91, 95, 104, 126, 127, 193
New Market Gap, 63, 69, 86, 94, 209
New Market-Gordonsville Turnpike, 33
New Market-Sperryville Turnpike, 33
New Orleans, Louisiana, 138
New York, 123
Newport, Page Co., Va., 126
Nicewarner, Erasmus, 127
Nichols, Will, 143
Nicholson, John, 166
Nicholson, Thomas, 166
Nicholson Hollow, 166, 167
Niederhonnefeld, Prussia, Germany, 144
Ninety-Six, S.C., 169
Nolin Creek, Hardin County, Kentucky, 46
Norfolk, Va., 158
Norfolk & Western RR., 189
North America, 14, 27
North Anna River, 16

Occoquon, Va., 87
Oetisheim, Germany, 146
Offenbacker/Overboker family, 29
O'Ferrall, Charles T., 127
Ohio, 122, 123
Ohio Valley, 171

Old Capitol Prison, Washington, D.C., 53
Old Homes of Page County, 207
"Old Sill" or "Drucilla" (slave), 38, 39
"Old Sorrel", 63
Old Southern Apples, 212
Old Stone Church (Clarke County, Va.), 39
Olinger, William H., 127
Opequon Creek, Va., 97
Orange & Alexandria Railroad, 87
Orange Co., N.C., 112
Orange Co., Va., 146, 149
Ordinance of Secession, Virginia's, 119
Ottowa Tribe, 25
Overall (Milford), Virginia, 41, 94, 96

Page, Colonel John, 30
Page, Elizabeth, 35
Page, James, 35
Page, Governor John, 30, 31
Page, Mann, 31, 35, 40
Page, Mann, I, 30
Page, Mann, II, 30
Page, Mary Mann, 30
Page, Matthew, 30
Page County Bank, 90
Page County Confederates, 118
Page County Confederate Veterans, 124, 125
Page County High School, 112, 126
Page County Men in Gray, 134, 136
Page County High School, 188
Page County Men in Gray, 192, 193
Page County Schools, 90
Page Courier, 81
Page Courier and Virginia Advertiser, 124
"Page Grays", 33rd Va. Inf., Co. H, 44, 55, 56, 78, 79, 106, 121
Page Milling Company, 213
Page News, 36, 213
Page News & Courier, 2, 38, 82, 140, 179
Page Power Company, 213
Page Valley Bank, 90
Page Valley Nurseries, 213

"Page Volunteers," 49, 53, 54, 57
Page Woolen Mill, 90
Painter Family, 144
Painter, Joseph, Sr., 128
Palatinate/Palatines – 10, 11, 12, 13, 32, 48, 146, 170
Pamunkey River, 16
Paris, France, 156
Parks, Richard Stewart, 53, 54, 140, 189
Pass Run, 42, 86, 218
Paxton, E.F. (Gen.), 79
Payne, William H.F. (Col.), 95, 96
Peachtree Creek, Ga., 121
Pence, Rebecca, 80
Pence, William, 79, 80
Pence, William A., 127
Peninsula Campaign, 58, 72
Penn, Davidson (Maj.), 65
Penn, William, 12
Pennsylvania, 13, 20, 21, 29, 123
Pennsylvania Dutch/German, 12, 220
"Peter" (slave and uncle to Bethany Veney), 43
Petersburg, Va., 76, 95, 168
Pfalz, 10
Philadelphia, Pennsylvania, 22, 28, 29, 144, 164, 170
Philadelphia Academy (University of Pennsylvania), 28
Phillips, William B., 33
Phillips Mills, 149
Pierson, John A., 75
Plantation of Ulster, 14
Point Comfort, Va., 158
Point Lookout, Maryland, 49, 56, 98, 115, 132
Pollock, George Freeman, 166, 167
Pope, John (Gen.), 71
Pontiac, Chief, 24, 25
Pontiac Conspiracy, 24, 25
Poplar Mills, 154
Port Gibson, Mississippi, 113
Port Republic, Virginia, 32, 69, 70, 120
Portals to Hell, 115
Portsmouth, Va., 168
Potomac River, 58, 76, 85
Powell, William H. (Col.), 103

235

Presbyterians, 15
Price, Berryman Zirkle, 127
Price, Gabrill L., 79
Price, Joseph M., 70
Price's Mill, 69, 70, 218
Printz, John, Sr., 42
Printz, Peter, 172
Protestants, 11, 14, 15
Purcell Artillery, 58
Purdom, Thomas, 168, 169

Quick, Nannie, 127
Quicksburg, Va., 126, 127

Raccoon Ford, 84
Ramey, Louis, 216
Rapidan River, 16, 84
Rappahannock County, Virginia, 53, 72, 166, 179, 213
Rappahannock River, 16, 146, 166
Rappahannock Station, Virginia, Battle of, 58
Raudenbusch, Hans Heinrich, 170, 171
Raudenbusch, Hans Peter, 170
Rawdon, Lord, 169
Reader, Michael, 29
Reader's Company, 29
Ream's Station, Va., 101
Red Bridge, 218
Red Gate Road, 78
Red River Expedition, 113
Redwell Furnace, 218
Reihen, Germany, 170
Rengsdorf, Rheinland, Prussia, Germany, 144
Reveberwein, Rev. Andrew, 22
Revolutionary War, 45, 46, 145, 148, 168, 169
Rhenish – 10
Rhine River, 12
Rhine River (Middle), 10
Rhineland, 20
Rhode Island, 105
Rhodes family, 24
Rhodes, Alexander H., 90
Rhodes, Frances Yager, 138
Rhodes, Mary Elizabeth, 90
Rice, Jacob W., 127
Richards, Aquilla, 45

Richards, Amelia "Emily", 45
Richards, Howard, 45
Richards, Joseph, 45
Richart, Captain, 74
Richmond *Examiner*, 104
Richmond, Virginia, 31, 91, 92, 105, 114, 136, 138, 168
Rickstacker, Anne, 171
Riedesel, Baron, 174
Rippetoe, William D., 55
Riverton, Va., 94
Roanoke College, 55
Robertson River, 146
Rochester, N.Y., 107
Rockingham County, Virginia, 21, 32, 46, 63, 131, 158, 159, 162, 163, 171, 172, 175, 179
Rockingham Turnpike, 32
Rodes, Robert E. (Gen.), 86
Rogers, William H., 140
Rohrer, Almira J., 122, 123
Rohrer, Jeremiah H., 122
Rohrer, Malinda, 122
Rohrersville, Maryland, 122
Roman Catholics, 14, 15
Rome, Georgia, 92, 93
Rome, Italy, 48
Romney, Virginia, 63, 92
"Rose" (slave), 34
Roots, 190
Rosen, Coiner, 126
"Rosewell", 30, 31
Rosser, Thomas Lafayette, 75, 87, 88, 140
Rosser-Gibbons Camp, No. 89, Grand Camp Confederate Veterans of Virginia, 140, 141
Rotterdam, 12, 144, 164
Roudabush, Jacob, Sr., 171, 172
Roudabush, Jacob, Jr., 172
Roudabush, John, 171
Roudabush, John Hiram, 172
Roudabush, Major Ashby, 172, 173, 213
Roudabush, Miller Elbea, 213
Roudabush, Peter William, 172
Roudabush, Virginia Belle McAllister, 213
Roudabush, Virginia Jackson, 172
Ruby, John C., 127

Rudacille, Philip, 31, 35, 40
Rudasiller, Jacob F., 75
Rudasiller, Thomas, 75
Rude's Hill, Shenandoah County, Va., 28, 107, 110, 126
Ruffner/Chapman House, 150
Ruop, Ursula, 146
Rumpenheim, Hesse, Germany, 174
Russell, Margaret Hill, 120
Russell, Robert Hill, 120, 121, 122, 123
Russell, Valentine, 120
Russell, William E., 127
Russell Co., Kansas, 216
Rust House, 50

Salisbury, N.C., 169
San Francisco, California, 105
Sangster's Station, Va., 87
Saratoga, N.Y., 174
Savannah, Ga., 122
Sheffield, England, 130
Schoharie County, New York, 48
Schultz, Rev. Christian, 22
Schwartz, Thomas E., 140
Scotch-Irish, 14, 15
Scotch-Irish Trust of Ulster, 15
Scotland, 14
Scott, Winfield, 51
Scots, 14
Scots-Irish, 14
Scots-Presbyterians, 14
Scottish, 14
Scottsville, Va., 110
Sears & Roebuck Co., 167
Secession, 47, 48, 49, 55, 61
Secessionville, S.C., 84
Seekford Cemetery, 23
Seekford, Jacob R., 38, 39
Seguin, Texas, 90
Sellers, John R., 169
Seminole Wars, 51
Semple, Robert, 205
Seneca, Kansas, 99
Seven Days Battles, 72
Shacklett, Fannie, 90
Sharpsburg, Maryland, Battle of (Antietam), 58, 77
Shawnee County, Kansas, 90

Shenandoah County, Virginia, 21, 26, 32, 62, 69, 75, 109, 144, 179, 200
Shenandoah, Florida, 217
Shenandoah, Iowa, 217
Shenandoah, Ga., 217
Shenandoah, La., 217
Shenandoah, N.Y., 217
Shenandoah, Ohio, 217
Shenandoah, Pa., 217
Shenandoah, Texas, 217
Shenandoah Iron Works, 44, 175
Shenandoah National Park, 166
Shenandoah River, South Fork, 32, 162
Shenandoah Valley Battlefields National Historic District, 217
Shenandoah Valley Railroad, 50, 189
Shenandoah, Va., 189, 216, 217
Shenk, Ambrose Booton, 55
Shenk, Henry C., 140
Shenk, John, 76
Shenk, Mary Jones, 55
Shenk apple, 212
Sheridan, Philip H. (Gen.), 76, 94, 95, 98, 208
Sherman, Mandel, 167
Sherman, William T., 51, 122
Sherman Silver Purchase Act of 1890, 131
Shields, James (General), 63, 64, 67
Shifflett, Edmond, 161
Shifflett, Millie Wyant. 161
Shiloh (Pittsburg Landing), Battle of, 52, 112
Ships:
    Anderson, 164
    Brotherhood, 164
    Dragon, 170
    James Goodwill, 22
    Mortenhouse, 162
    Scott, 146
    St. Andrew's Galley, 162

Shirley, O., 127
Shockoe Hill Cemetery, Richmond, Va., 104
Short History of Page County, 2, 16, 31, 63, 136, 143, 181, 193, 206

Shuler family, 38
Shuler, Emma Jane, 106, 110, 111
Shuler, John, 55, 106
Shuler, Mary Ann Kite, 55, 106
Shuler, Michael, 55, 78, 106
Shuler, N.W., 127
Shuler-Koontz Cemetery, Alma, 23
Sigel, Franz (Gen.), 72
Skyline, 166
Slavery, 26, 27, 34, 38, 40, 42, 44, 118
Slusher, Dallas, 76
Slusher, Sarah L., 99
Smith, Bentley, 143
Smith, Charles H. (Col.), 87, 88
Smoot, H.J. (Mayor of Luray), 124
Snyder, Daniel, 165
Somerville, Page County, Va., 65, 66, 108, 154
Sons of the American Revolution, 148
Sons of Confederate Veterans, 134, 141, 143, 192
Southern Claims Commission, 128
Southern Loyalists in the Civil War: The Southern Claims Commission, 128
Spanish American War, 152
Sperryville, Rappahannock Co., Va., 72
Sperryville Road, 86
Spitler, Abraham, 20
Spitler, Mann (Colonel), 59, 62
Spotswood, Governor Alexander, 18, 146
Spotsylvania County, Va., 146, 148, 166
Spotsylvania Court House, Virginia, 49, 53, 98, 99, 100, 132
Springfield, Illinois, 46
Springfield, Page Co., Va., 122
St. Bartholomew's Day Massacre, 156
St. John's Churchyard (Richmond), 31
St. Louis, Missouri, 19
St. Luke's Lutheran Church, Alma, 165
St. Paul's Lutheran Church, 175
Stanley, Va., 82, 165

"Star Spangled Banner," 125
Staunton, Va., 87, 214
Staunton National Cemetery, 214
Steadman, Major, 73
Steele, Mager William, 80
Stanardsville, Virginia, 17
Stanley Flour Mill, 213
Steinsfurt, Germany, 170
Stephens, Alexander Hamilton, 131
Steptoe War, 51
Stiegel, Charles B., 127
Stiehl, Catherine, 163
Stoever, Deitrich, 22
Stoever, Rev. John Casper, Sr., 22, 26
Stoever, Rev. John Casper, Jr., 22
Stoever, Magdalena Eberwein, 22
Stone/Holtiman/Brubaker Raid, 24
Stoneberger, Christina, 164
Stoneberger, Frederick, 165
Stonewall Brigade, 55, 120, 127
Stony Run, 165
Stover, Jacob, 19
Stover, John W., 141
Stover, Lena Gertrude, 138
Strabane Township, Pa., 171, 172
Strahl, Johan Conrad, 174
Strahl, Margaretha Seybel, 174
Strasburg, Virginia, 59, 64, 94
Strickler, Abraham, 89
Strickler, Benjamin, 128
Strickler, Colonel Daniel, 36
Strickler, Harrison Monroe, 76, 141
Strickler, Harry M., 2, 16, 31, 63, 143, 181, 193, 206
Strickler, Hiram Jackson, 89, 90
Strickler, Martin, 175
Strickler, Susannah Hollingsworth, 89
Strohl, Christian, 174
Strohl, Peter, 174
Strole Farm Road, 108
Strole, Christian, 162, 175
Strole, Elizabeth Kiser, 162
Stuart, James Ewell Brown "J.E.B." (Gen.), 77, 143
Stubblefield, George (Captain), 149
Sullivan, Jeremiah C. (Gen.), 65, 66, 218

Summers, George Washington (Captain), 106, 107, 108, 109, 110, 111, 126, 127
Summers, George Washington, Sr., 107, 108, 109, 110
Summers-Koontz Incident, 2, 100, 112, 197
Summers-Koontz Camp No. 490, Sons of Confederate Veterans, 82, 141
Summers-Koontz Roadside marker, 126
Swift Run Gap, 16
Swiss Immigrants, 18, 19
Swiss-German immigrants/settlers, 21
Switzerland, 11
Sycamore Mineral Springs, Kansas, 99

Talbot, Sir William, 17
Taliaferro family, 49
Tanner's Ridge, 33
Taylor, Elizabeth, 158
Taylor, Richard, 65
Taylor, Zachary, 51, 65
Tecumseh, Kansas, 90
Telling the Truth in History, 183
Texas, 90, 105
Tharp, William, 108
The Campaigns of Lieutenant-General N.B. Forrest, 52
The South, Its Products, Commerce, and Resources, 51
Thirty Years War, 11, 12, 170
Thomas, George Henry, 51
Thomas, Roland (Captain), 149
Thornton Gap, 33, 86, 87, 88, 212
Toledo, Ohio, 113
Torbert, Alfred T.A. (Gen.), 94, 95
Tories, 145, 205
Trappe, Pennsylvania, 28
Trenton, N.J., 145
Trevillian's Station, Battle of, 76
Triplett, Charles, 75
Tuebingen, Germany, 146
Turner, Nat, 34, 118
Turner Ashby Camp, U.C.V., 126
Tuscarora Tribe, 18
Twain, Mark, 211

Twenty-Five Chapters on the Shenandoah Valley, 16
Tyler, Erastus B. (Col.), 69

United Daughters of the Confederacy, 134, 143
UDC Cross of Military Service, 139
Ulster-Scots, 14
Ulster, Ireland, 14
Union Units:
   Dieckmann's Battery, 73
   13th Indiana Infantry, 65, 66
   14th Indiana Infantry, 120
   1st Maine Cavalry, 87
   1st (Maryland) Potomac Home Guard Cavalry, 198
   2nd Massachusetts Cavalry, Co. A, 96
   4th New York Mounted Rifles, 73
   22nd New York Cavalry, Co. H, 107, 109
   4th Ohio Infantry, 67
   6th Ohio Cavalry, 49, 73
   48th Ohio Infantry, 112, 113
   66th Ohio Infantry, 70, 121
   66th Ohio Infantry, Co. G., 120
   83rd Ohio Infantry, 113
   192nd Ohio Infantry, 107, 108, 113
   2nd Pennsylvania Cavalry, 87
   3rd Pennsylvania Cavalry, Co. H, 125
   8th Pennsylvania Cavalry, 87
   16th Pennsylvania Cavalry, 87
   26th Pennsylvania Emergency Regiment, 76
   68th Pennsylvania Infantry, 73
   73rd Pennsylvania Infantry, 73
   1st Vermont Cavalry, 65
United Confederate Veterans, 142, 143

United Daughters of the Confederacy, 134, 138, 192
United Daughters of the Confederacy Building, 138
United Kingdom, 15
United States House of Representatives, 29, 130
United States Military Academy (West Point), 51
United States Senate, 29
University of Virginia, 57, 90, 116, 151, 153
Upperville, Va., 87
Ups and Downs of a Confederate Soldier, 132

Valley Forge, Pennsylvania, 28, 149
Valley Guards, 91
Valley Pike, 69, 107
Veney, Bethany, 42, 43, 44
Verbena Mill/Farm, 70, 218
Veterans Administration, 84
Vienna, Virginia, 96
Vietnam Fund, 139
Virginia Department of Transportation, 126
Virginia Genealogical Web Project (VaGenWeb), 176
Virginia House of Delegates, 90
Virginia Military Institute, 89-92
Vicksburg, Mississippi, 63
Vicksburg Campaign, 113
Virginia Civil War Trails Markers, 77, 84
Virginia Civil War Trails, 218
Virginia Regimental Histories Series, 134, 135, 136, 137, 189, 192, 193
Virginia & Tennessee Railroad, 87
Virginia State Legislature, 151
Virginia State Library, 136
Virginia's Tidewater, 16
Von Graffenreid, Baron Christopher, 18, 19
Von Mosheim, Conrad Lorenz, 26
Von Steinwehr, Adolph Wilhelm August Friederich Baron (General), 49, 73
Walker, E.J. (Col.), 85

Waller Tazewell Patton Camp, S.C.V., 141
Walters, William, 75
Walton, M.L., 127
Wapping Heights, 85, 86, 218
War of the Grand Alliance, 11, 12
War of the League of Augsburg, 11, 12
War of the Palatinate, 12
War of Spanish Succession, 12
Warner, Mrs. I. Clifton, 139
Warren County, Virginia, 34, 94, 159, 179
Warren Rifles Chapter, U.D.C., 139
Warren, James W.T., 75, 140
Washington, D.C., 136, 148
Washington, George, 28, 30, 168, 171
Washington Artillery Battalion (Louisiana), 58
Washington, Carroll County, Ohio, 171
Washington Co., Md., 198
Wassamassaw Cavalry (Co. D, 2nd S.C.), 84
Wayland, John W., 16
Wayne, "Mad" Anthony, Gen., 149
Waynesboro, Virginia, 16
Weaver, Tilman S., 140
Weevils in the Wheat: Interviews with Virginia Ex-Slaves, 42
Westmont, N.J., 82
Wharton, H.M., Rev. Dr., 142, 143
Wheat, Charles C., 63
Wheeling, Virginia (W.Va.), 92
Weakley Hollow, 167
Whig Party, 171
Whistleberry, Sergeant, 83
"White Hall," 62
White House (The Fort), 21, 204, 205, 207
White House Bridge, 32, 63, 64, 69, 73, 92, 218
White House Ford, 73, 74
White's Comanches, 75, 76
White, Mrs. M.J.W., 139
Whitehaven, England, 166
Whitzel, Mary Magdalene, 172
Whitzel, Mary Tutwiler, 172
Whitzel, Peter, 172

Whortle Berry, Sergeant, 83
Whosoever Farm, 142
Wickham, Williams C., 94, 95
Wilderness, Virginia, Battle of, 55, 76, 106, 130
William E. Rudge's Son Press, 132
Williamsburg, Virginia, 31, 149, 174
Williamsport, Md., 85
Williamson, Thomas L., 127
Willow Grove Farm, 150
Willow Grove Mill, 100, 208, 218
Wilson, Captain, 65, 66
Wilson, James H., 94
Winchester, Virginia, 57, 61, 69, 77, 87, 105, 158, 174
Winchester, Virginia, Third Battle of (Opequon), 56, 94
Winnie Davis Cottage, 142, 143
"Winter King", 11
Wittenberg, Germany, 11
Wood, Mrs. Dewey R., 139
Wood, Vincent, 34
Woods, Jacob H., 127
Woodstock, Virginia, 28
Works Project Administration, 42, 43
Wright, A.R. (Gen.), 85
Wright, Silas K., 140

Yager, Christina Overall, 90
Yager, Nicholas Wesley, 47, 90
Yager, William Overall, 89, 90
Yager's Mill, 95, 218
Yates, Middleton Warfield, 76, 140
Yeager, Barbara, 147
York County, Pa., 170
York County, Virginia, 30
Yorktown, Va., 145, 149
Young, William Townsend, 53, 54, 200, 201
Yowell, Claude, 210

Zirkle, John, 178

About the Author

A native of Page County, Virginia, Robert H. Moore, II completed most of his undergraduate work at East Carolina University and received his Bachelor of Science degree in Liberal Studies from Excelsior College in 1995. He is currently in the process of completing his M.A. in History at Old Dominion University. A 10 ½ year veteran of the submarine force of the United States Navy, Robert has written seven books for the Virginia Regimental History Series and, in the last two years, has published *Avenue of Armies: Civil War Sites and Stories of Page County,* Virginia and *Gibraltar of the Shenandoah: Civil War Sites and Stories of Staunton, Waynesboro and Augusta County, Virginia.* He has also written extensively for magazines such as *Civil War Times Illustrated, Blue and Gray Magazine* and *America's Civil War.* For the past six years, Robert has also maintained the "Heritage and Heraldry" newspaper column (*Page News & Courier*) featuring the history and genealogy of Page County. Robert also serves on the History Committee for Virginia Civil War Trails and the Education & Interpretation Committee of the Shenandoah Valley Battlefields Foundation. A former chairman of the Page County Civil War Commission, Robert has played a role in securing funding for twelve Virginia Civil War Trails markers in Page County and has written texts for signs throughout the Shenandoah Valley. He is presently the Commander of the 4th Brigade, Virginia Division, Sons of Confederate Veterans and is also Commander of the Summers-Koontz Camp #490, Sons of Confederate Veterans in Luray. He currently resides with his family in Augusta County.

www.ingramcontent.com/pod-product-compliance
Lightning Source LLC
Chambersburg PA
CBHW062016220426
43662CB00010B/1359